HARVARD ECONOMIC STUDIES

I. The English Patents of Monopoly. By William H. Price. 8vo.

II. The Lodging House Problem in Boston. By Albert B. Wolfe. 8vo.

III. The Stannaries: A Study of the English Tin Miner. By George R. Lewis. 8vo.

IV. Railroad Reorganization. By Stuart Daggett. 8vo.

V. Wool-Growing and the Tariff. By Chester W. Wright. 8vo.

VI. Public Ownership of Telephones on the Continent of Europe. By Arthur N. Holcombe. 8vo.

VII. The History of the British Post Office. By J. C. Hemmeon. 8vo.

VIII. The Cotton Manufacturing Industry of the United States. By M. T. Copeland. 8vo.

IX. The History of the Grain Trade in France. By Abbott Payson Usher. 8vo.

X. Corporate Promotions and Reorganizations. By A. S. Dewing. 8vo.

XI. The Anthracite Coal Combination in the United States. By Eliot Jones. 8vo.

XII. Some Aspects of the Tariff Question. By F. W. Taussig. 8vo.

XIII. The Evolution of the English Corn Market from the Twelfth to the Eighteenth Century. By N. S. B. Gras. 8vo.

XIV. Social Adaptation: A Study in the Development of the Doctrine of Adaptation as a Theory of Social Progress. By L. M. Bristol. 8vo.

XV. The Financial History of Boston, from May 1, 1822, to January 31, 1909. By C. P. Huse. 8vo.

XVI. Essays in the Earlier History of American Corporations. By J. S. Davis. 8vo. 2 volumes.

XVII. The State Tax Commission. By H. L. Lutz. 8vo.

XVIII. The Early English Customs System. By N. S. B. Gras. 8vo.

XIX. Trade and Navigation between Spain and the Indies in the time of the Hapsburgs. By C. H. Haring. 8vo.

XX. The Italian Emigration of Our Times. By R. F. Foerster. 8vo.

XXI. The Mesta: A Study in Spanish Economic History, 1273–1836. By Julius Klein. 8vo.

XXII. Argentine International Trade under Inconvertible Paper Money: 1880–1900. By J. H. Williams. 8vo.

XXIII. The Organization of the Boot and Shoe Industry in Massachusetts before 1875. By Blanche E. Hazard. 8vo.

XXIV. Economic Motives. By Zenas C. Dickinson. 8vo.

XXV. Monetary Theory before Adam Smith. By Arthur E. Monroe. 8vo.

HARVARD UNIVERSITY PRESS

CAMBRIDGE, MASS., U.S.A.

HARVARD ECONOMIC STUDIES

PUBLISHED UNDER THE DIRECTION OF
THE DEPARTMENT OF ECONOMICS

VOL. XXV

LONDON: HUMPHREY MILFORD
Oxford University Press

MONETARY THEORY
BEFORE
ADAM SMITH

BY

ARTHUR ELI MONROE, PH.D.
ASSISTANT PROFESSOR OF ECONOMICS
HARVARD UNIVERSITY

CAMBRIDGE
HARVARD UNIVERSITY PRESS
1923

OP

PRINTED AT THE HARVARD UNIVERSITY PRESS
CAMBRIDGE, MASS., U. S. A.

TO THE MEMORY

OF

MY MOTHER

PREFACE

Few aspects of modern economic discussion have their roots so deeply in the past as the theory of money. Not only were most phases of it discussed before the time of Adam Smith, but some of our ideas concerning it may almost be called commonplaces since the beginning of the Modern Age. A knowledge of this material is, therefore, indispensable for a proper appreciation of the work of later writers. No survey of early monetary theory has been available in English, however, and no adequate one in other languages. This was brought home to me some years ago, when I was trying to evaluate the work of certain early American pamphleteers, and as a result I abandoned my original project and undertook the present study.

As will be clear from the table of contents, this is a history of theories rather than of theorists or of their times. The ideas of each writer, instead of being presented as a whole, have been considered in connection with various convenient and significant subdivisions of the subject. This heightens the impression of continuity, facilitates the comparison of ideas, and brings out relations which might otherwise escape notice. Brief general estimates of the work of particular writers are given in the several introductory chapters. To spare the reader the tedium of repetition and diffuseness considerable rearranging of scattered ideas has been necessary, but care has been taken not to read anything into a writer that is not consistent with his work as a whole. References to general and monetary history have been kept at a minimum; for, although such information often helps to explain the interests, policies, and even the errors of the writers of different times and places, it does not affect the validity of their reasoning, and its elaboration serves only to distract attention.

My thanks are due to Professor C. J. Bullock, who made invaluable suggestions at almost every stage of the work, and to Professors F. W. Taussig and A. A. Young, who read portions of the manuscript.

A. E. M.

Harvard University
February, 1923

CONTENTS

PART I

THE ANCIENT WORLD

PART II

THE MIDDLE AGES

PART III

THE BEGINNINGS OF THE MODERN AGE

PART IV

FROM DAVANZATI TO LOCKE

PART V

THE EIGHTEENTH CENTURY

PART I

THE ANCIENT WORLD

CHAPTER I

INTRODUCTORY

THE broad characteristics of method and approach which we associate with the economic thought in general of classical antiquity[1] are exemplified with but little modification by the monetary theories of that period. Separate treatises on the subject, in any modern sense of the term, were never attempted and probably never thought of; such scattered references as there were are found imbedded in works on ethics or politics, by some phase of which they were suggested, or in the discussions of the Roman jurists. Such a method of approach naturally tended to give to these discussions a distinctly ethical coloring, and to limit them to those aspects of the subject which seemed to be involved in the moral and political problems of mankind. Being written, moreover, by philosophers who felt, perhaps to some extent affected, a disdain for mean commercial interests, they were all the less likely to receive extended treatment. Centuries later a mercantile age made handsome amends for this early neglect, but not until the trying experiences of the Middle Ages had brought the importance of monetary problems painfully to the fore.

In this, as in so many other fields of Greek thought, the name of Aristotle (384–322 B.C.) is preëminent. In his crabbed and often obscure paragraphs are developed many important ideas on the subject of money — important not only because of the great insight which they reveal, but even more because of the profound influence which they have had on modern monetary theory through his devoted disciples, the Schoolmen. Plato's (427–347 B.C.) contributions were far less notable than those of his great pupil; and even the practical-minded Xenophon (445–355? B.C.) has left us little on this topic.

[1] See Trever, *Greek Economic Thought*, pp. 8–13.

The Romans added little to the analysis worked out by the Greeks. Like the Stoics and Epicureans, whom they followed, their philosophers had not much interest in economic questions, and the few points they noted refer more to archæological than to social aspects of the subject. The principal interest of the discussions in the *Corpus Juris* lies in the influence they exerted in later times.

CHAPTER II

GREECE

An explanation of the functions of money is a logical starting-point for theoretical discussions of this subject, and so we are not surprised to find the beginnings of such an analysis among Plato's meagre references to the question of money. In the *Republic* he notes the need of money "as a symbol, for the sake of exchange"; and in the *Laws* he remarks briefly that money "reduces the inequalities and immeasurabilities of goods to equality and measure."[1] Money, then, is a medium of exchange and a measure of value.

It was the second of these points, apparently, which most impressed Aristotle; for we find it clearly brought out in his *Ethics*, while the first point, though plainly implied in his *Politics*, is not directly stated. In the *Ethics* he explains that, in order to ensure proportionate equality as justice requires, "such things as are the subjects of exchange must in some sense be comparable"; some kind of measure must be provided in order to enable us to equate values. This is the reason for the invention of money. Later in the same chapter, he notes a third function, to which Plato had not referred, saying that money is "serviceable with a view to future exchange; it is a sort of security . . . that if we do not want a thing now, we shall be able to get it when we do want it." In other words, he recognizes money's use as a store of value.[2]

Closely related to the question of the functions of money is that of the effects on man and on society which may be traced to the use of money. Among the ancient philosophers and poets the belief was common that gold and silver had had a most baneful influence on the human race, that to the greed which they en-

[1] Plato, *Republic*, bk. ii, p. 242; *Laws*, bk. xi, p. 489.

[2] Aristotle, *Ethics*, bk. v, chap. 8; *Politics*, bk. i, chap. 9.

gendered could be traced crimes against every dictate of justice — a feeling concisely expressed in Virgil's famous line,

Quid non mortalia pectora cogis,
Auri sacra fames![1]

It is not always clear whether these denunciations are aimed at the use of money as such, or at the greed for wealth in general of which the desire for money is only an expression.

Aristotle, however, devotes considerable attention to this point in a characteristically difficult passage, and seems to hold that the use of money, by leading to retail trade, in which money itself is the goal of exchange, has so blinded men to the true limits of desirable acquisition, that they go on piling up coin under the impulse of their endless desires, some even assuming money to be wealth. Money thus serves to accentuate a bad tendency. It has also, in this way, given rise to the evil of usury, which he regards as "the most hated kind" of trade. On the other hand, by facilitating exchange, money promotes association and hence all life in society, which is indispensable to man's highest development.[2]

The origin of so important a convention as money is a question sure to engage the attention of the student of society; but it calls for such skillful analysis and for such a rich background of historical fact, that progress is bound to be slow. For the most part, we find little on this point in the classical authors except semi-mythological accounts of the inventors of money, which have no scientific value.[3]

In Aristotle, however, there are a number of suggestions which deserve notice. It is clear, he says, that barter preceded the use of money; and barter rests upon the "demand for mutual services which holds society together — for if people had no wants, or their wants were dissimilar, there would be no exchange, or it would not be the same as now." Thus, the fact that men have wants which can be satisfied by mutual services explains the existence of exchange. This explanation carries with it the implication that barter may not always be convenient, that the individual

[1] See also other references in Genovesi's *Lezioni di Commercio*, pp. 89, 90.

[2] Aristotle, *Politics*, bk. i, chaps. 9, 10; *Ethics*, bk. v, chap. 8.

[3] Babelon, *Origines de la Monnaie*, pp. 189, 202–204.

may not always readily find another with whom he can make an exchange. He does not draw this conclusion directly; but, as he goes on to point out how money enables us to procure what we want in the future, it seems probable that he had it in mind. This, as we shall see, is the way the Schoolmen interpreted the passage.[1] In the *Politics* he adds the further consideration that, since the necessaries of life are not easily carried about, money was adopted to diminish this inconvenience, when the inhabitants of one country came to be more dependent on those of another. At first the value of things adopted as a medium of exchange was measured by size and weight, but in the course of time people put a stamp on them to save the trouble of weighing, and to mark the value.[2]

As to how such customs developed, he really does not express an opinion; but as some of the phrases in the above-mentioned passages were made the basis of later theories on this point, they need to be considered here. The standard of measurement, he reasons, must be one upon which all agree; and he also declares that money exists, not by nature, but by convention. Now these expressions appear to mean simply that the medium of exchange, to be effective, must be generally accepted; and that the precious metals have this quality, not in the nature of things, but because of general esteem, which might change. They are not a theory of the introduction of money at all; but, together with other similar expressions, they were so interpreted.

Aristotle notes the existence in his time[3] of a theory, which we shall encounter again in later writers, that it is a matter of comparative indifference what material is used for money. Plato's reference to money as a "symbol or token"[4] seems to indicate that he was in sympathy with this view; and this conclusion is strengthened by his proposal, in the *Laws*, that for domestic trade a token-money established by law should be used, gold and silver being restricted to transactions with foreigners.[5]

With this view Aristotle, himself, does not agree. Instead, he heads a long line of "sound-money" advocates by limiting money

[1] See below, p. 22. [2] *Ethics*, bk. v, chap. 8; *Politics*, bk. i, chap. 9.
[3] *Ibid.* [4] *Republic*, bk. ii, p. 242. [5] *Laws*, bk. v, p. 313.

to materials that are "useful and easily applicable to the purposes of life." [1] His reason for this is probably to be found in the passage quoted above, where he says that money must be generally acceptable. Only a directly useful commodity would have this quality. In the same passage he adds that money, though its value is not always the same, has a more constant value than anything else.[2] From this it seems reasonable to infer that he considered stability of value a further quality to be desired.

Although the problem of the value of money was not the burning issue in classical times which it later became, it did not pass unnoticed. The first reference to it seems to be in Xenophon's *Revenues of Athens*. This, indeed, is only indirect, for he speaks simply of the value of gold and silver; but he seems to have the money use particularly in mind. Gold, he says, if it appears in great quantity, becomes much less valuable, and causes silver to bear a higher price; but silver does not show the same effect, the reason being that nobody ever had so much silver as not to desire more.[3] This last argument, it seems to me, would be advanced only by one who was thinking of silver as money, — of which, it may indeed be said, no one ever has too much, — while the reasoning with regard to gold considers the commodity aspect only. The universal acceptability of money has simply misled Xenophon into thinking that its value, that is, the value of silver, is not subject to depreciation; and he doubtless made the error all the more readily because of his desire to make out a good case in favor of silver-mining.[4] At any rate, it was not very successful reasoning, even for a first attempt.

Aristotle considers the value of money more specifically, and declares that it is subject to the same law as other things. This is a logical corollary to his statement elsewhere, to which we have already referred, that money is to be made of a useful commodity easily adaptable to the purposes of life. With the commodity character of money thus clearly in mind, he naturally assimilated

[1] *Politics*, bk. i, chap. 9. [2] *Ethics*, bk. v, chap. 8.

[3] Xenophon, *Minor Works*, pp. 254, 255.

[4] This seems simpler than Dubois's explanation that Xenophon considered depreciation in value possible only in case of superabundance, and believed silver to have an unlimited market. (Dubois, *Doctrines Économiques*, p. 52.)

it to his general theory of value. This theory, which he developed as a principle of justice rather than of fact, may be briefly stated as follows. An exchange is just when neither party to it gains or loses; the objects exchanged must be equal. Since they are of different sorts, however, they will have to be equalized by comparison with some common standard. This standard is the demand for mutual services which holds society together. The more important the service of a producer, the less of his product must be given for that of another producer.[1]

Besides these views on the value of money, we also find some tendency to regard it as a purely arbitrary matter, settled by legal enactment. Thus Aristotle remarks that some writers hold that money is a purely conventional thing, whose value and use would both disappear, if another commodity were substituted for it.[2] Genovesi says that some of the Stoics were of this opinion, and perhaps they are the ones to whom Aristotle referred.[3]

[1] *Ethics*, bk. v, chap. 8.
[2] *Politics*, bk. i, chap. 9.
[3] Genovesi, *Lezioni di Commercio*, p. 28.

CHAPTER III

ROME

THE references to monetary questions by the writers of Roman times are even more scanty and fragmentary than those we find among the Greeks. The Romans shared the unfavorable opinion concerning the influence of money on mankind, to which we referred in the last chapter, and some of their statements leave little doubt that they were distinguishing money from wealth in general. Pliny, like Aristotle, declares that, by giving rise to usury, money has opened a new field to avarice.[1] The distinction is also made in Plutarch's account of the introduction of iron money in Sparta by Lycurgus, as a means of checking avarice and crime.[2]

In discussing the law of sale, the jurist Paulus made what may fairly be called a real contribution to the analysis of the evolution of money. Without attempting to account for the custom of barter, merely asserting its existence in primitive times, he goes on to say that, since occasions where two persons can just satisfy each other's desires are rarely met (*sed quia non semper nec facile concurrebat, ut, quum tu haberes quod ego desiderarem, invicem haberem quod tu accipere velles*), a material was chosen to serve as a general medium of exchange. This point about the coincidence of wants is only implied in Aristotle's discussion of barter. It should be noted that Paulus apparently distinguishes no other function of money except that of a medium of exchange.[3]

The opinion of Aristotle that money should be made of a valuable material, which we find expressed or implied in most later writers, seemed to some commentators on the Roman law to be contradicted by certain phrases in Paulus, particularly his state-

[1] Pliny, *Natural History*, xxxiii, 14.

[2] Plutarch, *Lycurgus*, p. 94.

[3] Oertmann, *Die Volkswirtschaftslehre des Corpus Juris Civilis*, pp. 86, 87. The reference is to the Digest, bk. xviii, tit. 1, § 1.

ment that money confers ownership *non tam ex substantia quam ex quantitate*. This, however, seems to refer to an entirely different aspect of the question — the legal status of money in contracts; and it is rather in another much-debated expression that his opinion on this particular point is to be found. As Oertmann holds, the *publica ac perpetua æstimatio* which Paulus associates with money really implies about the same idea that Aristotle had expressed: money rests on public esteem, it must be a thing valuable in itself.[1] Except for the elder Pliny's admission that the durability of gold makes it peculiarly suitable for monetary use, whatever else may be said against it,[2] we find no discussion of this question until the time of the Schoolmen.

The passage from Paulus quoted at the beginning of the foregoing paragraph has also been interpreted as implying a fiat theory of the value of money.[3] Further support of this interpretation was found in the principle of the jurists that the same numerical sum must be returned by debtors that had been received,[4] and in their refusal to allow the money of the country to be treated as a commodity, that is, to be bought and sold.[5] Such a reading of these passages is misleading, however, it seems to me, for it loses sight of the fact that these writers were developing a juristic rather than an economic theory of money. They were concerned with the "paying power" rather than the "purchasing power" of money; and were not far wrong in concluding that in this respect — the only one with which the law has to do — the courts could not go behind the legal enactments, without destroying the essential character of money, and reducing it again to a commodity.

It has been thought by some that there was evidence of a somewhat different point of view in the decision of Valentinian and Valens that certain coins, struck by former princes, must be ac-

[1] Oertmann, p. 87. This is also the interpretation of Thomas, *Théories Économiques dans le Corpus Juris Civilis*, pp. 54, 55.

[2] Kautz, *Geschichtliche Entwicklung der National-Oekonomik*, p. 157.

[3] Genovesi, *Lezioni di Commercio*, pp. 27, 28.

[4] Thomas, *op. cit.*, p. 57.

[5] Pagnini, *Saggio sopra il Giusto Pregio*, p. 221.

cepted, if they contained the due weight and had not been altered;[1] but this implication is not clear. The decision is concerned in part with the legality of the acts of previous sovereigns; and, for the rest, is merely insisting upon the integrity of the coins as a condition for legal tender. It does not seem to indicate a belief that the value of a coin is identical with the value of its metal content.

[1] Thomas, *op. cit.*, p. 53.

CHAPTER IV

SUMMARY

Of the many questions which now engage the attention of writers on monetary theory, only five were discussed, even briefly, by the thinkers of the ancient world: the evolution of money, the functions of money, the influence of money on mankind, the qualities of the money material, and the value of money. On each of these the Greeks, and especially Aristotle, made a real beginning, working out analyses which later thinkers had only to develop.

Money's service as a medium of exchange and measure of value was clearly recognized, the latter function being stressed by Aristotle. He also referred to the use of money as a store of value. Money was believed to have had, on the whole, a bad influence on mankind, though it facilitates association and, hence, life in society. It was seen that exchange rests on the existence of mutual wants and that money enables traders to avoid the inconveniences which result from the dissimilarity of wants and the difficulty of transporting some wares. Some writers held that money might be made of any material; but Aristotle advocated the use of materials valuable for other uses, and implied that stability of value was desirable. He also opposed the view that the value of money is arbitrarily fixed, and considered it subject to the same laws as the value of other things.

Besides these positive contributions, Aristotle also left some scattered passages — notably his references to the conventional origin and status of money — which tended to confuse later readers and, as we shall see, hampered rather than helped them in the solution of their problems.

On only one of these five topics — the inconvenience of barter — did the Romans make any additions to the theory as developed by the Greeks, and on some they did not go even as far as their teachers.

PART II

THE MIDDLE AGES

CHAPTER V

INTRODUCTORY

THE six centuries following the downfall of the Roman Empire were for Europe a period of intellectual stagnation. The disorders of the barbarian invasions and the absorption of clerics in the problems of theology left little room for the liberal studies that had flourished in Greece and Rome. The love of learning was not entirely dead, it is true, and a few writers laboriously gathered the fragments of ancient learning into ponderous encyclopedic treatises; but they made no pretence of studying the phenomena of their own time, and had little interest in the progress of ideas. Science was utterly dormant.

The most important of these compilations was the *Etymologiæ*, or *Origines*, of the famous Bishop Isidore of Seville, who lived at the beginning of the seventh century.[1] This was a strikingly complete résumé of what was then preserved of the learning of the past (*nihil enim Isidorus intentatum reliquit*), and it long remained the chief source of information on scientific subjects. An earlier and less complete compendium of much the same sort was the *Institutiones Divinarum et Humanarum Lectionum* of Cassiodorus (480–575(?)), the verbose quæstor of Theodoric.[2] This also was read and quoted for centuries.

The references to money which we find in these writers have only an antiquarian interest. Lacking the works of Aristotle,[3] and being interested in the subject in its historical rather than its scientific aspect, they did no more than speculate about the derivation of the word, and reproduce the semi-mythological accounts that had been handed down by the Romans.

[1] For an account of Isidore's life and work, see Brehaut, *An Encyclopedist of the Dark Ages*.

[2] On Cassiodorus, see Hodgkin, *The Letters of Cassiodorus*.

[3] Before the twelfth century Aristotle was known to scholars only as a logician. — De Wulf, *Medieval Philosophy*, p. 139.

The twelfth century brought many changes to western Europe, and none was greater than the quickening of its intellectual life. Contact with Arabian, Jewish, and Byzantine philosophies opened up vast new fields of interest, the growth of schools and universities stimulated discussion, and the development of towns and commerce brought material questions more and more to the fore. The works of Aristotle, with the important beginnings of monetary theory which we have already noted, gradually became known to Western scholars. These tendencies culminated in the brilliant thirteenth century, the "golden age of Scholastic philosophy," but they continued to be a vital force for at least two centuries more.

Like other fields of thought, the theory of money made great advances during this period. The analyses of Aristotle, promptly adopted and soon elaborated, furnished a sound starting-point, while urgent new problems forced a discussion of far more monetary phenomena than had been considered by "the philosopher." In particular, the evils of debasement, from which the Greeks had been largely free,[1] attracted increasing attention, as princes resorted more and more to this source of gain, and as the spread of the "money economy" made a stable currency more imperative. This and related problems color every mediæval discussion of money.

These new developments are first to be noted in the work of the great Dominican, St. Thomas of Aquin (1225–74). Albertus Magnus, his teacher, had already made Aristotle's ideas familiar, by means of a rough paraphrase; but he had not tried to elaborate the ideas of the Greek master. St. Thomas, however, not only took the greatest pains to record Aristotle's views correctly, procuring new translations for this purpose, but he made a start at refining and expanding these views. His discussions of monetary problems, as of other economic questions, are not brought together in one place, but are scattered through the *Summa Theologica* and his minor works. Further progress in developing the traditional doctrine is found in other Scholastics, especially John

[1] Lenormant, *Organisation Politique et Économique de la Monnaie dans l'Antiquité*, pp. 171–178.

Buridan, who in 1327 became rector of the University of Paris, and who was perhaps the keenest analyst of economic matters in the Middle Ages. Secular writers also were beginning to discuss monetary questions.

The views of earlier writers were summed up and combined in the *Traictie de la Première Invention des Monnoies* (*circa* 1360) of Nicole Oresme, Bishop of Lisieux and a scholar of considerable distinction. As probably the first special treatise on the theory of money, and as an unusually clear and straightforward exposition of the Scholastic doctrine, this work undoubtedly deserves a distinguished place; but its originality has been overrated. On some points Oresme is inferior to Buridan, whose lectures he heard in Paris, and on others he reverts to the naïve accounts of Isidore and Cassiodorus. The great popularity of Oresme's treatise is attested by the number of manuscript copies and printed editions of which we have knowledge.[1]

From now on in this period there is little progress to report. In many respects the Middle Ages may be said to have come to an end with the fourteenth century; but in our particular field, mediæval problems and mediæval traditions continued to influence discussion even beyond the end of the fifteenth century. There was no abrupt break. We find no trace of novelty in the writings of Gabriel Biel (1430?–95); and even the *Tractatus contractuum et usurarum* of Molinæus (1500–66), which brought exile upon its author, belongs to the old tradition. The authors whom we shall consider in Part III as belonging to the modern age also leaned heavily on their Scholastic predecessors.

[1] For further details on Oresme, see Wolowski's edition of the *Traictie.*

CHAPTER VI

BUILDING ON TRADITION

It was not until the works of Aristotle became available — at first the *Ethics*, later the *Politics* — that the scholars of this period began to develop any clear ideas about money. Their early attempts were little more than "childish etymologies," as Jourdain expresses it. The road to knowledge, according to Isidore of Seville, is by way of words, and they are to be elucidated by reference to their origin. Applying this theory to money, he says that it is so called from *moneo*, meaning to advise, because it warns us against fraud in weight and composition. The piece is called *nomisma* because it bears the stamp of the prince. The pieces are called *nummi*, from Numa, a king of Rome, who invented them.[1] Cassiodorus is quoted by Oresme as writing that gold was discovered by Cutus and silver by Indus, two kings of Scythia, who for this reason were reputed divine.[2]

Isidore's statement that money contains three elements — metal, weight, and effigy — and that the absence of any one of these leaves it no longer money [3] has a little more significance. Underlying it, seems to be a vague idea that money is essentially a commodity, an idea which we shall meet frequently, later, in discussions of the value of money. Though far from an explicit statement of the commodity theory, it seems to be a groping in that direction.

With Aristotle's discussions in hand, the Schoolmen were soon able to develop a more impressive theory of money.[4] Like many later writers, they gave great prominence to money's service as a

[1] Jourdain, *Excursions Historiques et Philosophiques à travers le Moyen Age*, p. 426.

[2] Oresme, *Traictie*, p. 12.

[3] Brants, *Théories Économiques . . . des XIIIe et XIVe Siècles*, pp. 179, 180.

[4] Ideas like Isidore's continued to appear long after the works of Aristotle had become known. For example, the *De Regimine Principum* of St. Thomas (finished by another hand), bk. ii, chap. 13; and the reference to Oresme above.

measure of value.[1] It was not as a separate function, however, that this was emphasized; exchange is the real end sought in the use of money, and it is only as it serves this purpose that a measure of value is useful. The two functions are thought of together. St. Thomas, for example, follows Aristotle closely as to the need of a measure of values, but declares that exchange is the real purpose;[2] and Oresme, in his French version, refers to money as "instrument de preuver et marchander,"[3] but in Latin calls it simply "instrumentum permutandi."[4] Antonine of Florence in the next century gives the same impression.[5] Aristotle's idea that money serves as a store of value was handed on directly by these writers in the phrase "fidejussor futuræ necessitatis."[6] It is evident that, in these discussions, the Schoolmen did not improve appreciably upon the analysis of monetary functions which they found in the Greek philosopher.

Their conclusions as to the influence of money on men's ways were not wholly unfavorable. They noted that money is often the end sought in crimes and, believing that the sin of usury is simply a misuse of money, they were inclined to question whether such a source of evil should not be rooted out.[7] On the whole, however, opinion inclined to the side of Oresme, who held that there was a balance of good to the community, or to that of Luther, who reasoned that the evil is in us and not in money itself.[8]

In their treatment of the origin of money we are conscious of a great change in the intellectual background. Exchange, like everything else, is referred to a divine origin. Oresme, who doubtless reflects the ideas of his precursors, if he does not use their

[1] Some writers, as we shall see, mention no other function.

[2] "Pecunia autem, secundum Philosophum, principaliter est inventa ad commutationes faciendas," *Summa Theologica*, 2–2, *quæst.* 78, 1. Similar expressions are found elsewhere in his works: *De Usuris*, bk. i, chap. 9; *Exposit. in VIII Lib. Politicorum*, i, *lect.* 7.

[3] Oresme, *Traictie*, p. 9.

[4] *Ibid.*, p. 94.

[5] Ilgner, *Die volkswirtschaftlichen Anschauungen Antonins von Florenz*, pp. 90–92.

[6] St. Thomas, *Exposit. in X Lib. Ethicorum*, v, 9; *De Regimine Principum*, ii, 7.

[7] Endemann, *Studien in der Romanisch-kanonistischen Wirtschafts- und Rechtslehre*, vol. ii, pp. 170, 171.

[8] Oresme, *Traictie*, pp. 9, 10; Roscher, *National-Oekonomik in Deutschland*, p. 62.

words, says exchange arose from the fact that, after God had divided the earth and its goods among the sons of Adam, men and places often found themselves with a surplus or lack of some commodity. Barter was therefore resorted to.[1] There is more in this, however, than a mere change in intellectual method. There is some attempt to explain the existence of mutual wants, and to distinguish different sets of causes: not only men but places have surpluses which may be exchanged for the surpluses of others.

With regard to the inconveniences of barter, the Schoolmen went considerably further than Aristotle. Albertus Magnus gave a simple paraphrase of his ideas; but St. Thomas, in commenting on the *Ethics*, pointed out the difficulty which Paulus had mentioned, and which is barely implied in Aristotle: the possibility that the man whose surplus you desire may have no need of yours.[2] It is possible that this reflects some acquaintance with the Roman Law, though it is doubtless true, as Jourdain argues, that the influence of the jurists was nothing like that of Aristotle. Antonine of Florence also refers to this point.[3]

Buridan, showing marked originality here as elsewhere, gives, as further reasons for the necessity of money, the delay (*distantia temporum*) which must sometimes intervene between the disposal of one's surplus and the consumption of the things obtained for it, — which perishable goods could not endure, — and the natural indivisibility of many valuable objects. So great are these inconveniences, that the use of money is indispensable for the support of a population as great as that of his time.[4] His analysis is closely followed by Biel; [5] but Oresme, who was familiar with Buridan's thought, as we know, dismisses the subject with a brief reference to the "many difficulties" of barter.[6] Molinæus quotes Paulus, and adds that barter was further complicated by the difficulty of agreeing upon the value of articles to be exchanged and of avoiding fraud or extortion.[7]

[1] Oresme, *Traictie*, p. 8.

[2] Jourdain, *op. cit.*, pp. 430–432; St. Thomas, *Exposit. in X Lib. Ethic.*, v, 9.

[3] Ilgner, *op. cit.*, p. 90.

[4] *Zeitschr. für die ges. Staatswissenschaft*, vol. lx, pp. 459, 460.

[5] Boyss, *Tractatus Varii*, p. 1.

[6] Oresme, *Traictie*, p. 9.

[7] Molinæus, *Tractatus Contractuum et Usurarum*, no. 531.

On the difficult question of the evolution of the custom of using money, Aristotle's words proved confusing rather than helpful. The idea of an agreement, which seems to lurk in some of his expressions,[1] seems to be taken more literally in St. Thomas's statement: "Est enim condictum inter homines, quod afferenti denarium detur id, quo indiget";[2] and it was this interpretation which became familiar to the Schoolmen. Moreover, it was probably strengthened by the words of another classical writer, the Roman jurist Paulus, who, in an often-quoted passage, says that a material was chosen (*electa materia est*) to lessen the inconveniences of barter.[3] Some writers, however, reverted to the traditions preserved in Cassiodorus and Isidore about the reputed originators of money. Oresme, for example, writes simply "les hommes subtilz trouvèrent ung usaige plus legier, c'est assavoir de faire monnoie," and quotes from Cassiodorus about the inventors of it.[4] A similar point of view is found in Vincent de Beauvais.[5]

To Aristotle's statements about the development of coinage the Schoolmen gave greater precision, at least. St. Thomas does not add much when he speaks of avoiding the trouble of "measuring or weighing";[6] but Oresme specifies not only the trouble of weighing but also the difficulty of recognizing the quality of the metals, as the reasons for coinage.[7] Biel, however, refers simply to the danger of fraud and uncertainty.[8]

A more important elaboration of Aristotle's ideas is seen in the Scholastic discussions about the qualities desirable in the money material. St. Thomas not only repeated what the Greek philosopher had said about making money of materials useful in themselves, but added that the high specific value of the precious metals, making them easily portable, was a further reason for their use as money. Moreover, in his commentary on the statement in the *Ethics* that the value of money varies, though less than that of other things, he remarks that this hinders the money function and should therefore be reduced to a minimum,[9] thus

[1] See above, page 7.
[2] *Exposit. in X Lib. Ethic.*, v, 9.
[3] Oertmann, *op. cit.*, pp. 86, 87.
[4] Oresme, *Traictie*, p. 9.
[5] Jourdain, *op. cit.*, p. 431.
[6] *Exposit. in VIII Lib. Polit.*, i, 7.
[7] Oresme, *Traictie*, p. 17.
[8] Boyss, *Tractatus Varii*, p. 1.
[9] *Exposit. in VIII Lib. Polit.*, i, 7; *in X Lib. Ethic.*, v, 9.

making more definite the need of stability of value in the money material. The more obvious influence of debasement on the value of money, and inadequate theories of value in general caused this consideration to receive little or no further attention during the Middle Ages.

To this somewhat tentative analysis Buridan made important additions. Money should be made of precious material, he says, in order to facilitate transportation; durable, in order to serve as a store of value; divisible into small parts for lesser purchases; and capable of being impressed with adequate marks for identification.[1] Oresme follows Buridan pretty closely,[2] and Biel repeats his views almost word for word.[3] Although Antonine of Florence questions whether a valuable material is absolutely necessary,[4] the statement of Buridan may be said to have remained the accepted one for over a century, and the basis of all later discussion.

[1] *Zeitschr. für die ges. Staatswissenschaft*, vol. lx, p. 460.

[2] Oresme, *Traictie*, pp. 11, 13, 18.

[3] Boyss, *Tractatus Varii*, p. 1.

[4] Ilgner, *op. cit.*, p. 93.

CHAPTER VII

PRICES AND RELATED PROBLEMS

In some respects the subjects of the present chapter might have been included in the preceding one, for the Schoolmen had Aristotle's discussion of value to build on; but the great practical importance of these questions in the Middle Ages makes it desirable to treat them separately.

1. The Commodity Theory

Throughout the period covered by this study we meet, in one form or another, the theory that money is to be considered a mere commodity, stamped and certified by the state, to be sure, but subject to no special laws of value. Sometimes no further suggestions are offered as to how the values of commodities, of which money is but an example, are determined; but generally there are more or less elaborate references to the forces which govern value.

We have already seen that there seem to be vague gropings toward a commodity conception of money in Isidore of Seville, before Aristotle's theory of value had been expounded by the Schoolmen. Even after the spread of Greek philosophy, however, we find some comparatively simple discussions of prices. Thus, in 1308, Pierre Dubois, the famous jurist, complained to the king that, as a result of debasement, prices were much higher, since foreigners had regard only for the actual amount of gold and silver in the coins.[1] Here the commodity aspect of money is more clearly recognized, but it is not very definite.

Aristotle's theory was taken over without modification by the early Schoolmen. Albertus Magnus and St. Thomas comment on these passages in Aristotle, without adding anything of note in regard to money.[2] The influence of supply, which is only implied in Aristotle, is made a little clearer by St. Thomas's reference to

[1] Brants, *op. cit.*, pp. 188, 189.

[2] Schreiber, *Die Volkswirtschaftlichen Anschauungen der Scholastik*, pp. 51–53.

rarity as the cause of the high value of the precious metals,[1] and more particularly by Henry of Ghent, who says that the value of money varies, like that of other things, according to time, place, and especially according to the supply available.[2] Antonine of Florence also notes the influence of supply indirectly, in his remark that, when gold is hoarded, it becomes scarce, and more goods will be given for the same money.[3] Duns Scotus follows Albert and St. Thomas closely.[4]

Buridan elaborates these ideas very skillfully, and considers the case of money more specifically. "The value of money must be measured by human need," he says; "for although we do not need gold or silver for our necessities, still the rich need them for their luxurious purposes. And therefore we see that gold and silver in the mass are of the same value, or about the same, as in money." Since the value of other goods is similarly measured, we can compare them by observing their relation to money.[5] Heinrich von Langenstein repeats this theory almost literally, and Biel follows its ideas closely, but neither of them refers to Buridan.[6]

2. The "Valor Impositus"

Along with these purely theoretical aspects of the question the Schoolmen had to wrestle with a very practical one — the right of the prince to fix the values of coins. On the one hand, they were agreed that this was one of the most important attributes of the coinage prerogative.[7] Only in this way, they seem to have reasoned, could a stable and efficient measure of values be provided. Moreover, Aristotle seemed to support this view. In his statement that money rests on convention, the Greek word *νόμος*, which has a very broad meaning, was translated by the

[1] "Modicum de istis propter eorum raritatem valebat multum de aliis rebus." *Exposit. in VIII Lib. Polit.*, i, 7.

[2] Schreiber, *op. cit.*, pp. 132, 133.

[3] Ilgner, *op. cit.*, p. 97.

[4] Schreiber, pp. 153, 154.

[5] *Zeitschr. für die ges. Staatswissenschaft*, vol. lx, pp. 457, 458; Kaulla, *Moderne Werttheorien*, p. 59. Oresme does not follow Buridan here.

[6] *Zeitschr. für die ges. Staatswissenschaft*, vol. lx, p. 461; Boyss, *Tractatus Varii*, p. 2.

[7] See what is said on this in Chapter VIII.

Latin *lex* and interpreted to mean statute law, of which the prince was the source.[1] On the other hand, seeing all around them the mischievous results of this reasoning in practice, they could not ignore the conflict between this point of view and that set forth in the foregoing section.

At first this feeling showed itself in stipulations that money should be *proba* or *justa*; but these were vague, and still subordinate to the will of the prince, who was bound by them in conscience alone. Later writers grew more insistent; but progress in setting up standards of *probitas* was slow, and the *valor impositus* was still held to be final.[2] Of course, these well-meaning appeals to the conscience of princes did not clear up the confusion between the economic and the legal aspects of money, — its purchasing power and its legal-tender status, — but they were a move in the right direction.

Further progress developed from discussion of the practice of money-changing. As a result of the multiplicity of coinage authorities and the frequent debasements, the practice of exchanging or selling one kind of money for another became very common; and as it was, not unjustly, suspected of being frequently a cover for usury, the legitimacy of such transactions was soon called into question. A first step toward justifying the exchangers was made when St. Thomas Aquinas, applying Aristotle's distinction of the primary and secondary uses of things to money, concluded that, although money in its primary use was a measure of value only, it might in its secondary use be an object of exchange or sale.[3] Other arguments also were advanced, and opinion grew increasingly favorable. Once the secondary use of money as a ware was recognized, it was not long before the *valor impositus* was reduced in importance, while the *bonitas intrinseca* was given greater weight. It was a long time, however, before there was general agreement with the opinion of Budelius, that the intrinsic value was the more important.[4]

[1] St. Thomas, *Exposit. in X Lib. Ethic.*, v, 9.

[2] Endemann, *Studien in der Romanisch-kanonistischen Wirthschafts- und Rechtslehre*, vol. ii, pp. 172–178; Schreiber, *op. cit.*, pp. 192, 193.

[3] *Summa Theologica*, 2–2, *quæst.* 78, 1.

[4] Endemann, *op. cit.*, vol. ii, pp. 197–206.

Many writers tried to reconcile the two points of view. Buridan, for example, reasoned that the *valor impositus* is not considered in the establishing of the coinage system, "since, if there were no money and the king should make one . . . it would not be for him to determine how much an obol or denarius was worth"; but if, when there was already money current, he should make another, he might establish its price in relation to the former money.[1] The idea back of this seems to be that the king's function is not to determine the purchasing power of money, but merely to set up legally binding standards as to the relation between the different coins.

We begin to find a clearer grasp of the problem in the writings of Molinæus. The *publica æstimatio*, on which money depends, does not imply the word of the prince alone, he says, but also the consent and usage of the people, and the custom of commerce. Any other interpretation would be contrary to the very nature of money, whose stamp was adopted simply for the convenience of commerce, to relieve us of the trouble of testing and weighing. It is true, however, that, because of people's faith in the public stamp, money has greater utility from the *quantitas impositilia* than from its substance. The actual decision as to the relation between the extrinsic and intrinsic values of money rests with the government, subject only to the demands of equity and justice, that is, of conserving and facilitating all legitimate commerce. So long as money is legal, it must be accepted by all those subject to the same authority.[2] Although this discussion is vague in some respects, it seems to indicate that Molinæus was clear as to the strictly legal significance of the *valor impositus.*

3. The Theory of Price Changes

From the beginning of the twelfth century debasements of the coinage became more frequent and flagrant, and protests soon arose against them. The fact that the evils complained of were really a matter of the value of money was not very clearly brought

[1] Schreiber, *op. cit.*, pp. 188, 189; *Zeitschr. für die ges. Staatswissenschaft*, vol. lx, p. 456.

[2] Boyss, *Tractatus Varii*, pp. 314–322; Endemann, *op. cit.*, vol. ii, p. 204.

out in some of these discussions; but it is obvious that this idea underlay them, and so they may fairly be considered in this place.

As early as 1110, Guibert de Nogent condemned bad money; and from that time on, debasement is spoken of as a public calamity.[1] St. Thomas said it caused the same confusion that would result from changing the standard of weight.[2] In a memoir of 1300, Pierre Dubois declared to the king (Philip the Fair) that debasement had caused losses to his subjects with which the losses of war could not be compared. The revenues of the nobles and such classes had not increased, he explained, while the things they had to buy were double in price. A few years later he again protested in similar terms.[3] In the first of these memoirs he was of the opinion that the king was one of the few in the state who did not lose through debasement; but in the second he concluded that the king also suffered in the long run.

Oresme is more specific. Trade is much upset, he says, because of the uncertainty, and merchants cease coming to the country. Moreover, the fixing of pensions and various annual revenues in money terms is a special reason why the coinage laws should be changed as seldom as possible: when money is debased, the revenues of the prince and nobles "cannot be justly paid." A few money changers profit at the expense of the larger and more necessary part of the community. Often they have secret information regarding changes in money, and so are able to buy up goods while they are cheap, and become rich when prices rise.[4]

Molinæus does not accept this reasoning. If all money be raised proportionally, nobody in the same state is injured or does injury; for the prices of all things rise in the same proportion. The trouble comes when only part of the money is raised. Then prices do not rise proportionally, and those persons gain who happen to hold the raised pieces. When the weight of money is lessened, the value of the material is raised by so much; and, therefore, if a creditor should wish to have the defect in the material made good to him, he would receive too much value and

[1] Babelon, *Théorie Féodale de la Monnaie*, pp. 295, 296.

[2] Brants, *op. cit.*, p. 183.

[3] *Journ. des Econ.*, Dec., 1880, p. 453; Brants, *op. cit.*, pp. 188, 189.

[4] Oresme, *Traictie*, pp. 26, 60–63.

would have to give it back, leaving him the same number of pieces.[1] This, it is evident, is a rather questionable application of the *valor impositus*, of which we have already heard.

Although the effects of price changes were commented on by numerous writers during this period, there seems to have been little discussion of the process by which such changes worked themselves out. It was taken for granted, apparently, that prices rose because merchants asked more; at least, that is the explanation which we meet later, in writers who were familiar with the work of the Schoolmen. An exception, however, to this way of reasoning is to be noted early. Dubois seems to hold that debasement, by making it profitable to send out goods rather than money (which is no longer taken at its face value), leads to a greater demand for goods, and hence to higher prices.[2] This is a really acute analysis of the transition to higher domestic prices; and in an age when prices were much affected by the force of custom, it was of greater significance than later.

4. The Standard of Deferred Payments

The inequities which arise between debtors and creditors as a result of general changes in prices became so glaring during the debasements of the Middle Ages that there were many disputes as to what constituted just repayment in such cases. Neither Aristotle nor the Roman Law really offered much help to the mediæval writers in deciding the question;[3] but certain passages in these authors seemed to support the theory of the *valor impositus*, or legal value, which we have just considered. From this general theory of the value of money it followed, of course, that justice was done if the debtor repaid a sum whose legal numerary value was equal to that which he had borrowed. There was no attempt to distinguish between the legal and economic aspects of the question.

[1] Boyss, *Tractatus Varii*, pp. 319, 324.

[2] Landry, *Mutations des Monnaies dans l'Ancienne France*, p. 208 n.

[3] There is some evidence that the later Romans decided in favor of the strictly legal value of money in matters of this kind. Thomas, *op. cit.*, p. 57; Conigliani, *Questione Giuridica dei Pagamenti Monetarii*, p. 9.

It was not long, however, before the philosophers and canonists began to give weight to the *bonitas intrinseca* in their discussions of the value of money, and to reason, therefore, that in disputes of this kind the metal content of the coins repaid must be considered. This change of opinion was in time reflected in the attitude of the jurists also, especially in Italy, where the trouble was most acute. Accepting the general principle that the debtor should return a sum of money really equivalent to what he had borrowed, they began to give weight to the *current* value of the money; but the great practical difficulties of determining this led them to follow the canonists in accepting the intrinsic metal content as a sufficient criterion.[1] This, as Conigliani points out, was accurate enough in those days, when neither scarcity nor confidence served to enhance the value of coins. The principle of intrinsic value was at first applied only to payments in foreign money; but it was gradually extended to more and more cases, until it covered all except subsidiary money. In Italy and Germany it was widely accepted, but among the jurists of France and England it made no headway.[2]

Molinæus, whose rigid application of the *valor impositus* we noted in the last section, refused to follow the canonist reasoning as to the greater importance of the *bonitas intrinseca*, and held that, so far as the courts are concerned, the legal value must be accepted as final. On the other hand, he was plainly aware of the economic importance of the metal content of the coins, and was probably the first to make clear the distinction between these two aspects of the question.[3]

[1] Conigliani cites an isolated opinion of the canonists, which accepts current value as a basis of repayment (p. 11 n.).

[2] On all this, see Conigliani, *op. cit.*, pp. 7–25. Cf. section 2, above.

[3] Boyss, *Tractatus Varii*, pp. 314–322; Conigliani, *op. cit.*, pp. 28, 29.

CHAPTER VIII

OTHER NEW PROBLEMS

1. The Standard

Although there was little direct discussion regarding the standard, the general attitude of the Schoolmen seems to indicate acceptance of the established usage — bimetallism. Oresme's ideas may probably be taken as representative of the conclusions of earlier writers. More than one metal, he reasons, must be used, since gold is too scarce, and hence too valuable, to serve conveniently for small purchases.[1]

There is also little discussion of the ratio to be observed in coining money of different metals, and in tax and legal-tender regulations concerning such coins. In the *Hipparchus*, a dialogue long attributed to Plato, the ratio of 12: 1 is recognized as a matter of course;[2] but there is no attempt to explain or justify this, and the passage was doubtless unknown to the Schoolmen, anyway. Theoretical discussion was late in developing. Oresme, again, probably reflects the discussions of his predecessors in considerable degree. He stipulates that the proportion between gold and silver in the different coins should follow the "natural habitude or value"; and, in harmony with his general theory that the money of a state belongs to the people and not to the prince, insists that the community alone has the right to alter the ratio. The only reason for such an action would be a change in the supply of the metals.[3] The preoccupation of thinkers with the question of "just" and "natural" prices, and the lack of an adequate analysis of market value, checked further development of this idea for a considerable time. Biel follows Oresme without modification.[4]

1 Oresme, *Traictie*, pp. 14, 15.

2 Grote's Plato: *Hipparchus*, l. 231.

3 Oresme, *Traictie*, pp. 30–33.

4 Boyss, *Tractatus Varii*, p. 7.

2. The Coinage Prerogatives

The question of state control of coinage was never debated during this period. According to Roman Law, the right of coinage belonged to the emperor. The canonists, however, facing a very different political situation, held that it belonged to the Pope, Emperor, and every *supremus princeps*. No others might exercise it, unless the higher authority had granted it. Only under these conditions could the uniformity essential in a common measure be maintained.[1] Moreover, every country ought to have a money of its own. This honors the prince by bearing his image, and it is fitting that money, the *regula et mensura rerum*, should bear the image of the prince, the *regula hominum*. It is also more convenient.[2]

Oresme emphasizes the utilitarian rather than the legal aspect of the question. It was to avoid deception that coinage was placed in the hands of a public authority, he says; and the same reason establishes the undesirability of allowing vassals, and even foreign princes, to coin similar or poorer money. So important is this principle, that a people should fight for it if necessary. Having the disastrous effects of debasement all too vividly in mind, however, he is careful to qualify this statement by insisting that the money of a country belongs to the whole people. Its ownership is as clear as that of goods for which it is exchanged.[3] Biel follows Oresme pretty closely.[4]

This general agreement on the principle of state coinage was not paralleled by any consensus of opinion as to what charge should be exacted for the service. The legal right of the prince to collect seigniorage was early established by such diverse arguments as the right of property indicated by his effigy, the right to tax merchandise, and the inclusion of coinage in the royal patrimony — regarding it as part of the royal domain.[5] Many of the earlier debasements were defended by this last argument. Sim-

[1] Endemann, *op. cit.*, vol. ii, pp. 171, 172; Babelon, *op. cit.*, pp. 279–285.

[2] St. Thomas, *De Regimine Principum*, ii, 13.

[3] Oresme, *Traictie*, pp. 19–22.

[4] Boyss, *Tractatus Varii*, p. 7.

[5] *Revue d'Histoire des Doctrines Économiques et Sociales*, vol. v, pp. 343, 344.

ilar arguments were applied to the case of vassals and others holding the right from a higher authority. Not until the end of the thirteenth century did the law begin to recognize any limitations on the prince's right.

Of course, there were many protests before this against the evil results of the right in practice; but these were not against the principle itself, but against its abuse. In these discussions, it should be noted, it was not a question whether the prince might collect the expenses of coinage, but whether he might take any more, and if so, how much. At first the Schoolmen tried to steer a middle course between the danger of arbitrary exactions by the prince and the injustice or hopelessness of expecting him to bear the expenses himself, and appealed to his conscience. Thus St. Thomas recognizes the right of seigniorage, but urges that it be used with reserve and discretion.[1]

The ineffectiveness of such appeals, demonstrated by repeated abuses, gradually led to the formulation of more definite restrictions. The trend of the times appears in certain preliminary developments. Princes began to offer their protesting subjects various compromises, such as agreeing to give due warning of changes, to give the new money an easily distinguishable form, and, finally, to obtain the consent of the people or their representatives. As a result of these developments, there grew up the tradition that the right of seigniorage was subject to certain limitations — in particular, that the will of the people must control. According to Babelon, whose discussion of this topic is most illuminating, the first definite formulation of the right of the people is in the Apparatus of Pope Innocent IV (Pope 1243–54) on the Decretals, where the principle is laid down that the prince may not charge more than the actual expenses of coinage, except in cases of great necessity, and then only with the consent of the people. Perhaps the term "people" is not to be taken too literally in expressions of this kind; but the point is clear that the right

1 "Etsi liceat jus suum exigere in cudendo numisma, moderatus tamen esse debet princeps quicumque vel rex, sive in mutando, sive in diminuendo pondus vel metallum, quia hoc cadit in detrimentum populi, cum sit (moneta) rerum mensura." Babelon, *Théorie Féodale de la Monnaie*, pp. 315, 316. The reference is to the *De Regimine Principum*, ii, 13.

of seigniorage is beginning to be thought of in more qualified terms.[1]

This decision of the Decretals of course became the tradition of the Church, and the canonists insisted on it thereafter. Buridan seems to be satisfied to restrict profit-taking by the prince to cases of necessity;[2] but Oresme is more emphatic than Pope Innocent. Although the community, being the owners of the money, should bear the expense of its manufacture by paying an adequate seigniorage, of which any slight surplus may, indeed, be at the disposal of the prince, any further demands on his part must be regarded as tyranny, and contrary to natural and divine law. It is not enough, moreover, to say that the prince may take more in case of need, for he might pretend necessity; the people must decide. In case of real need, debasement is a cheap and equitable way of raising revenue, for he who has more pays more. It is also less likely to be resisted, because people do not feel it so much. In time of emergency these considerations may outweigh the objections.[3] Antonine of Florence and Biel accept Oresme's view.[4]

Some exceptions were taken, however, to this doctrine of the canonists, even as early as the fourteenth century. Bartolus, a contemporary of Buridan, held that money should be so regulated that it will be worth as much in bullion form as in coin, and saw clearly that this requires gratuitous coinage.[5] Molinæus also appears to object to all charge for coinage, saying that it is best to have the extrinsic value of the coins equal to their intrinsic value. This practice would have a double advantage: commerce could be carried on everywhere without the intervention of money-changers (*collybistarum*), and all temptation to counterfeiting would be removed, there being no profit in it. A third advantage might also be added, he continues, for under these conditions

[1] On all the above, see Babelon, *Théorie Féodale de la Monnaie*, pp. 289, 296, 297, 305–308, 315–332.

[2] *Zeitschr. für die ges. Staatswissenschaft*, vol. lx, p. 459.

[3] Oresme, *Traictie*, pp. 24, 48–59, 65–75.

[4] Ilgner, *op. cit.*, pp. 94, 95; Boyss, *Tractatus Varii*, p. 8. See also Schreiber, *op. cit.*, pp. 192, 193.

[5] Landry, *Mutations des Monnaies dans l'Ancienne France*, p. 70; Endemann, *op. cit.*, vol. ii, pp. 176, 177.

countries which have no mines can have as great abundance of money as others.[1]

3. The Coinage System

The problem of organizing the moneys of a country into an efficient system was opened up during this period, but there are only a few references to it. Oresme, without going into detail, advises that money should be of convenient shape and weight for handling, counting, and carrying, and with a durable impression that cannot easily be counterfeited. Early concern about a matter which later assumed the first importance among theorists and administrators — the maintenance of an adequate supply of money — is reflected in his principle that gold and silver should not be allowed in other uses until the money use is satisfied. He gives no indication, however, of what was to be considered a proper amount for currency purposes.[2]

More important for later theory were the discussions of the canonists concerning the status of the smaller coins. As these coins were peculiarly subject to debasement, the question presently arose whether a creditor must accept payment in such money. Thus Molinæus records that the Senate of Paris had decided this question in the negative, on the ground that such money was not made for carrying on commerce, but only for making change, and that it was inconveniently bulky in large sums. This reasoning did not appeal to Molinæus, but, on the whole, opinion was against him. Albertus Brunus, for example, says that in this question circumstances and customs must be considered; but that it is unreasonable to suppose that the creditor for a large sum expected to be repaid in small money;[3] and the citations of later writers indicate that this opinion had other supporters at the time.[4] The bad repute, moreover, of Molinæus — *ille Parisiensis* — among orthodox writers doubtless helped to minimize his influence. At any rate, it is enough for our purpose that this point was frequently discussed, and hence was likely to be familiar to later theorists.

[1] Boyss, *Tractatus Varii*, p. 317. [2] Oresme, *Traictie*, pp. 11, 12, 18, 19.

[3] Boyss, pp. 94, 95. [4] *E.g.*, in Klock, *Tractatus . . . de Ærario*, p. 515.

4. PRINCIPLES OF CIRCULATION

Among the most perplexing and disturbing of the currency disorders which troubled the Middle Ages was the disappearance from circulation of certain kinds of money. The earliest reference to this phenomenon seems to be the often-quoted lines of Aristophanes, in which he notes, without explaining, the fact that poor money seems to have taken the place of good in the city. "For neither do we employ these at all which are not adulterated . . . and alone correctly struck . . . but this vile copper, struck but yesterday . . . ," declares the chorus in the *Frogs*.[1] There is no other reference to it among classical writers, however, and even this can hardly be regarded as the statement of a general principle.

Henry of Ghent, who was the first of the mediæval writers to discuss the question, was interested in its ethical aspects, but his reasoning shows a clear grasp of the economic considerations involved. When the state allows or orders many kinds of coins to circulate together, it may happen, he says, that the value relations are so fixed, that one coin is worth more, on the basis of its weight, than its established price. In this case the possessor will be justified in withdrawing it from trade and disposing of it by weight, unless such action is prohibited. This discussion leaves no doubt as to the real cause of the disappearance of certain coins, but it makes no attempt to analyze the process further.[2]

Still more puzzling was the disappearance of one of the metals from circulation, which was particularly annoying when the extracted coins were the standard money of the country, in which people were accustomed to express accounts and contracts. As early as the fourteenth century, we find evidence that the problem was receiving attention. In a memoir written by some unknown mint-master we are told of the danger of not "adjusting gold and silver," since in such a case, as he expresses it, "sometimes silver eats gold, sometimes gold eats silver." [3]

[1] Aristophanes, *Frogs*, lines 718–725.
[2] Schreiber, *op. cit.*, p. 134.
[3] Brants, *op. cit.*, p. 189.

As a recognition of the existence of a tendency — an "economic law" — this is better than Oresme's reference to the difficulty. Nowadays, he complains, everyone presumes and offers to sell his gold or silver money according to his will, disregarding the price set by the prince. Thus it has come about that no one can get gold except according to the will of the owner, who sells it just like other riches, which is exactly contrary to the primary purpose for which money was instituted. And "par ceste tollérance, se part et diminue l'or d'ung pays et se transporte en ung autre, où il se aloue à plus hault pris." [1]

In discussing the effects of debasement he makes some interesting points. As a result of this practice, he says, gold and silver leave the country for places where they will have a higher value; and outsiders, moreover, coin the inferior pieces and bring them in. This attempt to describe and analyze the process by which the better coins were extracted is of great interest; for not only does it probably express ideas already held in Oresme's time, — by his own admission he is no innovator, — but its viewpoint will be seen to underlie many later discussions. Several points in it are to be noted. The better pieces are declared to be lost through export; and except for the hint of some kind of an exchange, in the clause "where they will have a higher value," no motive is established for this sending away of treasure; we are not told what the exporter gets for his money. In the second place, there is supposed to be a kind of replacement process, through the sending in of debased coin made abroad. It is not implied, however, that this has any connection with the export of good coins just mentioned; and there is no explanation of how the foreigners dispose of these coins, in order to reap the gains which Oresme assures us they obtain. The working of purely domestic influences is ignored.[2]

This tendency to place the blame on foreigners, and to assume that the displaced coins are exported, although an inadequate explanation, even for those times, was a more accurate description of conditions than it would be to-day. The absence of free coinage probably did encourage counterfeiting among foreigners who wished to pay debts in the less valuable coins; and the disor-

[1] Oresme, *Traictie*, p. 22.

[2] *Ibid.*, pp. 59, 60.

ganization and mysteriousness of foreign exchange doubtless increased the possibilities of this method of taking advantage of coinage irregularities. In part, however, these ideas are only a reflection of the general distrust of foreigners; and despite the deterrent effect of heavy penalties, the activities of the prince's own subjects were by no means a negligible factor in the coinage disorders.

An attitude much like Oresme's appears in a report made in 1412 to Charles VI, by the authorities of the University of Paris, in which it is asserted that, through the diminution in the fineness of the coins, "la bonne monnaie est expulsée, car les changes et les Lombars cueillent tout le bon or, et font payement de nouvelle monnaie."[1] This differs, however, from Oresme's account, by implying that the export and import of coin were in the same hands, and somehow involved in commercial transactions. As a description of what was going on, this shows considerable insight; but it leaves much to be desired in the way of explanation of the facts.

Molinæus seems to refer to the phenomenon, but is not clear, and it is open to question whether he grasped the full significance of the discussion. If the extrinsic value of the money exceeds the intrinsic, he says, a country having no mines will be relatively flooded with bad money, for outsiders will bring in proportionately less money and take away proportionately more goods for it. Hence the country will become poorer in the "sinews of war and the state."[2] This may not refer to a displacing process at all, but merely to the reduced value of the money received for exports.

5. The Problem of Reform

Although the mediæval scholars were not much concerned with questions of practical policy, we find a few references, toward the end of the period, which indicate that such questions were beginning to attract attention. In Oresme's discussion of alteration of the coinage some general principles are laid down which have some bearing on the problem of reform. The imprint of money

[1] Brants, *op. cit.*, p. 189. [2] Boyss, *Tractatus Varii*, pp. 317, 318.

may be changed, he holds, only when it has been counterfeited, or when the old is too worn for further use. The names of money should never be changed, for it confuses the relation between the pieces. Coins of a new weight should be introduced only under new names, for double measures are abominable to God. The material should be changed only when there is not enough of the metal formerly used. These negative principles, however, are all obviously aimed against the abuse of the royal coinage prerogative, and give little positive help for cases where currency disorders make some remedy imperative.[1]

Somewhat later Biel touched on a different aspect of the problem. It would perhaps be better, he remarks, to correct the coinage ratio by coining gold pieces lighter, in order that revenues and prices established in the case of other things may remain unchanged and nobody be defrauded. The new pieces should have a distinctive form, and the currency of the old pieces need not be forbidden.[2]

Molinæus, with the characteristic intemperance of language which doubtless contributed to making his doctrines anathema among the orthodox, declares that the idea that it is good to raise the value of a certain kind of money under some circumstances, — for example, when a large amount of it has been exported from the country, — "is so stupid as to fill one with amazement." Foreigners will not for that reason bring any more of such coins back, or any more quickly, but will take away all the more goods for what they do bring. They don't need our goods any more because gold is dearer, but simply get them cheaper.[3] I need hardly remind the reader that Molinæus's name is not conspicuous among the early expounders of "Gresham's Law."

[1] Oresme, *Traictie*, pp. 30–43.
[2] Boyss, *Tractatus Varii*, p. 5.
[3] *Ibid.*, p. 320.

CHAPTER IX

SUMMARY

All the analyses worked out by the writers of Greece and Rome were adopted during the Middle Ages, after the works of Aristotle had found their way to western Europe, and many received interesting elaboration. The statement of the functions of money was not appreciably improved; but the origin of money, especially the inconvenience of barter, and the qualities desirable in the money material, were explained more fully and clearly. Much of this advance is to be credited to John Buridan of the University of Paris. The influence of money on mankind began to be regarded somewhat more favorably.

Aristotle's theory of value was made the basis of mediæval discussions of this topic, and gained some in precision in the hands of the Schoolmen; but the apparent conflict between this theory and the legal theory of the *valor impositus* long puzzled thinkers. Gradually, however, the *valor impositus* came to be subordinated to the *bonitas intrinseca*.

The important consequences of changes in the value of money, which Aristotle had not mentioned, were forced upon the attention of the writers of the Middle Ages by the serious debasements in the twelfth and following centuries. From the beginning of the fourteenth century it was recognized that certain classes — the receivers of fixed incomes and other creditors — were adversely affected by the price changes which result from the currency disorders. With regard to the question of deferred payments under these conditions, there was a difference of opinion, some holding that the legal value should be the only factor considered, and others arguing that the debtor was bound to repay a sum containing as much fine metal as he had received, with the latter point of view gaining ground. Molinæus, however, stood by the former opinion, distinguishing clearly between the legal and the economic aspects of money.

Other new problems also engaged the attention of the Schoolmen and canonists. The question of the standard was merely broached, tacit acceptance of the bimetallic *status quo*, and inadequate ideas about market value serving to side-track discussion. The coinage prerogatives, however, especially seigniorage, were discussed at considerable length, writers gradually coming to agree that the prince might not collect more for coinage than enough to cover expenses, except in emergencies, and then only with the consent of the people. In this point of view the canonists were strengthened by the interpretation given the Decretals by Pope Innocent IV.

The canonists also began a discussion, important for later theory, concerning the treatment to be accorded fractional coins, which, being especially subject to debasement, were likely to be refused by creditors. The general conclusion was that such money was not intended for commerce, and therefore creditors could not be required to accept it.

A final problem brought to the fore by the coinage disorders was that of the disappearance of certain coins from circulation. By the fourteenth century it was perceived that this was the natural result of economic considerations, and some attempt had been made to analyze the process by which the more valuable coins are extracted. In general, it was believed that such money was exported, and foreign counterfeiters were held to be chiefly responsible.

The question of procedure in reforming the currency, destined to occupy a large place in later discussions, was barely hinted at.

PART III

THE BEGINNINGS OF THE MODERN AGE

CHAPTER X

INTRODUCTORY

THE sixteenth century saw great changes in the intellectual, economic, and political life of western Europe. Although the break with the past was not wholly abrupt, as we saw in Chapter V, certain new tendencies became so conspicuous as to justify us in regarding this period as the beginning of a new era. Prominent among these was the development of secular influences. The Scholastic and canonist traditions still lived, as shown by such writings as the *Tractatus Contractuum et Usurarum* of Molinæus, which we considered in Part II; but they were now overshadowed by the interests and activities which had been revived by the Renaissance. The study of ethics and politics was no longer left to ecclesiastics; more and more attention was given to science; business and commercial interests came rapidly to the fore. Great discoveries and dynastic rivalries had far-reaching effects.

All these tendencies are reflected in the development of monetary theory. Some of the doctrines of the past were handed on without significant modification; but many were elaborated and refined, and some were quite transformed. There was a marked change in point of view. Instead of treating monetary questions incidentally, in connection with ethical questions, as was so generally the case in the Middle Ages, the writers now began to study the phenomena more as problems in practical statecraft, to pay more attention to technical details, and to express their ideas in the more general phrases of abstract science. Even the ideas which they accepted without change generally gained in clarity in their hands.

The tendency toward secularization is plainly seen from a survey of the important names of the period in our field: they are all laymen. First in point of time comes Copernicus. The coinage of Poland and Prussia being in great disorder, the King of Poland had consulted about the matter with various advisers, among them Copernicus. The ideas advanced by the latter were embodied a little later (1526), at the request of the King, in a brief treatise, *Monete Cudende Ratio*. Although this does not mark any great advance over the best work of the Schoolmen, it is notable for its detached scientific point of view, and for its clear-cut statement of some principles which earlier writers had been inclined to express in more tentative form.

The controversy over the Saxon coinage reform, which arose a few years later (1530), is of less importance for the development of the theory, but of considerable historical interest. When Albert and Ernest, sons of the Elector Frederick, divided Saxony between them in 1481, it was arranged that their mining and coinage prerogatives should continue to be exercised in common. Friction presently developed, especially after the succession, in the Ernestine line, of Johann der Beständige, who opposed the sound money policy of the Albertines. The question was vigorously debated by two anonymous pamphleteers, of whom the supporter of the Albertine faction was by far the more capable. His work displays a fairly clear grasp of some important economic principles, but neither improved nor added to the ideas of the Schoolmen.

The important *Discourse of the Common Weal of this Realm of England* (about 1550), now generally attributed to John Hales, contains many striking references to the question of money, which show that the writer was conversant with the best thought on the subject and clearly understood most of the monetary phenomena of his time. Behind its quaint and often picturesque language we can discern a point of view and a range of interests quite different from what we saw in the writings of the Scholastics.

By the middle of the century Europe was beginning to feel the effects of the new supplies of the precious metals from the mines of America, and prices were rising markedly. At first, the explanation of the rising prices was naturally sought in the cause with which people had already become familiar — debasement; but it was not long before it was seen that this was inadequate, that the plentifulness of gold and silver was causing their value to fall. Though suggested by earlier writers, this point was first made clear by Jean Bodin, in his *Réponse aux paradoxes de M. de*

Malestroit touchant l'encherissement de toutes les choses et des monnaies (1568). Monetary questions are also treated in his *Six Livres de la République* (1576), sometimes following the best tradition, but often with marked originality and independence. The great reputation of this work caused Bodin's ideas on monetary questions to become widely known among later scholars.

The growing importance of business men and business interests is shown by the two names with which we end this survey, Bernardo Davanzati and Gasparo Scaruffi, both Italian merchants. The former had many literary interests, having prepared a translation of Tacitus and a history of the Reformation in England under Henry VIII; and he was famous for the vigorous Italian prose style which he had carefully developed. In 1582 he published a brief *Lezione delle Monete*, which on some points is of the first importance. An English translation of it was published in 1696. Scaruffi, who, besides his work as merchant and banker, was for some years assayer of the mint at Reggio, published in 1582, under the curious title *Alitinonfo* (from Greek words meaning "true light"), a treatise covering many practical questions in detail. Some of his suggestions were very bold, especially for those times; and although the work is not very important on its theoretical side, these practical discussions lend it great interest.

CHAPTER XI

TRADITIONAL DOCTRINES

PROGRESS in monetary theory during the sixteenth century did not always follow the lead of earlier writers. Some points which the Schoolmen had taken over from Aristotle and elaborated with much pains received little attention; and some of their tentative solutions of new problems remained undeveloped.

The functions of money, when mentioned at all, are treated along Aristotelian lines, the measurement of values being stressed, but conceived as a phase of the process of exchange.[1] Hales repeats the idea of a store of value by calling money a "storehouse of anie commoditie ye would haue," [2] and, from his references to Aristotle in this part of the dialogue, appears to be following him on this point.

Hales also repeats in vigorous style the idea that the evils supposed to arise from the use of money are really the result of our own defects. It is quite true, he admits, that money "drives men to all kinde of mischeife," but one might as well complain that iron and steel are the "instrumentes of muche murder and slaugheter amonge men." It would be as fatal for a nation to give up all its gold and silver as to abandon its tools and weapons. The trouble comes from the "evell usinge" of money.[3] This is the opinion of Davanzati also.[4]

Except for Nifo's elaboration (1531) of Aristotle's statement of the difficulties of barter, — he was a profound student of the Greek philosopher,[5] — we meet no discussion of the origins of money in this period till the time of Hales.[6] His remarks about

[1] This is the impression given by Copernicus (*Monete Cudende Ratio*, p. 49); Hales (*Discourse*, p. 73); Scaruffi (*Discorso*, pp. 141, 142); Bodin refers only to the measurement of value (*Six Bookes*, p. 687).

[2] Hales, *Discourse*, pp. 73, 114.

[3] *Ibid.*, pp. 114, 115.

[4] Davanzati, *Lezione*, p. 36.

[5] Fornari, *Teorie Economiche nelle Provincie Napolitane*, vol. i, p. 105.

[6] Reference should perhaps be made to Copernicus's statement (*op. cit.*, p. 51) of the purpose of coinage, in which he follows Oresme.

early methods of exchange show a knowledge of what had been written about this since Aristotle. He says the practice of barter, which is said to have existed "in the time of homer," must have been "verie cumbersome," since it "would Require muche cariadge of wares up and downe," and "hard weare it readely to find that the one might paie the other of equall valew." The perishability of commodities, moreover, is a further source of difficulty in barter.[1] Agricola has a similar discussion, giving three arguments to show the superiority of the use of money over barter: money is more adapted to the equalizing of values; it is generally cheaper to transport; and finally, many people may not need our wares, although we need theirs.[2]

Davanzati's treatment of this question is quite interesting. Men, he writes, need several things for the preservation and maintenance of life; but, as no climate produces all things, and no one is fit for all trades, it arises that no man toils for himself alone, and all good things are communicated and enjoyed by means of trade. After pointing out the inconveniences of barter, in about the same terms that had been used by earlier writers,[3] he goes on to say that "necessity, the mother of inventions, taught men to choose a place, where many meeting from different parts with their commodities might the more easily supply one another," and thus arose fairs and markets. The convenience of these opened men's eyes to a greater, "that as they had chosen a place, so they might appoint some thing and make it equivalent to all others," and they accordingly agreed that everything might be given or received for a certain quantity of money. Gold and silver were at first used in unwrought pieces, as they came to hand; but, "as additions are easily made to inventions," they were next weighed, and still later stamped to show their weight and fineness without further test. The earliest coins bore the figure of a sheep, "the riches of the ancients consisting then in their flocks."[4]

[1] Hales, *Discourse*, pp. 47, 48, 71.

[2] Roscher, *National-Oekonomik in Deutschland*, p. 51.

[3] Perhaps it is significant that he fails to mention Aristotle's point about the necessity of equating values, in view of the decline of the latter's prestige during the Renaissance.

[4] Davanzati, *Lezione*, pp. 22–26.

A little later appeared the curious theological interpretations of Spangenberg, which, though of no value as theory or history, are interesting examples of a method which was probably fairly common in some quarters. The oldest coins, he says, bore ships and a Janus-head, undoubtedly because Noah wished thereby to set up an eternal remembrance of his rescue. Janus is Noah himself, who belonged to two ages. The ox on many coins is a reminder that we should not esteem trade and money too highly and thereby neglect agriculture, which is more important.[1] One would hardly think, in reading these passages, that a thousand years had passed since the time of Isidore of Seville.

There was little attempt to improve upon what earlier writers had said about the qualities needed in the money material. Nifo stresses the point, implied in Aristotle, that it is to ensure general acceptability that money should be made of a valuable material;[2] and Hales gives an excellent version of the ideas developed by the later Schoolmen.[3] The latter also refers to the idea, met as early as the time of the Greeks, that it makes no difference what money is made of.[4] Bodin's remark that the uncertain price of copper in all places makes it unfit for money probably indicates that he considered stability of value desirable in the material used for money.[5]

Although there were great advances in the analysis of the value of money, as we shall see, only one writer of this period showed any grasp of an equally important value problem: the ratio between the metals. Hales merely declares that the proportion between the metals cannot be changed by any prince, or it would have been done long ago by some needy ruler. It is still what it was in the time of "Diuinus plato." [6]

[1] Roscher, *op. cit.*, pp. 168, 169.

[2] Fornari, *op. cit.*, vol. i, pp. 105, 106.

[3] "Thearfore weare the mettalles of gould and siluer devised, as wares in so small weight most in value, and least combersome to carie, and least subject to detriment or hurt in the cariage therof, and maie be cut and devided in most peices and porcions with out anie losse, . . . apteste to Receave forme or marke, and most currant in all places." Hales, *Discourse*, pp. 71, 72, 74, 75.

[4] *Ibid.*, p. 69.

[5] Bodin, *Six Bookes*, p. 691.

[6] Hales, *Discourse*, p. 109.

Bodin, however, recognized more clearly that the question of the ratio is really an aspect of the general problem of value. Though he thinks it has continued at 12:1 with striking regularity for some two thousand years, he admits that there have been variations, and that these may occur from changes in the supply, or in the demand for the metals in the arts. Such variations are very gradual, however, and consequently we may reasonably insist that the same ratio be followed in all countries. A general trade over the world cannot allow any great alterations except by common consent.[1]

Even after Bodin's time, very crude views persisted. Scaruffi, for example, declares that the ratio 12:1 is sufficiently proved by "Divine Plato's acceptance of it," and that it is ordained by God: there are always fewer of the more precious things.[2] We shall meet similar ideas later.

The mediæval opinion that coinage should be in the control of the sovereign found full acceptance in the sixteenth century. Copernicus believes such control an indispensable condition for general acceptability;[3] and Bodin includes the right to coin money among the attributes specified in his famous theory of sovereignty.[4] Davanzati's reasoning that private citizens may be suspected of fraud, but not the prince "who is the father of all,"[5] is reminiscent of Oresme.

These statements of the sovereign's right to coin money were often accompanied by warnings regarding its exercise. Copernicus declared that a necessary preliminary to currency reform is the cessation of coinage by a great number of mints. A diversity of mints prevents uniformity in the value of money, for it is difficult to supervise them. There should be a single mint in the land of each sovereign.[6] Bodin agrees with this reasoning.[7] That the trouble here referred to was common appears from the comment of the reformer Zwingli, that it is a wonder the privilege had not been granted to the tinkers.[8]

[1] Bodin, *Six Bookes*, pp. 690–692.
[2] Scaruffi, *Discorso*, pp. 84, 175.
[3] Copernicus, *op. cit.*, pp. 67–69.
[4] Bodin, *Six Bookes*, pp. 175, 176.
[5] Davanzati, *Lezione*, p. 30.
[6] Copernicus, *op. cit.*, p. 67.
[7] Bodin, *Six Bookes*, p. 696.
[8] *Zeitschr. für die ges. Staatswissenschaft*, vol. xvi, p. 612.

The problem of deferred payments under an unstable currency was not discussed at much length during the period, but such references as we find appear to follow the Canonist tradition. Thus Copernicus recognizes the need of providing for difficulties of this kind when a reform of the coinage is undertaken, and cites a decree at Malburg in 1418, which specified how the payment was to be made in such a case.[1] Hales also points out this need, and suggests that a change in contracts proportional to the change in the coinage should be arranged for.[2] Both these statements, it is evident, imply agreement with the Canonist view that the *bonitas intrinseca* must be considered — that an equal weight of metal should be returned by the debtor. Bodin recommends that, after a recoinage, rents and other fixed money dues should be paid "eu esgard a la valeur que tenoit le sol au temps quelles furent constituees"; [3] and Scaruffi made a similar suggestion with regard to debts.[4]

[1] Copernicus, *op. cit.*, p. 79.

[2] Hales, *Discourse*, p. 119.

[3] Bodin, *Les Six Livres de la Républqiue*, p. 699.

[4] Scaruffi, *Discorso*, pp. 103, 104.

CHAPTER XII

THE VALUE OF MONEY

1. Early Discussions

During the first half of the sixteenth century the theory of prices underwent no great change. The tendency to minimize the importance of the *valor impositus* and to identify the value of a coin with the value of the metal in it, which we noted above (Chapter VII), continued to make headway; and as a result of the growing seriousness of debasement, it came to occupy the foremost place in discussions of prices. Less attention was given to the causes which govern the value of the money material, while more emphasis was placed on the effects of alterations in the weight of the coins.[1] The effects of debasement were by no means universally understood,[2] but they were generally recognized by the theorists.

Copernicus agrees with the general principle we have just outlined, but points out some qualifications. The value of a coin "has the goodness of the material as a basis," it is true, but it may be somewhat more or less than the value of the material. The latter happens when money is "too much multiplied," that is, when so much money has been coined that men seek bullion more. This reasoning obviously applies only to cases where neither free coinage nor freedom to melt the coin exists, but he does not mention either of these qualifications. Other considerations may also affect the value of a particular coin, as in the case of the Hungarian ducats, which, though not quite pure, exchange weight for weight for pure gold, because of the value of the guaranty con-

[1] The legal value was not without supporters, as shown by such writings as Molinæus, *Tractatus Contractuum et Usurarum*, referred to in Part II. Grimaudet also seems to favor the legal theory. Bodin de Saint-Laurent, *Les Idées Monétaires et Commerciales de Jean Bodin*, p. 78.

[2] Thus, in 1506, Louis XII complained of the high prices at which gold and silver were being sold, and blamed the goldsmiths and other merchants. (*Rev. d'Econ. Pol.*, vol. xv, p. 2.) The high prices were doubtless largely due to currency disorders.

veyed by their stamp. It remains true, however, that the metal content of the piece is of the greatest importance.[1]

In the Saxon coinage controversy of 1530 the unknown supporter of the Albertine policy makes much of this. The value of money is measured according to what it "selbst von Silber und Metall in sich hatt und hellt." The coinage stamp, or the temporary opinion of the populace, makes no real difference; for, eternally as nature, a grain of silver remains what it is. Proof of this can be seen in the action of merchants. They regard the silver content of the pieces, not their number, and hence they charge less when one pays them in good, that is, heavy, money: there is as much silver in the fewer coins they receive. This is the reason for the high price of silver nowadays; it is paid for in bad money. Hence the proposal to coin money lighter, according to the greater price of silver, is an "eigennützigerr vortheilhafftiger griff." As often as you changed the coins, silver would rise, and this would continue till the coins became "eitel kupffer."

He barely hints at the causes which determine the value of the metal itself. This is in his rejoinder to his opponent that high prices are not caused by lack of money but quite the contrary, "denn wer kein gelt hat der keufft selten thewer." Here he seems to recognize the influence of supply on the value of the metals — for the value of money is simply that of the metals. There is, moreover, just a suggestion of the influence of demand in his remark that the value of silver could not be raised unless it were esteemed more highly in all nations, for only then would there be no market where the merchant could get more silver for his wares. He seems to be thinking of some kind of agreement in the above reasoning, however, and not much importance can be attached to it. Finally, we should add that he appears not to grasp the full significance of this price theory, for he gives increase of population and lavish consumption as further causes of high prices.[2]

[1] Copernicus, *op. cit.*, pp. 51, 53, 63, 73.

[2] Lotz, *Drei Flugschriften*, pp. 10–16, 98–114; Zielenziger, *op. cit.*, pp. 138–155; Roscher, pp. 108–110. The influence of quantity had apparently been touched upon earlier in this controversy, for the supporter of Duke Ernest mentions the action of the merchants at Zeitz, who protested against flooding the country with money, on the ground that this would cause its value to fall. (Lotz, p. 62.)

As may be inferred from the reference to him in the above paragraph, the supporter of Duke Ernest was much inferior to his opponent. He seems to ascribe high prices to such diverse causes as peace, prosperity of mining, good money, bad money, plenty of money, lack of money, and monopoly, and it is impossible to give an intelligible account of his views. The one idea that seems at all definitely held is that the value of the coins should be so fixed as to correspond accurately to the market "price" of silver.[1]

2. The Price Revolution

By the middle of the century Europe had begun to feel the effect on prices of the great supplies of the precious metals from the New World. The cause, however, of these disturbing changes was not at first understood, partly, I believe, because of the almost exclusive emphasis which had been placed on the demand aspect of the value question, and partly because of the more obvious influence of debasement on prices. Some writers, indeed, mentioned the coming of the new supplies, only to ignore their influence a few pages later when discussing prices. In the case of Frank, this is the more readily accounted for, as Roscher says, because of the fact that he considered the value of money to be a matter of human opinion;[2] but in Agricola the inconsistency is not so easily explained, for he not only mentions the American discoveries, but develops a clear-cut theory that the value of the metals depends upon the uses to which they can be put, and their scarcity.[3] Perhaps his failure to note the influence on prices of the new supplies is due to his failure to emphasize the identity of the value of money and that of its metal content.

It was exclusively this last aspect of the question, on the other hand, which interested John Hales. The rise in prices he considers due simply to debasement. When the prince, he says, tried

[1] Lotz, pp. 40–48, 54. He also gives just a hint of the influence of quantity on the value of the precious metals, saying that silver was formerly cheaper because the supply from the mines was larger; but he does not connect this idea with the theory of prices at all. (*Ibid.*, pp. 58–60.)

[2] Roscher, *op. cit.*, pp. 94, 95.

[3] *Ibid.*, pp. 51, 52; *Zeitschr. für die ges. Staatswissenschaft*, vol. xvi, p. 606.

to stamp half a pound as a pound, the coins circulated till it was discovered, and then their value fell to half; and thus we see that, with the few undebased pieces still in circulation, one can buy as many things as of old. This is largely due to the fact that foreign merchants, who do not come to buy in the country, and hence disregard our rating of the new money, raise their prices when the metal in the coins is diminished.[1]

The same point of view is found in the *Paradoxes* of Malestroit, which called forth Bodin's famous reply. His principal thesis is that, although prices are higher in France than formerly, goods are not really dearer, because they sell for no more gold or silver than formerly. He does not say explicitly that prices are higher because there is less metal in the coins, but that would seem to be the implication. It is not clear, moreover, whether he regarded this as a normal result, for he adds that in these matters kings have always had to follow the "disordered will of the people."[2]

What seems to have been the first reference to the influence of the American supplies of the metals has been pointed out by Bodin de Saint-Laurent in Noël du Fail's *Balivernes et contes d'Eutrapel*, published in 1548. In this work the author remarks, almost parenthetically, "du temps de Lupolde, ce qui coûtait cent sols vaut ce jour dix livres, ce qui est à cause des pays nouvellement trouvés et des minières d'or et d'argent que les Espagnols et Portugais en apportent."[3] A similar passage has been noted by Professor Merriman in Gómara's *Annals of the Emperor Charles V*, probably written about 1557. Prices, he says, were much lower in 1500 than now, "á causa, segun mi juizio, de la mucha plata y oro que de las Indias á nos han venido."[4] Neither of these tantalizingly brief statements of such novel doctrine appears to have attracted any attention.

The first writer to make clear the connection between the rise of prices and the abundant importations from the mines of America, and the first to give due emphasis to the influence of the available supply of the precious metals was Jean Bodin. This was first

[1] Hales, *Discourse*, pp. 42, 43, 77, 78, 104, 107.

[2] Bodin de Saint-Laurent, *op. cit.*, pp. 15, 16, 85.

[3] *Ibid.*, pp. 34, 35.

[4] Gómara, *Annals*, pp. lii, 162.

brought out in his *Réponse aux Paradoxes de M. de Malestroit touchant l'encherissement de toutes choses et des monnoyes*, published in 1568. Malestroit, as we have already said, ascribed the rise in prices wholly to debasement, and Bodin first demonstrated that the diminution in the weight of the coins was by no means commensurate with the change in prices. For this change he assigns five causes: the greater abundance of gold and silver, monopolies, scarcity of commodities, indulgence of kings and lords, and debasement. The first is the "principal and almost only" cause, and he is proud of having discovered an idea on so important a subject.

This effect of increased supply, it is important to note, he regards as neither peculiar to money nor unprecedented in history. The same thing, he declares, happened in Rome when Paulus Æmilius and, later, Julius Cæsar brought great stores of the precious metals to the city from foreign countries. Then as now it was the abundance of gold and silver "qui cause le mépris d'icelui et la cherté des choses prisées." To make the matter clearer, he gives examples from other commodities, and recalls how the Queen of Sheba brought so many precious stones to Jerusalem that they lost almost all value, while the Spaniards found that in the New World hammers and knives were much more valuable than pearls, because they were so much scarcer. Thus the value of gold and silver is considered subject to the same laws as other commodities, and the value of money is simply that of the metal of which it is made.

Although Bodin was doubtless acquainted with the Scholastic discussions, which had emphasized the influence of demand upon value, he almost entirely neglects this aspect of the problem. The only reference to it is his remark that unless princes punish the lavish use of gold in plate, gilding, and the like, the price of gold must rise.

Three of the subordinate causes of high prices which Bodin mentioned — monopoly, scarcity, luxury — are not so properly causes of general high prices as of high prices for particular commodities, and it might, therefore, seem that in mentioning them along with debasement and abundance of the precious metals he was confusing two different questions. This, however, I do not believe to be the case. In the first place, he assigned these causes to account for a particular situation, and in such a discussion these considerations are relevant; in the second place, he himself refers to the distinction to be made, and speaks of the change in the supply of gold and silver as operating independently of the "particular changes which cause the prices of things to rise above the ordinary, as in the case of provisions in time of famine." [1]

Bodin has been called the first great quantity theorist, and the impressive roll of later adherents of this theory has been cited as evidence of the extent of his influence.[2] The first of these two statements seems to me misleading. It is true that he was the first to give the influence of quantity on the value of the precious metals the importance it deserved; but he in no way implied that this was at all different in kind or in degree from the effect on values in general. The content of the modern "quantity theory" is quite different, however, and it is by no means true that any one who believes in the influence of quantity on the value of money is to be classed as one of its supporters. The second statement contains more truth, though perhaps not in just the sense that the author intended. Bodin's emphasis on the influence of quantity seems undoubtedly responsible for the rise, a little later in the century, of a theory which wholly subordinated the influence of demand, and held, moreover, that changes in the supply showed their effects in a way which was essentially different from that observed in other commodities. These writers are the real ancestors of the modern "quantity theory."

The immediate effect of Bodin's theory, especially in the field of practical affairs, was negligible. Not only did current opinion explain the prevailing high prices by very different causes, but legislation went contrary to his reasoning. In 1575 a petition addressed to Henry III took substantially the same view as Malestroit, and so does Garrault three years later. Debasement and similar practices are blamed for the rise in prices, but there is no hint as to the causes determining the value of the money metal.[3]

[1] Bodin, *Six Bookes*, pp. 666, 667, 692; Bodin de Saint-Laurent, *op. cit.*, pp. 17, 20–29, 84, 85.

[2] Dubois, *Hist. des Doctr. Écon.*, pp. 185, 186.

[3] Bodin de Saint-Laurent, *op. cit.*, pp. 35 *ff*.

The first evidence of Bodin's influence appears in an anonymous *Discours sur les causes de l'extrême cherté qui est aujourd'huy en France et sur les moyens d'y remédier*, published in 1574. This contains such obvious borrowings from Bodin that it has been attributed to him by some. It is doubtful if this is true, for the author so far misunderstood Bodin's theory as to give, as a further cause of high prices, the gathering of great quantities of the precious metals in plate, etc. In 1580 appeared a *Traicté des finances de France*, perhaps by the same author as the above *Discours*, which likewise contains whole phrases copied from Bodin.[1]

Outside of France the first to apply this reasoning to explain the rise in prices seems to have been W. S., the unknown individual who, in 1581, published as his own a revised version of John Hales's *Discourse of the Common Weal*. The most notable of the revisions was the addition to the causes of high prices of "the great store and plenty of treasure." It is, of course, impossible to determine whether this change was due to the influence of Bodin; but it seems reasonable to think that the rather unskillful W. S. did not develop the idea independently. This is the more probable in view of the fact that Bodin's works had certainly already reached England. Bodin had been there, and had been received at court; his famous work on the *Republic* (in which these ideas are mentioned incidentally) was quite widely read there; and, finally, he himself tells us that his *Réponse* to Malestroit was translated in 1569 by order of the English Chancellor — a point which seems to have been overlooked in discussions of this question.[2]

Fourteen years after the publication of Bodin's *Réponse* to Malestroit, appeared Davanzati's *Lezione delle Monete*, in which the relation between the supply of money and its value is worked out in a new way. "All these [earthly things which satisfy men's wants] are, by the consent of nations, worth all the gold (and in this I include silver and copper) that is wrought: therefore all men covet all the gold to buy all the things, to satisfy all their wants, to be happy. The parts follow the whole: therefore, how

[1] Bodin de Saint-Laurent, *op. cit.*, pp. 40–43.

[2] *Ibid.*, pp. 43, 44; Bodin, *Six Bookes*, p. 691.

much of a man's happiness . . . depends on a thing, so much is it worth of all his gold and labor." The value of coins is identical with that of their metal content, for the seller of a commodity expects so much metal in return, not so many stamps or pieces.

This line of reasoning is not worked out further, but the implication seems to be that changes in the supply of the money metals would cause proportionate changes in their value. Davanzati does not reason quite consistently, however, for he remarks, only a few paragraphs later, that, when all the gold in Peru and the Indies has been transported into Europe, it will become a drug, and either some scarcer material must be found to make money of, or barter will be returned to. This conclusion would not seem to follow from the principle that all goods are worth all the gold, silver, and copper, but rather from a consideration of the influence of demand upon the value of the metals.[1]

[1] Davanzati, *Lezione*, pp. 32, 35, 40 *ff*.

CHAPTER XIII

NEW LIGHT ON OLD PROBLEMS

1. The Coinage Prerogatives

The general acceptance by mediæval writers of the principle of collecting seigniorage, at least to cover the expense of coinage, was not paralleled in the writers of the sixteenth century. Copernicus would have the coins contain enough alloy to offset the expense of manufacture, but he opposes any profit-taking even for emergencies, thus breaking with Scholastic tradition.[1] Hales, however, conceded debasement in case of great need.[2]

Bodin, although he held that the prince is bound by the law of nations not to alter money to the loss of his subjects or of foreigners, thought it would be better to lay a tax on the people to pay the expenses of the mint, and give up seigniorage altogether.[3] Davanzati advocates the same course more explicitly. To take away all temptation to seeking gain through debasement, the simplest plan is to command that money be so regulated that it may pass without expense from bullion into coin and back. This, to be sure, puts the expense on the mint, but it is no different from paying for soldiers, magistrates, and other public services.[4]

Davanzati's very enlightened view did not win immediate favor. Although Scaruffi concedes that the prince may bear all or part of the expense of the mint, for the honor and glory of it, he thinks it would be preferable to collect payment from those who have the coining done. For this plan he claims several advantages. It is fair, because it puts the expense on those to whom the coinage is a direct convenience; it will encourage the manufacture of coins of greater fineness; and will diminish fraud, complexity, and confusion. In any case, however, the expense should not be deducted from the coins, for this is usually abused; and,

[1] Copernicus, *op. cit.*, p. 69.

[2] Hales, *Discourse*, pp. 87, 115–117.

[3] Bodin, *Six Bookes*, pp. 687, 696.

[4] Davanzati, *Lezione*, pp. 45, 46.

moreover, since the expense is not in proportion to the value of the coins, its deduction would upset the ratio between the metals and between the various coins. And finally, an expected objection is met by the assurance that the expense would be too small to deter people from bringing their bullion to be coined, especially when they would be free to try to get their loss back in trade.[1]

2. The Coinage System

Interest in the problem of the general organization of the coinage system did not develop till after the Middle Ages. The more serious and puzzling difficulties presented by debasement occupied the attention of the Schoolmen so fully that they were entirely content to accept the tolerably satisfactory status quo in this matter. Minters and treasury officials, no doubt, discussed it from a technical point of view, as they did other kindred subjects, but they have left nothing except their practice to indicate their opinions.

Bodin, however, believed that systematic regularity in coinage practice would help to relieve the abuses to which the money of all countries was so frequently subjected. He favored the adoption of three coins bearing different marks, the second weighing twice as much as the first and the third twice as much as the second. These should be coined of both gold and silver, a gold piece being worth twelve silver pieces of the same weight and stamp. This simple arrangement would obviate much confusion and fraud. Since poor people need even smaller coins, and since some people might be deterred from acts of charity if there were no smaller coins which they could give, it may be advisable to coin copper also, though it rusts badly, or to arrange for further subdivisions of the silver. That the feasibility of this scheme depended on a stable ratio between the metals did not worry him, for, as we have seen, he attached great significance to what he belived to be the age-long persistence of the ratio of 12:1 between the metals. He resolutely opposed any exceptions to the uniformity of this scheme, and in reply to the argument that certain pieces of base silver should be coined to avoid too heavy copper

[1] Scaruffi, *Discorso*, pp. 101–111, 148–151, 218–229.

ones, he declared this would be very prejudicial, for it would enable coiners to deceive the common people, for whom these smaller pieces are made. And he shrewdly adds that debasement would probably not stop with the smaller coins.[1]

To Scaruffi the need of uniformity appeared to be in a different connection. He conceived the idea of a kind of universal monetary standard, an "imperial money," to which the moneys of all states, though called by other names, perhaps, should correspond and be reducible. This imperial money should consist of three values: the lira of twenty soldi, the soldo of twelve denari, and the denaro of two bagattini. These were to be based on the standard pound in use at Bologna; an ounce of gold being equivalent to seventy-two "lire imperiali" and an ounce of silver to six lire. Such a system would provide a single, just, public, and common measure for all kinds of contracts and payments.[2] This truly ambitious but practical and sensible plan — the 12:1 ratio is not essential to it — probably never had a chance of acceptance in Scaruffi's time; and, as nations developed a stronger and stronger sense of independence, it was apparently forgotten. It is interesting, however, as an unexpectedly early expression of the ideas which in modern times received a trial in the Latin Union.

The technique of coinage was discussed in greater detail than Oresme had devoted to it. Copernicus was interested in the question of alloying the precious metals. This he considers desirable for three reasons: alloyed coins are less exposed to melting for goldsmiths' purposes, they can be made in smaller fractions of convenient size, and they are more durable.[3] Bodin concedes the need of alloy to render the metals more durable and workable, but says that beyond a legally fixed maximum no mixture whatever of the metals should be allowed. This standard should be twenty-three carats for gold and silver and for plate as well as coin. The greater ease of recognizing the pure metal will greatly reduce the possibility of fraud, both in plate and money, and the goldsmiths will no longer care to melt coin, as they do when they

[1] Bodin, *Six Bookes*, pp. 689–691, 697.

[2] Scaruffi, *Discorso*, pp. 90–92, 136, 137, 142, 143, 160–162.

[3] Copernicus, *op. cit.*, p. 51.

may make plate of less fineness of it. Preventing the mixture of gold and silver will also spare the loss of the latter, which, because of the great cost of refining, is not counted in gold of fourteen carats and finer.[1]

The practice of alloying was not universally approved. Agricola, famous as the "father of mineralogy," argued that pure gold and silver would be everywhere accepted and hence be a much greater convenience to commerce as well as the best form of treasure. Foreigners bring in their goods more readily to a country using such money, and the king's revenues profit by the increased volume and value (the money being better) of the customs. Native goods are sold dearer and foreign goods cheaper than is the case when the money is not pure.[2]

As for the form of the coins, Bodin is of the opinion that it would be better to have money cast in the form of a medal, like that of the ancients, instead of following the practice of minting. This is not only cheaper and easier, but it produces coins of better shape and more uniform thickness. These are harder to counterfeit with base metal, since the greater bulk of a given weight of base metal renders it more easily distinguishable among good coins of uniform size. Minting superseded casting when the scarcity of metal rendered it necessary to make coins very thin, and this reason no longer exists. At any rate, no pieces weighing more than half an ounce should be coined, for their thickness makes them too easy to counterfeit.[3] Davanzati is also in favor of a return to the casting of coins, for reasons that are practically identical with those of Bodin.[4]

Bodin and Davanzati likewise agreed that foreign money should not be freely current, the latter suggesting that certain officers be appointed to receive foreign money and pay the owner its value in domestic money.[5]

[1] Bodin, *Six Bookes*, pp. 687–689, 696.

[2] *Zeitschr. für die ges. Staatswissenschaft*, vol. xvi, pp. 616–619.

[3] Bodin, *Six Bookes*, pp. 689, 698–700.

[4] Davanzati, *Lezione*, p. 48.

[5] Bodin, *Six Bookes*, p. 696; Davanzati, *Lezione*, p. 43.

3. The Principles of Circulation

Mediæval writers, as we have seen, recognized the existence of a tendency for bad money to displace better money from circulation, but they did not make much progress in explaining the process. The matter was somewhat cleared up during the period we are now considering.

Copernicus, like Oresme, treats this problem as one aspect of the debasement evil. It is very inadvisable, he says, to introduce a new and poorer money, for it will drive out the older good money. Goldsmiths and other dealers pick out the better coins, and melt them to sell the silver, "receiving from the ignorant more silver with the same sum of money." [1] He is not interested, however, in what becomes of the melted coins, and does not discuss the part played by export and foreigners in their disappearance. The suggestion that the extraction of the better coins is facilitated by the ignorance of some holders of them seems to be made here for the first time.

Shortly after this, the unknown advocates in the Albertine-Ernestine coinage controversy wrestled clumsily with the problem. The champion of the Ernestine policy declares that, as a result of the superfluity of too good money, all the good money "has become pennies"; the merchants have picked it out and melted it, because they obtain their silver cheaper that way. Cheap foreign coins are put into circulation at more than their real value. Though obscurely expressed and illogically reasoned, this statement is as accurate in its facts as that of the supporter of the Albertines. The latter replied that it might be true that good money was being melted, but that the worst offenders were counterfeiters, and minters who needed silver in order to make debased money. Merchants could have no object in doing it, for they could not gain unless they exchanged bad money for good, which was strictly forbidden.[2]

Hales's frank and incisive language leaves no doubt that he is aware of the nature of the difficulty. Foreigners, he says, tend to bring us those things that are cheap among them and dear with us.

[1] Copernicus, *op. cit.*, pp. 57, 63. [2] Lotz, *Drei Flugschriften*, pp. 44–46, 100–102.

This is particularly brass, not in pots and pans, indeed, but in coins like ours, of which they can afford to give more for goods than we. "To what purpose should they bringe silver or gold hither, whearas the same is not estemed?" In other words, foreigners will pay in cheap money for the goods they buy. The explanation of the phenomenon as the consequence of commercial transactions, rather than the wiles of money-changers, marks a considerable advance in this phase of the discussion. With regard to the disappearance of the better coins he makes equally shrewd observations, pointing out how the merchants "perceivinge what was to be wonne theare in beyonde the sea, raked all the old coyne for the moste parte in this realme, and founde the means to haue it caried ouer." For this reason, it is impracticable to try to reform the coinage while leaving the poor coins in circulation. For it is well known that goldsmiths and others, when there was no "dew proportion kept betewne the coines," "apperceavinge the new coyne of gold to be better than the new coine of siluer that was made to countervalew it, piked out all the gold . . . and layde that aside for other uses." [1]

Shortly after this was written, but before it was published, Sir Thomas Gresham in a letter to Queen Elizabeth gave the explanation of this phenomenon which led Macleod to apply the name "Gresham's Law" to the statement of this economic tendency. "Ytt may pleasse your majesty to understande," he writes, "thatt the firste occasion of the fall of the exchainge did growe by the Kinges majesty, your latte ffather, in abasinge his quoyne ffrome vi ounces fine to iii ounces fine. Wheruppon the exchainge fell ffrome xxvi *s.* viii *d.* to xiii *s.* iv *d.* which was the occasion thatt all your ffine goold was convayd ought of this your realme." In some respects this is not as good as the statements of earlier writers; it puts too much emphasis on the relation of exchange to the outflow of the undervalued coins. Later in the letter, indeed, he says in so many words that exchange is "the cheffest and richist thing to restore . . . your reallme to fine gowld and sillvar." [2]

[1] Hales, *Discourse*, pp. 32, 33, 44–46, 78, 79, 106.

[2] Burgon, *Sir Thomas Gresham*, vol. i, pp. 484, 485.

Bodin, being interested primarily in the question of prices, gives only brief attention to the present topic. Counterfeiters, minters, and merchants, he says, "draw the good money out of the countrey, and coine baser in another place," whenever coins of greater intrinsic value are issued at the same rate as poorer ones, or when a country coins money "of better weight" than that of its neighbors. This second case, of which he gives numerous illustrations, seems to refer to instances where foreign coins of less value circulated on a par with the domestic money, but it is not made clear. He simply says, for example, that in converting the "testons" of France into testons of Flanders there is so much gain per livre. Even if no money is exported, however, the prince's subjects "always have good means to melt, alter, and falsify both gold and silver coin, if there be diversity of standard." Goldsmiths use the better coins to make plate of less fineness, which they sell at a higher rate than the law allows.[1] Thus Bodin gives weight to the domestic influences which Oresme had missed, and makes somewhat clearer how the exporter of good money expected to make his profit.

There are many discussions of this topic among Italian writers from this time on. Davanzati makes himself somewhat clearer than Hales. When silver is debased, he says, the price of gold (that is, in terms of silver or ideal money) must rise, or the common proportion between them could not hold; all the gold would be bought up and carried where it was worth more.[2] Scaruffi notes that under a coinage system based simply and honestly on the weight of the coins, such as he advocates, no one would carry gold or silver out of the country, for there would be nothing to gain by it; nor would any one import foreign coin to have it recoined. He also refers to the necessity of regulating the prices and rates of money in order to prevent the metals from being "transported from place to place"; but he is obscure and unsatisfactory.[3]

[1] Bodin, *Six Bookes*, pp. 694, 695.

[2] Davanzati, *Lezione*, pp. 41, 42.

[3] Scaruffi, *Discorso*, pp. 148, 149, 207, 208.

4. The Theory of Price Changes

Although the problem of the value of money received considerable attention during the Middle Ages, no one, apparently, had taken the trouble to discuss just what was meant by changes in this value or how such changes were to be measured. Few discussions, indeed, are found in the whole period covered by this study, and none of these attempt or suggest anything like the refined statistical methods now used.

Bodin's fundamental idea is that changes in the value of money can be determined only by comparing the prices at different times of a commodity whose value may be considered fairly stable. Accordingly he objects to Malestroit's attempt to reason on the basis of the prices of velvet, and points out that this commodity was formerly very scarce and hence more valuable than now, so that its price would now be lower but for the fall in the value of money. The best evidence of general price changes is afforded by the price of lands. This is better even than grain prices, for the value of grain varies according to good and bad seasons, while lands "can neither increase nor diminish nor be changed in their natural excellence." [1]

This way of reasoning about the matter seems not to have appealed to Davanzati, and he is rather hopeless of obtaining information on this point. To be always acquainted with the proportion which things bear among themselves and with gold, one would need to look down from Heaven. As it is, we can scarce discover the things around us.[2]

The spread of price changes was explained by Hales along what were probably conventional lines. Since traders give no weight to the names of the coins, but consider only their actual metal content, they promptly raise prices when the coinage is debased. Thus we have to "paie dearer for everie thinge that we haue from beyonde the seas," and therefore "must sell againe as deare oure thinges, or els we should make ill bargaines for oure selves." [3]

The effects of price changes, which had been perceived fairly

[1] Bodin de Saint-Laurent, *op. cit.*, pp. 18, 19.

[2] Davanzati, *Lezione*, p. 33.

[3] Hales, *Discourse*, pp. 79, 80.

clearly by the Schoolmen, were enlarged upon by their successors. Copernicus repeated St. Thomas's point that debasement causes confusion like that which results from changing the standard of weight, and declares it is one of the four principal causes of the decadence of kingdoms: it not only hinders trade, but it causes all arts and industries to decline. He also seems to see its unfavorable effect on creditors, but is not at all clear on the point.[1]

The sturdy supporter of the Albertine faction, in the Saxon coinage controversy, makes much of the harm done to trade, and of the loss sustained by creditors. Some merchants favor debasement, he says, in order to profit by the money they have on hand, but they forget that on the great sums owed to them they would lose much more, when they had to accept payment in the debased coin. Noblemen, moreover, would lose; for although the prices of all things would be higher, the peasants would insist on following the numerary value of money (Einen gülden vor einen gülden achten), and rents would be paid in debased money. Either debtors must pay proportionately more, or creditors must suffer a corresponding loss; there is bound to be dissension in either case. The miners, too, would be defrauded, for they are compelled to sell their silver to the government at a fixed price, which will be less if paid in debased coin.

He appears to forget the prince's position as creditor, merely protesting that debasement lets foreigners off free, and robs the citizens of a part of their property. He does not ignore the effect on the prince's revenues entirely, however, for he points out that bad money, by lessening trade, will diminish the income from customs.[2]

His opponent tried to answer these arguments, but his discussion is unintelligible.[3] Osse, who was at court while the controversy was going on, follows the spokesman of the Albertine faction pretty closely.[4]

[1] Copernicus, *op. cit.*, pp. 49, 61–67.

[2] Lotz, *Drei Flugschriften*, pp. 6–12, 16–22, 86–94.

[3] *Ibid.*, pp. 26–34.

[4] Zielenziger, *Die Alten Deutschen Kameralisten*, p. 167.

Hales is quite clear as to the effects of the rise in prices caused by debasement. Changing the names and qualities of the coins, he says, causes great confusion in accounts and contracts. As a result of the higher prices, the holders of farms and the like at old rentals gain, when money is debased; while the landowners lose. The latter have nothing to sell at higher prices to recoup themselves for their greater expenses; they have only income, which is fixed for considerable periods. This is true also of all those who have their "Lyvinges and stipendes rated at a certeyntie." Only those who live by buying and selling come out even.

He also brings out Oresme's point about the king's revenues, and declares that he is especially injured by the rise in prices. Since all the treasure of the realm must come into his hands every few years, he cannot escape loss. As a result, his treasure will be diminished and the country endangered in case of emergency, particularly if supplies have to be purchased abroad.[1] It is evident that this discussion marks a great advance in financial theory since the time of Oresme.

After Hales's time we meet references to the question more frequently. Malestroit saw that receivers of fixed incomes, among them the king, were injured by debasement.[2] Bodin declared that, as a result of this practice, nobody could "make a true estate of what he hath," contracts, taxes, wages, rents, etc., were uncertain, while nothing could more afflict the poor. He also called attention to another interesting financial aspect of rising prices. Those who wish to restore taxes to what they were under Louis XII forget, he says, that prices are higher now, as a result of the great supplies of gold and silver from America. The burden of taxes is now really lighter.[3] Davanzati pointed out that the "credit and estates" of the citizens would be diminished in proportion to the debasement, since they would receive that much less gold and silver. The prince would be among the sufferers.[4]

[1] Hales, *Discourse*, pp. 17, 18, 33–35, 77, 80, 81, 86, 107, 108.

[2] Bodin de Saint-Laurent, *op. cit.*, p. 84.

[3] Bodin, *Six Bookes*, pp. 666, 687.

[4] Davanzati, *Lezione*, p. 40.

5. The Problem of Reform

As the principles of circulation began to be understood, thinkers came to see that these must be considered when planning a reform of the currency. Until the sixteenth century, however, we find only undeveloped references to the question, and these have a different point of view. Copernicus is very definite on this point. When a new and better money is issued, he says, it is necessary to demonetize the old and forbid its use entirely (*vetus aboleatur ac prorsus intereat*), in order to prevent the old from destroying all the advantage of the new. The former should be made exchangeable at the mint at its intrinsic value. It would not do to allow this money to circulate at a reduced rate, as some have suggested, for the multiplicity of different values would be so great that it would be impossible to fix them all accurately and great confusion would result. Every citizen should bear a little loss in order to obtain the greater gain.[1]

Hales has the same opinion as Copernicus with regard to the impracticability of reforming a part of the coinage only, because of the extraction of the better coins; but he differs as to the other measures to be adopted. In the first place, he suggests a proclamation ordering that after a certain date all coins should circulate according to the old rate, and in the second place, he proposes that the king agree to give an equal sum in money of the old standard for all of the debased (newer) money which is brought to the mint. He admits this would be a big expense to the king, but declares it would be money well spent and be to his ultimate advantage, for it would restore the loss which his revenues suffered through debasement. As for the objection that there would not be enough gold and silver for the country's needs at the restored rate, he answers that the additional amount needed would come partly from the king's own treasure, partly from people who would turn over old coin or plate to the mint, and especially from exports of staples. There might also be some resort to barter.[2]

[1] Copernicus, *op. cit.*, pp. 69–71.
[2] Hales, *Discourse*, pp. 105, 106, 110–113, 116.

CHAPTER XIV

SUMMARY

The writers of the sixteenth century showed comparatively little interest in some aspects of the theory of money which the Schoolmen had discussed with considerable success. Their analyses of the functions of money are brief and conventional, as were their discussions of the qualities desirable in the money material; and their accounts of the origin of money, though sometimes interestingly elaborated, represent little advance in ideas. They agreed readily that coinage should be a public function, and went somewhat further than their predecessors by urging the importance of confining coinage to a few mints. Though much impressed by the inequities arising from changes in the value of money, they offered no suggestions for regulating deferred payments, and made few references to the problem. Their ideas regarding the ratio between the money metals were, with the exception of Bodin's, crude and inadequate.

The price revolution, at first misinterpreted, eventually stimulated an important advance in the theory of the value of money; the influence of supply, which hitherto had been little attended to, now being given its due weight. This new development was at first only a continuation of the commodity theory, but it led to a new analysis in which the value of money was treated in a special way — the "quantity theory."

The limitations on the coinage prerogative, which the Schoolmen had cautiously developed, were boldly increased, the two most distinguished writers during the period being frankly in favor of gratuitous coinage. Even those who did not go as far as this were inclined to deny the theory that seigniorage might be a suitable source of revenue in emergencies.

A characteristic evidence of the growing influence of secular interests in the sixteenth century is seen in the increased attention given to the technical aspects of monetary theory. The form and fineness of the coins were discussed in considerable detail, and careful proposals for introducing system and uniformity into the chaotic currencies of Europe were formulated.

On two topics which the Schoolmen had discussed at some length — the principles of circulation and the theory of price changes — the writers of the early modern period gave clearer statements of the general tendencies, and more complete analyses of the different factors involved. Thus the influence of logical commercial motives and of domestic agencies was pointed out in the discussions of circulation; and the effects of rising prices were seen to involve general as well as particular considerations, public as well as private losses in contractual relations.

Although only two writers discussed the problem of reforming the currency, the sharp contrast between their suggestions and the references to this topic among the Schoolmen shows the growing importance of practical problems in this period. In particular, these writers warned of the necessity of having regard for the principles of circulation when introducing coins of a weight or fineness different from the old.

PART IV

FROM DAVANZATI TO LOCKE

CHAPTER XV

INTRODUCTORY

THE full product of the tendencies which were beginning to stand out in the period we have just studied appeared during the century that followed, in the triumph of the political and economic philosophy which we know as Mercantilism. Considerations of commercial power and national greatness now came to dominate social philosophy, and thinkers applied themselves with increasing zeal to the practical problems of economic life.

Among these problems none seemed of more pressing and fundamental importance than those concerned with money, *nervi rerum*, an indispensable factor in national prosperity.[1] In consequence, monetary theory was widely discussed — in special treatises, in works on political theory, in essays on trade and commerce, in encyclopedic compilations of political and business lore, and in tracts on contemporary problems. Practical questions of policy continued to receive much attention; for coinage disorders were by no means at an end, and a rapidly developing commerce demanded a better mechanism of exchange.

As a background for these discussions, the writers of the seventeenth century had a considerable body of theory and tradition, which, although not very well systematized, extended to nearly every phase of the subject. This they utilized fully, making improvements as to form and content at many points; but they made only one noteworthy extension of the theory — the analysis of velocity of circulation. In the following chapters, therefore, the ideas discussed are arranged with reference to their place in a general theory of money, rather than to differences in the emphasis which they received during these years.

Early in the period appeared a number of discussions of practical problems, which reflect the frequent embarrassments to

[1] *Cf.* what is said below, in Chapter XXXVII, on the place of money in Mercantile thought.

which the small Italian states were subjected as a result of currency disorders. Conspicuous among these, from the standpoint of general economic theory, is Antonio Serra's *Breve Trattato delle Cause che Possono Far Abondare li Regni d'Oro e d'Argento dove non sono Miniere* (1613), a title prophetic of later discussions. Its principal purpose was to refute the arguments of De Santis that the scarcity of money was due to the high exchange, and it is in no sense a general treatise on money; but it contains shrewd comments on various topics. Written while the author was in prison on a charge of coining, the work was unnoticed by his contemporaries.

Among the other authors of this group we may mention Gasparo Thesaurus, a senator of Piedmont, whose *Tractatus Novus et Utilis de Augmento ac Variatione Monetarum* (1607) contains a few interesting suggestions; Gian Turbolo, director of the mint at Naples, whose point of view is much like Serra's, but often confused and obscure; and Romeo Bocchi, author of two volumes (1621) on money which develop novel ideas on some points.

During these early years discussions of monetary theory also appeared in treatises on general political theory. Montchrétien's *Traicté de L'Œconomie Politique* (1615), famous as the first to use this title, contains nothing notable on money, and what little there is appears to be drawn from Bodin. The writings of Georg Obrecht (1617) also show the influence of Bodin. Grotius's *De Jure Belli et Pacis* (1625) makes a few references to monetary questions, mostly along conventional lines.

By this time English merchants had begun to realize their ambition to play a large part in the trade of the world, and men of affairs were discussing the principles of commercial success. A lively controversy developed between the bullionists, who advocated restrictions on the export of the precious metals, and those who urged the theory of the general balance of trade. In the course of these discussions was written the great classic of Mercantilism, Thomas Mun's *England's Treasure by Forraign Trade*, which was largely a reply to Gerard de Malynes, a supporter of the bullionist policy. Although written before 1628, it was not published until 1664. During these years there appeared also some widely-read compendiums of general commercial information, such as Malynes's *Lex Mercatoria* (1622) and the *Merchants Mappe of Commerce* (1638) of Lewes Roberts, another famous merchant. These contain some references to monetary questions, which, though they contribute nothing to the theory, are interesting as evidences of the spread of certain conventional doctrines.

More important for monetary theory than any of these is the *Discourse of Coin and Coinage* of Rice Vaughan. This very able work, the first monograph on this subject in English, was written about 1630, but was not published till 1675, after the author's death. It compares favorably with the best work of the Continental writers who had preceded, and doubtless contributed to the prestige which English economic writings were beginning to enjoy.

In Germany also there was increasing interest in economic questions, particularly as related to national policy. The work of the Cameralists, as these writers are called, was generally encyclopedic in character, and their ideas rarely display much originality; but they show how the doctrines developed by English, French, and Italian writers were being taken up in other countries. In the *De Nummis* of Jacob Bornitz (1608) various questions are discussed, more in the spirit of the Scholastics than of Bodin, though the latter is referred to. The massive discursive treatises of Maximilian Faust (1641) and Kaspar Klock (1634, 1651) were presently followed by more systematic works, which reflect the influence of more modern forces. Seckendorff's *Der Teutsche Fürstenstaat* (1656), the first of the kind to be written in German rather than Latin, and the writings of Conring show the new tendency. Then came the work of a distinguished Austrian group, the ingenious and enterprising Johann Becher, whose *Politischer Discurs* appeared in 1668; his son-in-law Philip von Hornick, whose *Oesterreich über alles, wann es nur will* (1684) was long popular as an exposition of Mercantile doctrine; and Wilhelm von Schröder, whose *Fürstliche Schatz- und Rentkammer* (1686) was strongly influenced by the work of Mun.

Far more important developments were taking place elsewhere, during these later years. In Italy, about 1680, Geminiano

Montanari, professor of mathematics and astronomy at Bologna, later at Padua, wrote a work of outstanding quality — *Della Moneta* — which for subtle reasoning and penetrating analysis had few equals during this century. In England, Sir William Petty, in many respects the ablest economist before Cantillon, was already occupying himself with economic questions. Most of his work was in the field of "Political Arithmetick," to use his own phrase, but he considers a good many monetary problems incidentally, often with important results; and he published one tract on the subject, *Quantulumcunque concerning Money* (1682), which shows him "very nearly at his best." [1]

Toward the end of the century the condition of the English coinage was a source of increasing concern to business men and public officials. The silver coins, in particular, were in a wretched state, and the gold guinea was the best coin left in circulation. In consequence, the price of guineas rose to thirty shillings. Proposals for reform were presently advanced, and developed a sharp difference of opinion: between those who wished to scale down the weight of the standard silver coins, on the ground that the "price" of silver had risen, and those who urged the retention of the old standard of weight and fineness. In 1695 the former policy was advocated by William Lowndes in a report from the Treasury. This report brought forth John Locke's famous *Further Considerations concerning Raising the Value of Money*, and numerous other pamphlets. In the course of these discussions many points of monetary theory were covered. There were also further discussions of trade and commerce in these years, often with important references to money.

Prominent among these writers of the last decade of the century were Nicholas Barbon, a man of advanced views on many points, but sometimes guilty of very specious reasoning; John Cary, author of popular works on trade; and John Pollexfen, distinguished for his sound views regarding paper money. Some of these works were published a little later than Locke's *Considerations*, but they all show his influence and may properly be included in this part of our study.

[1] Hull's edition of Petty's economic works, Introduction, p. lxix.

CHAPTER XVI

THE ORIGIN AND FUNCTIONS OF MONEY

1. The Origin of Money

The concept of mankind's development from an earlier and simpler "State of Nature," which became familiar to the world of thought during this period, is reflected to some extent in the theory of money. Pufendorf, who did much to spread this doctrine in the field of politics, traces the origin of money to the multiplicity of wants which arise as nations "degenerate" from their primitive simplicity, and which render the more natural process of barter too cumbersome.[1] The influence of this way of thinking is seen also in Davenant's analysis. Mankind, he says, at first subsisted by their labor, and from what the earth produced; but when their corruptions brought in fraud, avarice, and force, men built cities and set up governments to protect themselves, and so great numbers were confined to small space. They were then compelled to resort to trade for those things which their own limited resources could not afford them.[2] A similar point of view is probably to be implied in Cary's reasoning that the growth of pride and luxury led to an extension of men's desires, and this in turn led to exchange.[3]

Roger Coke, in 1696, gave a new turn to the discussion. Since most things, he writes, must be prepared before they can be used, and since no man can prepare things by himself alone, but all live in "mutual Commerce," exchange is necessary.[4] As we shall see later, this tendency to emphasize the interdependence of men becomes stronger in the next century.

Apart from these few discussions, we find little mention of this phase of the subject. A few writers refer briefly to the advan-

[1] Pufendorf, *The Law of Nature*, p. 466.

[2] Davenant, *Works*, vol. i, pp. 348, 349.

[3] Cary, *An Essay on the Coyn and Credit of England*, p. 4.

[4] Coke, *A Treatise Concerning the Regulation of the Coyn of England*, p. 2.

tages of the division of labor;[1] but in general these advantages are taken for granted.

The inconveniences of barter, which had been analyzed with care by earlier writers, received even less attention than the foregoing topic. In fact, the few versions we find are incomplete and compare unfavorably with those of Davanzati or Hales.[2] Urgent problems of another sort and the practical interests of business men tended to push questions like this into the background.

The idea that the use of money rests on an agreement continued to dominate monetary theory till well along in the eighteenth century. A few writers made vague incidental references to the "invention" of money;[3] but the agreement concept, strengthened, no doubt, by the contract theory of the state, which gained so many adherents during these years, encountered no direct opposition in the period we are now considering. Its appearance in the works of English, German, and Italian writers shows how generally it had been accepted.[4] None of these discussions deserves special mention.

Meanwhile, without refuting the agreement theory, another analysis had been developed. The first use of money, says Vaughan, was as a pledge; for, since one of the parties to an exchange was often unable to repay the other exactly, the corruptions of man's nature soon gave rise to the use of pledges, in order to put exchanges on a more secure basis.[5] The same idea appears later in Locke[6] and Asgill. The latter goes on to say that at first men used as pledges "particular tokens between one man and another," till by degrees silver and gold, having acquired a value

[1] Clement, *A Discourse of the General Notions of Money, Trade, and Exchanges*, pp. 3, 4; Asgill, *Several Assertions Proved*, p. 9.

[2] Bornitz (see Roscher, *op. cit.*, p. 187); Roberts, *Merchants Mappe of Commerce*, p. 46; Coke, *op. cit.*, pp. 2, 3; Pufendorf, *Law of Nature and Nations*, p. 466; Vaughan, *Discourse of Coin and Coinage*, p. 3.

[3] Montchrétien, *Traicté de l'Œconomie Politique*, p. 175; Barbon, *Discourse concerning Coining the new Money lighter*, p. 17.

[4] Roberts, *Merchants Mappe*, p. 29; Pufendorf, *Law of Nature*, p. 466; Vaughan, *Discourse*, p. 6; Locke, *Works*, vol. v, p. 22; Cary, *Coyn and Credit*, p. 5; Doria (see Fornari, *Teorie Economiche nelle Provincie Napolitane*, vol. i, p. 346).

[5] Vaughan, *Discourse*, pp. 1, 2.

[6] Locke, *Works*, vol. v, p. 22.

for other uses, became the common pledge of the world.[1] This idea of a gradual development is an advance over earlier writers, and seems to indicate that the agreement theory was losing its hold.

The development of coinage was not much discussed. Salmasius, famous for his writings on usury, continues along the lines indicated by Davanzati, with slight modifications. To remedy the inconvenience encountered in exchanging articles of small value, the masses of metal were first cut into small pieces, then it was decided to make these of a certain weight, and finally to stamp the weight on them.[2] Cary gives a similar account.[3] Faust adds that the figure of the prince is stamped on coins to inspire respect in would-be counterfeiters,[4] thus giving a new turn to the old idea that the effigy of the prince ought to deter the wicked.

According to Vaughan the stages of development were somewhat different. The first step after the simple use of the metals by weight was to put a stamp on them to show their fineness. It was not till later that the stamp was used to indicate both weight and fineness.[5]

2. The Functions of Money

Like the topics treated in the foregoing section, the functions of money were not extensively discussed. The service as a measure of value continued to be emphasized, and generally in close connection with the process of exchange, as in earlier writers.[6] This also is what seems to be implied in the description of money as "counters," which is met occasionally.[7]

The development of the idea of money as a mere measure of value, apart from its use in exchange, is hard to trace. Petty

[1] Asgill, *Several Assertions Proved*, pp. 8, 9.

[2] Salmasius, *De Usuris*, p. 455.

[3] Cary, *Coyn and Credit*, p. 6.

[4] Faust, *Consilia pro Ærario*, p. 123.

[5] Vaughan, *Discourse*, pp. 12–15.

[6] Klock, *Tractatus . . . de Ærario*, p. 128; Pufendorf, *Law of Nature*, p. 466; Schröder (see Zielenziger, *Die Alten Deutschen Kameralisten*, p. 307); Petty, *Economic Works*, vol. i, p. 183; Conring (see Roscher, *op. cit.*, p. 260); North, *Discourses upon Trade*, p. 529; Pollexfen, *Discourse of Trade*, p. 23.

[7] Davenant, *Works*, vol. i, p. 355; Asgill, *op. cit.*, p. 9.

seems to have something of the sort in mind when he doubts "whether in that sence [a uniform measure of value] there be any Money, or such Rule in the World"; [1] and Mun's reference to money as "not only the true measure of all our other means in the kingdom, but also of our forraign commerce," [2] is apparently of like import. Locke, however, seems to have been the first to make the distinction at all clearly. Money, he says, while the same quantity of it is in use in a country, is really a standing measure of things, and alterations in their price are truly in their value with relation to each other.[3] In this conception the idea of a medium of exchange would not seem to be involved.

Aristotle's point, that money serves as a store of value, was not mentioned very distinctly in these years. It is only implied in North's remark that money is "a proper fund for a surplus of stock to be deposited in," [4] and in the idea of money as a pledge, which appeared frequently after Vaughan made it the basis of a theory of the origin of money.[5]

3. The Reactions of Money on Man and on Society

The influence of money on human motives, though relatively little discussed, was viewed rather unfavorably. According to Vaughan, a too plentiful supply of money increases vanity and wantonness, since the great commutability of all things for money enables every fancy to be gratified.[6] Pufendorf attributes to money a direct increase in covetousness. As long as riches consisted of cumbersome goods, the difficulty of managing and preserving them checked the desire to get more and more.[7]

More thought was given to the influence of money on economic life. Mun's reference to the general belief that money is the "life

[1] Petty, *Economic Works*, vol. i, p. 183.

[2] Mun, *England's Treasure*, p. 149.

[3] Locke, *Works*, vol. v, p. 44.

[4] North, *Discourses upon Trade*, p. 530.

[5] Vaughan, *Discourse*, p. 1; Locke, *Works*, vol. v, p. 22; Asgill, *Several Assertions Proved*, pp. 8, 9; Barbon, *Discourse of Trade*, p. 16; Pollexfen, *Discourse of Trade*, p. 23.

[6] Vaughan, *Discourse*, p. 58.

[7] Pufendorf, *Law of Nature*, p. 469.

of trade"[1] shows the trend of early Mercantile opinion. Presently more specific statements began to appear. Pufendorf regarded money as instrumental in promoting "the more improved and cultivated Way of Living";[2] and Montanari, calling money the greatest invention of the human mind, says that he might elaborate the gains made by humanity, from the use of money, "both in the sciences and arts, whose increase depends entirely on the communication of peoples, and in the conveniences which render life less disastrous."[3] Barbon makes the ingenious suggestion that money is necessary for the exchange of the great mass of things which are used in refined communities, for the need of these is so slight that men would not bother to barter for them.[4] Vaughan followed Aristotle in saying that money gave rise to retail trade and thus to usury.[5]

[1] Mun, *England's Treasure*, p. 137. This is also the implication of the numerous variations on the theme of money as "nervi rerum," which we find in the Cameralists. See Zielenziger, *op. cit.*, pp. 122, 124, 379.

[2] Pufendorf, *Law of Nature*, p. 466.

[3] Montanari, *Della Moneta*, pp. 17–19.

[4] Barbon, *Coining the New Money Lighter*, p. 93.

[5] Vaughan, *Discourse*, p. 2.

CHAPTER XVII

SOME QUESTIONS OF POLICY

1. The Qualities Desirable in the Money Material

The opinion, dating back to Aristotle, that money should be made of a valuable material seems to underlie the general theory of this period, but few direct references to it are found. These make it clear that the purpose of the requirement is to ensure general acceptability.[1]

Grotius elaborated the idea that the money material should be stable in value. That which is the standard of other things, he says, ought itself to be constant, and such are gold, silver, and copper, for they are almost always of the same value in all places.[2] Pufendorf and Locke reason in the same way; [3] but it can hardly be said that there was general recognition of this requirement.

Two new points were brought out during these years, neither of which attracted any attention. Barbon gives, as one of the advantages of gold and silver for money, the fact that they are harder to imitate than most other things would be.[4] At about the same time Asgill made a suggestion which reflects the growing influence of commercial ideals, declaring that money should be such that mere delivery gives title.[5] I have seen no other references to these points till the eighteenth century.

In contrast to these discussions were a few passages supporting an equally old doctrine — that it makes little difference what material is used. Barbon writes that, since the value of money "arises from Publick Authority," it may be made of any material

[1] Faust, *op. cit.*, p. 124; Pufendorf, *Law of Nature*, p. 467; Cary, *Coyn and Credit*, p. 5.

[2] Grotius, *Rights of War and Peace*, p. 305.

[3] Pufendorf, *Law of Nature*, p. 469; Locke, *Works*, vol. v, p. 47.

[4] Barbon, *Discourse of Trade*, p. 17.

[5] Asgill, *Several Assertions Proved*, p. 12.

which is convenient and cannot easily be counterfeited. This ignores entirely some of the qualities insisted upon by other writers, and reduces the others to a very minor position. He does admit, however, in another place, that the universal value of gold and silver is a convenience in trade.[1] Davenant says that men might agree to set up anything instead of gold and silver as money.[2]

Between these two extremes stood a small group of writers who held that either view might be correct, according to circumstances. Salmasius reasons that, although the prince or the state can give money of any material an arbitrary value within the state's own boundaries, outsiders' objections must be considered, or the trade of the nation will be ruined.[3] Hobbes, similarly, extends his absolute theory of sovereignty to include money, and declares that between the subjects of a state any material may be made money. Between nations, however, gold and silver are the most convenient money, since they are highly valued everywhere.[4] Pufendorf follows Salmasius closely.[5]

2. Problems of the Standard

The bimetallic status quo begins to meet opposition in the seventeenth century. The first instance of the new point of view, that I have seen, was in Bocchi, who says that, because of the difficulties which arise from an incorrect ratio between the metals, it would be better to use gold alone, but for the fact that the supply of that metal is inadequate.[6] The practical conclusion is about the same that we found in Bodin and Oresme, it is true, but the preference in theory for monometallism seems significant.

Petty comes out more strongly. The world measures things by gold and silver, but principally the latter; "for there may not be two measures, and consequently the better of many must be the onely of all." Since the proportion of gold to silver varies, he ex-

[1] Barbon, *Coining the New Money Lighter*, p. 13; *Discourse of Trade*, p. 17.
[2] Davenant, *Works*, vol. i, p. 444.
[3] Salmasius, *De Usuris*, pp. 456, 457.
[4] Hobbes, *Leviathan*, p. 193.
[5] Pufendorf, *Law of Nature*, p. 468.
[6] Graziani, *Le Idee Economiche degli Scrittori Emiliani e Romagnoli*, p. 51.

plains later, only one of them can be "a fit matter for money." [1] Locke is equally emphatic. Since the ratio between the precious metals must, in the nature of things, be variable, they cannot be the measure of commerce together; for such a measure must be invariable, and keep the same proportion of value in all its parts.[2]

We also begin to meet expressions of preference as between the precious metals. Bocchi, in the passage just referred to, appears to consider gold more desirable; but in England there was a different attitude. Vaughan says that such a proportion between gold and silver should be kept that both will abound, but especially silver, for the greater part of the commerce of the kingdom, and about all inland trade is carried on in that metal.[3] Petty's point of view is similar, as we have just seen; and Locke declares that, although gold may and should be coined, it is "not the money of the world nor fit to be." [4]

These statements, it is evident, do no more than insist on the maintenance of the conditions to which English business had been accustomed for years. Some advance toward a more reasoned choice is made by Cary, who explains that silver was adopted as money because it was plentiful enough to satisfy all needs of trade, divisible into smaller parts than gold, easily tested, and not too bulky.[5] The next year Pollexfen tried his hand at the question, with no more conspicuous success. Gold is not so serviceable as silver, he argues, because those who have it are not willing to make payments with it, but are inclined to hoard it, unless they can have more for it than it is worth.[6] This reasoning doubtless reflects Pollexfen's observations during the disordered period before the great recoinage, but he does not seek to connect it with the working of "Gresham's Law," which he understood fairly well. As a general principle, of course, it is of little value.

On the question of the coinage ratio some crude ideas persisted.

[1] Petty, *Economic Works*, vol. i, pp. 44, 183.
[2] Locke, *Works*, vol. v, pp. 102, 103, 151.
[3] Vaughan, *Discourse*, p. 71.
[4] Locke, *Works*, vol. v, p. 151.
[5] Cary, *Coyn and Credit*, p. 5.
[6] Pollexfen, *Discourse of Trade*, pp. 33, 34.

It was frequently assumed that the ratio 12:1, which had come down from ancient times, was invariable.[1]

The operations of the money changers, however, made such reasoning seem inadequate, and some attempts were made to carry the analysis further. Bodin's point, that the common estimate of the nations must prevail, found several supporters. In 1609 an unknown writer, probably a mint official, explained that no fixed ratio was possible, because of the necessity of conforming to one's neighbors,[2] and a few years later Serra said that the ratio depended on custom, including that of near and distant countries with which the country has trade.[3] Klock and Vaughan also stress the importance of the opinion of neighboring states.[4] Vaughan goes on to say that, although the true ratio is difficult to determine, that of 12:1 has the advantage of agreeing with Spain's and being the most convenient of numbers for computations.

Petty applied his general theory of value to the question of the ratio. Although often set only by popular error, this really depends, he says, on the respective quantities of land and labor required in the production of the metals. He also seems to attach considerable importance to the general opinion of nations.[5]

Montanari saw more clearly what was the really important aspect of Bodin's analysis. The relation between the metals depends simply upon the quantity of them in the hands of men which is destined for commerce, and the esteem which men have in bartering them. These factors might change, of course, from such causes as new supplies from America, consumption of the metals in non-monetary uses, and the drain of the metals, especially gold, to the East. History does not support Bodin's claim that the ratio has been pretty constant for two thousand years.[6]

[1] Bornitz (see Roscher, *op. cit.*, p. 188); Turbolo, *Discorsi e Relazioni*, p. 191; Bocchi (see Gobbi, *L'Economia Politica negli Scrittori Italiani*, p. 171); Malynes, *Lex Mercatoria*, p. 205. Bornitz gives, as the principal reason for the greater value of gold, the medicinal virtues of the "aurum potabile."

[2] *Revue d'Histoire des Doctrines Economiques et Sociales*, vol. ii, p. 23.

[3] Serra, *Breve Trattato*, p. 160.

[4] Klock, *Tractatus . . . de Ærario*, pp. 511, 515; Vaughan, *Discourse*, pp. 72–74.

[5] Petty, *Economic Works*, vol. i, p. 44, vol. ii, p. 444.

[6] Montanari, *Della Moneta*, pp. 74, 75, 89, 306–309.

Locke, though opposed to the double standard, as we have seen, was in favor of coining gold to show its weight and fineness. In his earlier writings he was of the opinion that these coins should be left to the rating of the market, but later he conceded that they might have a price set on them, but below the market value. With such a price they could not be forced on any one to his loss, and holders would doubtless insist on full market value in paying them out.[1] A plan of this kind was adopted after the recoinage, but the guinea was rated too high, and hence tended to displace silver. This evidently is what Locke wished to avoid by fixing the permissive ratio at less than the market value of gold. He wished to ensure the maintenance of the silver standard. The whole scheme, however, shows how hard it was for even a professed monometallist to break away from the old tradition.

Although the conclusions of Montanari and Locke show that the concept of market value was now pretty well incorporated into the theory of the coinage ratio, there were exceptions which continued older modes of thought. Barbon's statement that "the par between gold and silver is uncertain," but that gold "is generally coined nearer the market rate than silver,"[2] seems to indicate hazy ideas on the subject, to say the least. Pollexfen says common consent has fixed the ratio.[3]

3. The Coinage Prerogatives

The juristic tradition of the sovereign's right to control coinage continued to be fully accepted during this period. To the authority of the Roman Law and the canonists was now added that of Bodin's widely read treatise; and although many writers do not trouble to specify it, we find it frequently.[4]

[1] Locke, *Works*, vol. v, pp. 101, 102, 151, 152.

[2] Barbon, *Coining the New Money Lighter*, p. 33.

[3] Pollexfen, *Discourse of Trade*, p. 18.

[4] Bornitz (see Zielenziger, *op. cit.*, p. 122); Keckermann, *Systema Disciplinae Politicae*, p. 329; Montchrétien, *Traicté*, p. 176; Faust, *Consilia pro Ærario*, p. 123; Seckendorff (see Zielenziger, *op. cit.*, p. 352); Vaughan, *Discourse*, p. 84; Montanari, *Della Moneta*, pp. 269, 270. Montanari adds that the only country where private persons are allowed to coin money is Russia. This is because of the small number of foreigners there, whom it is so difficult to keep from making counterfeit money (pp. 35, 36).

The liberal views of Bodin and Davanzati regarding seigniorage made but slow progress during the following century. Most of the writers were merely belated followers of the Scholastic tradition, or not much interested in the question. Mariana, Keckermann, Bornitz, Faust, and Klock approve a coinage charge to cover expenses and to furnish revenue in public emergencies, but only Bornitz insists on the consent of the people as a protection.[1] Biblia thinks the expense of manufacture may well be deducted from the coins.[2] Bouteroüe, whose statement that the prince is not the proprietor of money is reminiscent of Oresme, says that seigniorage is legitimate only "when it is moderate and produces more honor than utility." Picard is probably right in his view that this means that the prince should collect seigniorage merely as an affirmation of sovereignty.[3] Vaughan favors seigniorage on the ground that it recompenses the state for the cost, acknowledges sovereignty, and helps prevent the melting and export of money.[4] Obrecht and Seckendorff seem to hold that the prince is bound mostly by his conscience.[5]

The newer ideas were not wholly without influence, however. Tilemann Friesen, Bürgermeister of Göttingen, in his *Müntzspiegel* (1592), though not sure of his ground, is inclined to think money should have the "inner virtue" of being equal to the goods for which it exchanges, even if its stamp should disappear.[6] It is not clear whether he saw that this involved gratuitous coinage. Thesaurus and Schröder, however, support such a policy definitely, the latter being the first to make this proposal in Germany.[7]

England's adoption of gratuitous coinage in 1666 was due to no such reasons as we have seen in the theorists, but merely to the hope of attracting money to the country to remedy the existing

[1] *Journ. des Econ.*, January, 1870; Keckermann, *op. cit.*, p. 331; Zielenziger, *op. cit.*, p. 123; Faust, *op. cit.*, pp. 217, 955; Klock, *op. cit.*, p. 512.

[2] Fornari, *op. cit.*, vol. i, pp. 272, 273.

[3] *Revue d'Hist. des Doctr.*, vol. v, pp. 357, 358.

[4] Vaughan, *Discourse*, p. 11.

[5] Small, *The Cameralists*, p. 52; Zielenziger, *op. cit.*, p. 353.

[6] Roscher, *op. cit.*, p. 149.

[7] Thesaurus, *Tractatus Novus et Utilis*, pp. 12, 13; Zielenziger, *op. cit.*, p. 308.

scarcity.[1] Nor did experience with the plan tend to influence opinion favorably. In fact, there was something of a reaction in England. North is frankly hostile, and declares that, by adopting a law which so facilitates melting, "the Nation hath been abused, and made to pay for the twisting of Straw, for Asses to eat." [2] Locke also thought that ease of melting was an objection, and favored charging the owners of the bullion one half the expense of coining.[3] Briscoe, however, maintained that the "intrinsic value" of the coins should not be diminished by even the charge for coinage.[4]

In other countries also opinion favored some charge for coinage. Montanari first disposes of the sovereign's claims by arguing that the coinage prerogative confers so much honor by diffusing his name and fame, that he can hardly expect to enjoy it for nothing, and still less to make a profit from it. On the other hand, it is a "useless exactness" to coin money of such weight and fineness that not even the expenses of the mint are deducted, for this causes the money to be recoined less fine or lighter elsewhere. It is true the Spaniards and Genoese follow this plan, but it is because they get the metals cheaper, and find it advantageous to increase the demand for their money by allowing foreigners this profit. The better way is to give domestic money a value slightly above the intrinsic. This will not hinder its acceptance by foreigners, since practically all princes regulate their money the same way.[5]

[1] Shaw, *History of Currency*, pp. 220, 221.
[2] North, *op. cit.*, p. 532.
[3] Locke, *Works*, vol. v, pp. 90, 199.
[4] Briscoe, *Discourse on the Late Funds*, p. 44.
[5] Montanari, *Della Moneta*, pp. 106, 107, 269–272, 330, 351.

CHAPTER XVIII

THE COINAGE SYSTEM

1. General Considerations

The proposals of Bodin and Scaruffi for a simpler and more uniform currency system received scant attention from later writers. In 1608 Coquerel outlined a plan which somewhat resembled Bodin's. The basis of currency should be the "Henrique d'or," divided into halves and quarters, and the "Henrique d'argent," similarly divided.[1] Obrecht's demand for an "Einheitsmünze" in the whole land, as a remedy for the bad condition of the currency, though it suggests Scaruffi's scheme, was probably in no way influenced by it.[2] Bocchi, however, was doubtless influenced by Scaruffi. He does not refer to him, but he knew his work, and makes very similar suggestions. It would greatly help commerce, he says, if princes would agree on the adjustment of money, that is, as to its valuation, and as to its quality and quantity. There should be no difficulty, he thinks, in effecting such an agreement.[3]

With the exception of these, the few later writers who considered this question at all were interested in other aspects of it. Bornitz explains, somewhat more elaborately than Bodin, that copper will have to be coined, for the sake of the poor, in those isolated countries which are so destitute of precious metals that these have a very great value there; and adds that a "firm and proper relation" should be maintained between the different kinds of money in order to prevent debasement. It should be so arranged that as many as possible of the larger pieces will be worth an even number of the smallest.[4]

Montchrétien, likewise, points out that small coins of base metal must be provided, lest certain transactions (like Bodin, he thriftily includes acts of charity) be checked. There should, how-

[1] Bodin de Saint-Laurent, *op. cit.*, p. 92.

[2] Zielenziger, *op. cit.*, p. 187.

[3] Gobbi, *op. cit.*, pp. 175, 176.

[4] Roscher, *op. cit.*, pp. 188, 189.

ever, be as few kinds of coins as possible.[1] Barbon also mentions the advantage of copper for use in small coins. Being less valuable than gold and silver, it makes coins that are larger and easier to use.[2]

2. The Form of Coins

Through the works of Bodin the conventional arguments in favor of alloying the precious metals had become familiar to scholars. Bornitz approves the practice, provided it is done with due consideration for the common law of nations, that is, merely to increase durability and help cover the cost of coinage; and, like Bodin, recommends that goldsmiths be required to use the same fineness in their wares as is used at the mint.[3] The note of caution in this passage is a common one. Serra warns against the danger of counterfeiting when alloy is used,[4] and Montchrétien urges that the metals be kept as pure as possible, since every alteration savors of corruption.[5]

Petty accepts these arguments and elaborates them somewhat. Alloying makes coins easier to handle and more durable, prevents melting by goldsmiths, and export by foreigners. Neither of the last two uses can be made of money except at a loss to those who do so; for in melting, the value of the alloy and the expense of refining are lost, and in foreign countries "the local value of the Piece perisheth, the intrinsick leaving him to loss." More alloy than is necessary for durability, however, is debasement, and it makes the coins easier to counterfeit, because of their less distinctive sound and color. Even the minimum amount of alloy has the disadvantage of causing a loss in case a recoinage is necessary, for the alloy is lost when the coins are melted.[6] One of Montanari's general rules of coinage requires that coins should be made as fine as possible. It has always been the finest coins that have enjoyed

[1] Montchrétien, *Traicté*, pp. 178, 179.
[2] Barbon, *Coining the New Money Lighter*, p. 15.
[3] Roscher, *op. cit.*, p. 189.
[4] Serra, *Breve Trattato*, pp. 145, 146.
[5] Montchrétien, *Traicté*, pp. 176, 177.
[6] Petty, *Economic Works*, vol. i, pp. 85, 86.

the greatest popularity and confidence, being harder to counterfeit.[1]

Barbon, on the other hand, asserts that the only reason for using alloy was to conceal the mystery of the Mint, in order to check counterfeiting, but adds that it also prevents the melting of coins, "upon a sudden rise of Bullion." This last point is based on Barbon's acceptance of a rather common fallacy, of which we shall hear more later — that the "price" of bullion might change independently of changes in the coinage.[2]

Some writers appear to object to any use of alloy, but they form a small minority. Thesaurus, like Agricola, thought that the universal acceptability of pure money made it a much better medium of trade.[3] Faust objects to mixing the metals, even in small coins.[4]

Biblia suggested an ingenious scheme as a means of checking the great evil of clipping, against which the authorities had long contended in vain. The face of each coin should be divided into two concentric circles, the outer stamped with the true value of the unclipped piece, and the inner containing more than half the metal but stamped with less than half the true value. The law should provide that these shall pass for their full value till the outer circle is clipped, and then at the value stamped in the inner circle. If clipped to the inner circle, they should pass as a mere commodity by weight.[5]

Bocchi stresses the importance of making coins of uniform weight, and says that imperfections in this respect make money uncertain as a measure, encourage counterfeiting, impede trade, expose the poor to imposition, and cause the good money to be exported.[6]

Faust adopts Bodin's proposal for a return to the casting of coins, and gives the same reasons.[7] Later in the century, Locke also criticized the practice of coining with the hammer, advocat-

[1] Montanari, *Della Moneta*, pp. 274–283.

[2] Barbon, *Coining the New Money Lighter*, p. 22.

[3] Gobbi, *op. cit.*, p. 162.

[4] Faust, *Consilia pro Ærario*, pp. 606, 607.

[5] Fornari, *op. cit.*, vol. i, pp. 265, 266.

[6] Graziani, *op. cit.*, p. 51.

[7] Faust, *Consilia pro Ærario*, p. 607.

ing the new method of milling. Hammering gives less protection against melting, since there is great inequality in the pieces and the heavy ones are likely to be picked out for that purpose. Moreover, there is greater danger of counterfeiting and clipping; for the tools of the older method are simple and the operations easily hidden, while the uneven form of hammered coins makes clipping less obvious.[1] The anonymous "Lover of his Country," who published a pamphlet on the coinage in 1696, agreed that milling was the only way to check clipping, which is "the gainfulest Sin that ever was invented, and sits the easiest upon the Sinner's Mind." [2]

3. Subsidiary Money

Many important suggestions concerning the regulation of fractional currency were made during this period. The later canonists, it will be remembered, had generally held that a creditor could not be required to accept more than a limited amount of small coins. Thesaurus not only referred with approval to laws limiting payment in small money to a certain fraction of the total, but drew a further conclusion from the reasons which had been adduced in support of this practice. Since this money is used only for making change and for small payments, it will be a good idea to coin only a small amount of it, in order to avoid one of the forms of debasement, an abuse to which small money is frequently subjected.[3] Thus we find suggested in a tentative way two of the restrictions now imposed on subsidiary money — limited legal-tender and limited coinage.

Support of one or both of these restrictions is met frequently after this time. Serra, in one respect, goes a bit further, and not only recommends that the quantity be limited according to the needs of the country, but explicitly concedes that this supply may be debased, a practice which Thesaurus had treated merely as a *fait accompli* — an abuse to be avoided. In this way, Serra thinks, the prince can gain considerable revenue; and although

[1] Locke, *Works*, vol. v, pp. 91, 92.

[2] *The Regulating Silver Coin*, p. 14.

[3] Thesaurus, *op. cit.*, pp. 33, 34, 98, 99.

there would be danger of counterfeiting, it would be easy to provide against other bad effects. Unfortunately, however, he declares that his present work is not the place to discuss these questions, and leaves us in the dark as to his further ideas on the subject.[1] Malynes notes that in 1622 in the United Low Provinces no one was required to receive in payment of sums of over one hundred guilders more than the tenth penny in certain small moneys.[2]

Faust improves somewhat on Thesaurus by showing an interrelation between the two restrictions which the latter had favored, and thus puts the limitation of legal tender on a more logical basis. As a protection against one of the forms of debasement, small money should be coined only according to the need for it in daily use, and no merchant should be compelled to accept it in payment. This second provision, he points out clearly, will serve to keep the quantity of such money within proper limits.[3] Klock, however, though he very probably knew Faust's work, merely follows Thesaurus's argument in favor of restricting the amount of small money.[4]

Petty adds some precision to the demand for a restriction of the supply of small coins, and, like Serra, concedes their debasement. Farthings and the like should be limited, he says, to about twelve pence per family; or, if this seem too arbitrary, by "considering the smallest Piece of Silver Money current in the Nation; which how much lesser it is, by so much lesser may the Number of Farthings be," since the use of farthings is only to make up payments in silver. Although these coins, as indicated above, may be debased, this should not be carried too far. The gain that is made thereby should be part of the king's revenue. This idea that subsidiary money may be made a source of revenue, which had already been mentioned by Serra, was doubtless suggested by the familiar use of general debasement for that purpose; but it is by no means the same thing, and, as we shall see, might be approved by men who strongly opposed debasement.

1 Serra, *Breve Trattato*, pp. 146–148.

2 Malynes, *Lex Mercatoria*, p. 210.

3 Faust, *op. cit.*, p. 850.

4 Klock, *Tractatus de Ærario*, p. 515.

Petty also considers another factor in the use of small coins. Those tokens which are coined "for Exchange in retailing by particular men" are not base, he holds, provided those who issue them are responsible and able to take them back and give silver for them; but it does not occur to him to suggest that this safeguard might be used to guarantee from abuse similar coins issued by the state.[1]

Montanari is interested in the revenue possibilities of this money. There are two reasons, he argues, why the prince can make it a source of greater gain: it is used only in small domestic trade, and whatever its goodness, it is practically banished by foreign princes, who wish for themselves the profit to be made on it. This resource must be used with discretion, however. No more should be coined than can be kept in circulation among the people for small needs; for an excess causes a scarcity of gold and silver, which are needed for large and foreign payments. These then go to a premium and all the inconveniences of debasement follow. There is also a limit to the extent to which small coins may be overvalued, for too great possibilities of gain will stimulate counterfeiters; but the greater expenses of the latter leave the prince considerable leeway. Not only are their operations likely to be less efficient, but, since their employees risk their lives, they must be paid high wages. On the other hand, it is unwise to coin small money at intrinsic value, allowing for coinage cost, for in this case it may make its way into foreign countries, only to be banished later, and return to plague its inventor, who has meanwhile coined a new supply. This will cause a scarcity of gold and silver, for, in sending back these small coins, foreigners will exchange them for other money, till the latter stands at a premium.[2] Skillful as some of this reasoning is, it is inferior to the earlier discussions, in that it provides for no safeguards except the prince's judgment as to the ultimate advantage of himself and his people.

[1] Petty, vol. ii, pp. 445, 447, vol. i, pp. 35, 85.

[2] Montanari, *Della Moneta*, pp. 107–117.

4. Foreign Money and Other Regulations

The question of the circulation of foreign money continued to attract attention. Many writers agreed with Bodin and Davanzati that it should not be permitted; and, in order that this might not hinder international trade, it was proposed that exporters should deposit security binding themselves to turn any foreign money they might receive for their goods over to the government, in exchange for domestic coin in proportion to the metal content of the foreign. In 1602 this advice was followed in France, and it soon led to a monetary crisis. There was much foreign money in France, and although the decree was intended to cause this to be recoined, the coinage charges were so high that money was hoarded.[1]

Serra argued that the circulation of foreign coin deprives the prince of coinage revenue, and exposes the subjects to fraud by other princes.[2] Montchrétien took a similar stand, saying that the admission of foreign money "invites our neighbors to send many bad payments."[3]

Some writers, however, did not agree with this reasoning. Thesaurus held that the best way to deal with such money was not to deny it currency altogether, but to compute its true value and order it to circulate only at that rate. This, he said, would cause less hard feelings between states and would keep out the worst money very effectually.[4] Obrecht also favors this plan, but his reason for it is obscure.[5] Vaughan is another advocate of such a regulation. The best way to deal with foreign money, he says, is to make it current "by the Ounce," at a rate so proportioned that Spanish money shall be given a value "as great as may answer the charge of coinage, without allowing anything for the King's Tribute." In other words, it should pass by weight for slightly more than its intrinsic value, but not as much as it passes

[1] *Revue d'Hist. des Doctr.*, vol. ii, pp. 11, 14.
[2] Serra, *Breve Trattato*, p. 143.
[3] Montchrétien, *Traicté*, p. 175.
[4] Thesaurus, *Tractatus Novus et Utilis*, pp. 36, 37.
[5] Zielenziger, *op. cit.*, p. 187.

for in Spain. Not being current by tale, it would, he believes, largely find its way to the mint in time.[1]

A few writers, despairing of preventing clipping, suggested that all money should pass by weight. Vaughan thought this would prevent foreigners from culling the heavier pieces, or attracting a country's money by raising its value. The government stamp in this case would be merely a guaranty of fineness.[2] Faust makes the same proposal.[3] Locke thought that clipped money should be subject to this regulation. It brings loss to those who happen to hold such money when the law goes into effect, but there is no practicable way to recompense them.[4]

The problems involved in operating the mint were occasionally discussed. Bocchi advocates farming out (*appalto*) the mint, because direct state management has proved inefficient.[5] Vaughan considers the "remedies" and testing of money. The first cause of "unequality of the coinage," he declares, is the greatness of the remedies, both in weight and fineness, and he thinks this may be an indication of special favors granted to mint-masters. Furthermore, the method of testing by sample to determine the remedies opens the way to further inequalities.[6] Faust and Klock follow Bodin in urging a reduction in the number of mints; and the former is in favor of reserving to the prince the right to purchase all gold and silver.[7]

[1] Vaughan, *Discourse*, pp. 87, 88.

[2] *Ibid.*, pp. 215–220.

[3] Faust, *op. cit.*, p. 850.

[4] Locke, *Works*, vol. v, pp. 147, 202.

[5] Graziani, *op. cit.*, pp. 51, 52.

[6] Vaughan, *Discourse*, pp. 91–94.

[7] Faust, *op. cit.*, pp. 247, 850; Klock, *op. cit.*, pp. 513, 514.

CHAPTER XIX

THE VALUE OF MONEY

1. Commodity Theories

Of all the theories of the value of money advanced after Bodin's time, none gained so many adherents as that of Bodin himself; and, moreover, the writers of the next hundred years followed his example further by emphasizing the influence of supply almost exclusively. Many of the discussions are of a most elementary character and hardly as good as Bodin's, but some deserve extended consideration.

As already pointed out, Bodin's ideas made rather slow progress at first, and some of his influence appears in the development of the "quantity theory" rather than the commodity theory itself. After the unknown reviser of John Hales's *Discourse of the Common Weal*, the next writer to adopt Bodin's reasoning appears to be Campanella, who seems to grasp the idea that an abundance of money causes high prices, though his statement is far from clear.[1] In 1600 an anonymous "conseiller et advocat général du Roy en la Cour des monnoies" stated the theory in terms much like Bodin's, giving it as his opinion that the rise in prices was due in part to debasement, but largely to the increase of gold and silver, which causes a given quantity of these metals to exchange for less of other goods whose supply has not been increased so much.[2] Scipion de Gramon, in "Le denier roial," also agrees with Bodin, and takes up the arguments of Malestroit which had occasioned Bodin's *Réponse*. To evaluate things, he says, is to compare them with something else of the same value; and since silver has fallen in the esteem of men because of the great quantity of it, we must give a greater weight as the equivalent in value of other

[1] Fornari, *op. cit.*, vol. i, pp. 171, 172. I am unable to say whether Campanella was acquainted with Bodin's work.

[2] Bodin de Saint-Laurent, *op. cit.*, pp. 44, 45.

commodities.[1] Montchrétien, who borrowed much from Bodin, refers to this idea also; but his remarks leave it uncertain how well he understood it. If it be objected, he says, that commodities can never be as cheap again, because of the great quantity of gold and silver from America, he would answer "that the essential value of things is immovable, not the accidental price, which depends on several things," and that prices do not always follow the changes in money. This conclusion is true enough, but one cannot but feel somewhat suspicious of the reasoning on which it is based.[2]

Outside of France we now find further examples of this reasoning, mostly brief or vague. Turbolo seems to adopt it, but his discussion is so confused that it is hard to say what he did think.[3] P. Sancho de Moncada, in his *Restauracion politica de Espana*, appears to be the first Spaniard after Gómara to explain the price revolution in this way.[4] Malynes considers both debasement and plenty of money causes of high prices, but he does not develop any reasoning in support of this opinion.[5] Salmasius's statement is pretty vague, but probably reflects ideas quite like the foregoing. The value of money depends on that of the metal of which it is made, and this is determined by the market — "ex pervulgato mercimoniorum usu." [6]

Vaughan's discussion is more elaborately reasoned than any yet considered in this chapter. There are only two certain and constant causes, he finds, of the increased price of all things: namely, the great abundance of gold and silver of late, and the "raising" of money; and as long as these causes persist, the rise of prices will continue, though it may be checked for a time. Other causes, such as scarcity, war, and depopulation, may cause changes in prices, but the effects will be temporary, and not all in the same direction.

[1] Bodin de Saint-Laurent, pp. 45, 46; Dubois, *Précis*, p. 185 n.

[2] Montchrétien, *Traicté*, p. 257.

[3] Turbolo, *op. cit.*, pp. 196, 197; Gobbi, *op. cit.*, pp. 190, 191; Fornari, *op. cit.*, vol. ii, pp. 284–286.

[4] Bodin de Saint-Laurent, *op. cit.*, p. 48.

[5] Malynes, *Lex Mercatoria*, pp. 45, 206.

[6] Salmasius, *De Usuris*, p. 456.

The first of these two fundamental reasons for high prices follows from the obvious principle that gold and silver must grow cheaper as a result of abundance, like other things; for it cannot be claimed that modern luxuries provide a use for the additional supply: ancient times had the same vanities as we.[1] The second reason is closely related to the first. The proportion which gold and silver bear to other things rests upon the "general consent of neighboring nations." Raising the value of money by a particular nation in no way affects this, and therefore it leads to a proportionate rise in prices.

This dependence of the value of gold and silver upon the consent of nations is apparently what underlies his conclusion in regard to the scarcity of money. One of the reasons for this condition he finds in the fact that England's supply of the precious metals has not increased as fast as prices in general. Although she does "draw some drops of this *Indian* spring, whereof *Spain* is the Cistern," they are got "upon hard terms and conditions." The kingdom has more money but is relatively poorer.

In general, then, Vaughan bases the value of money on the general influences of supply and demand. There is just a hint, however, of another factor. Since all other nations, he says, must get their silver from Spain, they must always value it higher than Spain, according to their greater or less distance away. This would seem to point to the influence of cost of production; but no more is made of it, and it is not brought into relation with the other theory.

Not only general prices, but the prices of other moneys, are raised by debasement. Whenever base money is current at more than its real value, the price of full-valued standard pieces is raised by the people despite severe penalties, and usually more than in proportion to the debasement. In this the people are right, for, although there be half as much fine silver in a base coin,

[1] I cannot agree with Hoffmann's statement that Vaughan follows Davanzati's idea of the equivalence of all goods and all money. Vaughan speaks of the "Proportion between Money and the things valued by Money," but this is apparently to be taken as a definition of price rather than as a theory of the value of money. Hoffmann, *Geldwertltheorien*, pp. 20, 21.

it is not worth half as much as a fine coin, because of the relatively large expense of extracting the silver.[1]

There was no progress and little discussion on this point from the time of Vaughan to the end of the century. Klock recognized in the precious metals a scarcity, labor, and use-value ("quia rara vena proveniunt, quia labore magno opere proferuntur, & præparantur, partim quia summam præstant humanæ vitæ utilitatem"), but he draws no significant conclusions as to prices from these ideas, and seems to attach most importance in this respect to clipping and counterfeiting.[2] Thomas Mun also stresses the alteration of money as a factor in the determination of prices, and seems to think that this is due to the influence of foreign trade. It is not the denomination of coins which is respected, he says, but their intrinsic value; and so, if strangers find our coin raised, they will demand higher prices. He does recognize the influence of quantity on the value of the precious metals, however, remarking that "all men do consent that plenty of mony in a Kingdom doth make the native commodities dearer." In making this admission, Mun was, of course, making a wide breach in the Mercantilist doctrine of the importance of "treasure"; but, as we shall see when we consider this topic, he was not so inconsistent as might appear.[3] Pufendorf gives a straightforward statement of the influence of supply without really making any improvement. Since the money metals are often brought into commerce as commodities, their value, or "natural price," must rise or fall according to their scarcity or plenty; and the "eminent price" of the metal (that is, its value as money) must follow this natural price, for it is unreasonable that a given quantity of silver should bear one value as a commodity and a different value as money.[4]

The writings of Locke at the time of the recoinage stimulated some discussions which accepted his practical conclusions, but apparently did not accept or appreciate his arguments for the "quantity theory."[5] One of the more elaborate of these discus-

[1] Vaughan, *Discourse*, pp. 8, 50, 51, 67, 68, 105–109, 124–134, 148, 149, 170–175.

[2] Klock, *op. cit.*, p. 510; Roscher, *op. cit.*, p. 215; Zielenziger, *op. cit.*, p. 128.

[3] Mun, *England's Treasure*, pp. 138, 149, 151.

[4] Pufendorf, *Law of Nature*, p. 470.

[5] See below, p. 111.

sions is that of Clement. Silver and gold, he begins, are capable, like other commodities, of rising and falling in price and may be said to be of more or less value according to their plenty or scarcity. Nothing that any nation can do will raise the value of bullion in the face of the great supplies that have come from America. He then turns to consider the effects of alteration, and other corollaries of the general principle that the value of a coin is simply that of its metal content. Domestic prices, he points out, must rise when money is raised, or the country will lose on its trade with foreigners, who will of course disregard the raising. Like Locke, he holds that when there is a demand for bullion for export, its price will rise somewhat above coined money "because of the Penalty and Hazard that attends the Melting or Transporting the latter." [1] Davenant remarks briefly that "gold and silver being the measure of trade, all things are dear or cheap as that sort of wealth is wanted or abounding." [2]

Pollexfen's discussion also gives relatively scant attention to the fundamental question of the value of the metals. Plenty of money, he says, "will always produce variety and plenty of Chapmen to purchase," and hence cause prices to rise; while scarcity of money will always have the contrary effect. Money in this statement is evidently to be taken as synonymous with gold or silver, for he makes it plain elsewhere that he recognizes no distinction between the two values. As it is unlikely that, if three quarters of an acre were by law called an acre, it would exchange for as much silver as before, so it is unlikely that three quarters of a crown piece, when called a crown, should exchange for as much land as before. If our prices don't rise, we shall be selling our goods at one rate and buying from strangers at another, for they will raise their prices in proportion to the raising of our money, to secure themselves against losses such as they suffered on debts contracted before. If they do not find it expedient to raise prices proportionately, they will not scruple to alter the quality of their goods. As to the price of bullion, it is unnatural and accidental that coin bartered for bullion should differ considerably in value. When coin may not legally be exported, people will pay a slight

[1] Clement, *op. cit.*, pp. 7, 25, 30–32.

[2] Davenant, *Works*, vol. i, p. 160.

premium if necessary, in order to obtain bullion for shipment. And finally he notes an often-ignored qualification by pointing out that goods and foreign exchange will not rise when clipped money begins to circulate, as long as there is a still larger quantity of unclipped available.[1]

Despite the great prestige of Bodin's work, there were many discussions after his time which seem to ignore the influence of supply and demand on the precious metals and to imply that price changes result simply from changes in the weight of the coins. Serra remarks that the principal disorder which would be caused by lowering the weight of the coins would be the rise in prices;[2] while Bornitz merely declares that money is esteemed "according to its goodness and full weight."[3] Similar brief references are found during most of the seventeenth century, but most of them do not deserve special mention.[4] The anonymous "Lover of his Country," whom we have already quoted, notes a qualification of some interest. Although the value of money must conform closely to the "real" value of the coins, this need not be entirely a matter of the fine metal content. The "real" value may exceed that of the metal, provided the extra value is settled upon "an unquestionable Security applicable to every particular person's Use," such as a Parliamentary fund.[5]

In striking contrast to the foregoing commodity theories was the cost-of-production theory of Sir William Petty, who applied to money the ingenious discussion of value with which students of the latter subject are already familiar.[6] Having laid down the principle that the value of a day's labor is the amount of food which that labor can cause land to produce in addition to the spontaneous product of nature, he proceeds to the conclusion that a quantity of silver produced by a given amount of labor will be

[1] Pollexfen, *Discourse of Trade*, pp. 10, 11, 16, 17, 25–31, 43.

[2] Serra, *Breve Trattato*, pp. 157, 158.

[3] Zielenziger, *op. cit.*, p. 122.

[4] Bocchi (Gobbi, *op. cit.*, pp. 166, 167); Christian de Spaignart (Roscher, *op. cit.*, pp. 178, 179); Lohneysz (Zielenziger, *op. cit.*, p. 458); Faust (*Ibid.*, p. 127); Bouteroüe (*Revue d'Hist. des Doctr.*, vol. ii, p. 24); *Considerations about the Raising of Coin*, pp. 4, 5, 16–19; Cary, *Coyn and Credit*, p. 11; Coke, *Treatise*, p. 13.

[5] *Regulating Silver Coin*, p. 77.

[6] Sewall, *Theory of Value before Adam Smith*, pp. 70–73.

equal to the food produced by the same amount of labor — "one is the natural price of the other." The amount of labor required is not to be taken in any narrow sense, however, but includes labor indirectly involved, such as that of transportation. Thus an ounce of silver, which in Peru would be equivalent to one day's food, may be worth four days' food in Russia because of the expense of freight and the like. From this reasoning we may conclude that, if the discovery of better mines should make it possible to procure two ounces of silver as easily as one was obtained formerly, "then Corn will be as cheap at ten shillings the bushel, as it was before at five shillings, *cæteris paribus*." [1]

Besides these fundamental considerations, the possibility of the influence of other factors on the value of money is also hinted at. Copper money "*ad valorem* in workmanship and matter both together" is not to be considered debased, unless the number of such pieces be excessive; for in that case the workmanship, "being of no other use but to look upon," becomes base by being too common. Here there seems to be just a suggestion of the influence of cost of coinage and of scarcity in giving coins a value somewhat greater than their metal content. The first of these ideas is also touched upon in a later passage, where he says that English merchants, in exporting English coin to trade with, "will be considered for the Manufacture of the new Money, besides the Metal of it." The second idea is also referred to again. If only a hundred of the handsome Britannia half-pence had been coined, he says, their beauty and rarity would have raised their value to over five shillings, though as metal they were not worth the half-penny they pass for. And finally it appears that the value of the silver itself may rise or fall from other causes besides changes in the cost of production. This seems to be implied, for example, in his statement that silver is not a stable measure, because men turn coin into plate whenever it pays them to do so; and also in his remark, dropped incidentally, that one of the reasons for the

[1] Hoffmann is in error in saying that, since Petty did not take rapidity of circulation into account, his theory implies the equivalence of all money and the goods in circulation. Not only was Petty a pioneer in the discussion of circulation, but it is misleading in any case to state his theory in this way. (Hoffmann, *op. cit.*, p. 35. He had apparently not read some of Petty's most important works.)

greater stability of the value of silver is the artificial character of the proportion between silver and such a commodity as corn, one being naturally useful and the other in itself unnecessary. No further explanation is given, but apparently the reference is to the different effect on value of changes in the supply of goods demanded for such different purposes. If this interpretation is correct, it indicates that the principles of value set forth in the last paragraph apply to the "natural" or long-run value of silver, and that deviations from this may occur as in the case of other goods.

These principles lead him to the same conclusions with regard to debasement that we have seen in other writers. Suppose a silver vessel weighing twenty ounces, he says; would the maker exchange it for a sum of money containing only eighteen ounces? It is the same with other commodities, though not so obvious; and if money is debased or raised, prices will rise in proportion.[1]

2. The Quantity Theory

The first writer to treat the question of prices along the lines begun by Davanzati was another Italian, Montanari. His discussion is of great interest. The value of money is due to the fact that men desire to exchange commodities in order to satisfy their wants. If men had no wants, and consequently had no occasion to make exchanges, money would be of no use. The wants of men, therefore, measure the value of goods, and also the value of money, which must correspond to these goods. From these considerations he is led to subscribe to the opinion of Davanzati "that all the commodities in commerce between men, taken together, are worth as much as the gold, silver, and copper, coined and in circulation." The reason these metals have this unique privilege, it appears later, is that they alone have become by common consent — "jus delle genti" — universally acceptable in exchange for commodities.

Although this theory was doubtless suggested by the work of Davanzati, to whom it is attributed, it differs from his in three important respects. It definitely limits the goods side of the

[1] Petty, *Economic Works*, pp. 50, 51, 85–90, 181–183, 440–443.

equation to those in commerce, and it limits the other side of the equation to coined money in circulation. It must be confessed, however, that Montanari seems quite unaware of the importance of these qualifications.[1] He also attempts more than Davanzati in the way of proof. If a city, he says, were cut off from all commerce with outsiders for a long time, and as a result found itself with fewer commodities, but with much gold and silver, it is plain that people would have to pay high prices. If only certain commodities were scarce, their price alone would rise, but the whole supply of goods would still be equal to all the money. Similar reasoning applies to the case of an isolated province; and since commerce is now so widespread that the most remote provinces are "linked together by a chain of gold and gems," we may say that all the gold, silver, and copper coined and in circulation is the price of all the commodities bought and sold among these nations. This may fairly be said to be the first clear-cut statement of the quantity theory.

In thus qualifying Davanzati's statement of the theory, Montanari had improved it logically, but at the same time he introduced a further complication. Since the metals of which money is made have many non-monetary uses, in which their value does not depend on quantity alone, it is necessary to harmonize these two sets of influences, and to discover to what extent the monetary value is dependent on the non-monetary value, or *vice versa*. Although Davanzati's theory did not raise this question, since it made *all* the metals equal all the goods, he unconsciously gave weight to the influence of the demand in the arts, as we have seen. Montanari, on the other hand, not only so modifies the statement as to make the question logically unavoidable, but he recognizes the fact in a fairly explicit way. In one passage he reasons that, if there were more money in circulation and no more goods, people would pay more for commodities or retire some of their money for other uses; and elsewhere he says that if men had less buying to do, less gold and silver would be used for money, and they would

[1] He is commonly taken at his word, and said to have followed Davanzati without modification. (*E. g.*, Kaulla, p. 112; *Handwörterbuch*, p. 774.)

be more plentiful for other purposes.[1] In these outside uses he gives full weight to the influence of utility. More explicit discussion of the question appears in his treatment of the problem of the ratio between the metals. He points out, accurately enough, that if they were used only for money, and were always in commerce, their relative values would depend simply on their respective quantities, but their use for other purposes makes it necessary to consider other factors.

Piecing together these ideas, we may conclude that he held that the exchange value of a coined piece of metal depends simply on the quantity of such pieces in circulation; that the exchange value of the same amount of metal uncoined depends on other factors also; and that the values in the two uses tend to be equalized. In this sense we may say that the true price of a thing "consists simply in the equality of esteem which men have for it and for a given amount of gold or of silver."

On the basis of the above principles, he draws some important conclusions with regard to particular monetary questions of his time. In the first place, it follows that the prince cannot, except in the case of small coins exclusively for domestic use, disregard the actual metal content of coins in fixing their relative values. In the second place, it is evidently incorrect to say that a coin is worth more because it passes for more imaginary money or for more debased small money; the amount of metal in it is the real criterion, and hence we should say rather that the imaginary or base money is worth less. Sometimes, however, because of the great fineness of a certain coin, or because of great confidence in the state which issues it, a coin may be worth slightly more than its actual fine metal content.[2]

The first appearance of this theory outside of Italy is in Becher's *Politischer Discurs*. He holds simply "dasz alle Güter zusammen gerade so viel wert seien, als Gold und Silber in der Welt gefunden werden." As this does not include the qualifications added by

[1] He does not note the possibility of the converse of this, probably because it implies free coinage, which was as yet unknown.

[2] Montanari, *Della Moneta*, pp. 45–48, 67–69, 82–84, 94–96, 104–141, 290–300, 338–342.

Montanari, and as the latter's work had not yet been printed when Becher wrote, it seems entirely probable that he drew his inspiration from Davanzati. Such influence from Italian sources is by no means unlikely in the case of such a many-sided character as Becher.[1] His son-in-law, Hornick, uses similar expressions, also without Montanari's qualifications, but is not very specific. Dividing economic goods into two classes, he places in one category gold and silver, "alsdie in ihrem Werth und Nutzen allen andern Dingen gleich kommen." It should be noted, however, that he is not here discussing the value of money.[2]

John Locke, the first Englishman to adopt the quantity theory, followed a somewhat different line of reasoning. The value of money, it should first be noted, is a special case. Money has the nature of a commodity, in that it serves as a medium of exchange, which use is a valuable one; but it differs from other commodities in that it serves us almost entirely by exchange, and seldom by consumption. Now the market value of all commodities varies according to changes in the "proportion between their quantity and their vent," but because of the above peculiarity of money, its vent is "always sufficient, or more than enough." People are always ready to accept money without bounds, since it serves them only by exchange. Therefore, the value of money is determined solely by its quantity. The "vent" of money, it is evident, is the goods that will be given for it; and hence Locke arrives at the conclusion that the value of money in general is the quantity of all the money in the world in proportion to all the trade, while the value of money in any country is the "proportion of present money to present trade."

In this statement of the theory, it is evident that, like Montanari, Locke limited the goods term of the ratio to those actually in trade. He was also in substantial agreement with Montanari as to the other limitations. In the first place, although the foregoing reasoning would apply to any money which was universally acceptable in exchange for commodities, Locke was clearly of the opinion that the precious metals alone, and particularly silver,

[1] Erdberg, *Johann Joachim Becher*, pp. 52, 53.
[2] Hornick, *Oesterreich über alles*, pp. 23, 24.

possessed this quality. Mankind has by common consent made these metals the pledges for use in their dealings with each other, and in all contracts silver is not only the measure, but the thing bargained for also. Moreover, it is apparently only with the metals coined and in circulation that we are concerned in speaking of the ratio between money and goods; for in statements of the theory in other places he speaks of the "value of silver considered as money," and the value of the gold and silver "used in commerce." It must be admitted, however, that he is not always careful to make these qualifications, and sometimes seems to imply that all the precious metals are equal to all the goods. These, however, are very likely only careless slips.

This carelessness may account for his failure to consider another point alluded to by Montanari — the influence of the non-monetary uses of the metals, in which their value is not determined solely by quantity. It is more probable, however, that this omission is due to Locke's belief that this influence was comparatively negligible. This would seem to be implied in the statement, already quoted, that money "serves us by exchange, almost never by consumption." One might also add, that even for those who sought gold or silver for consumption, their possible monetary use was a factor of considerable importance.

The theory as already developed by preceding writers carried the implication, though it was never expressed, that changes in the quantity of money would cause proportional changes in its value. In Locke this is made more explicit, and he remarks, for example, that since there is now ten times as much silver in the world as before the discovery of the West Indies, it is now "nine tenths less worth"; that is, it will exchange for nine tenths less of any commodity which "bears the same proportion to its vent" as formerly.

These general principles suggest some conclusions of a more specific character. Most important is that concerning the relation between debasement and prices. If the precious metals alone are universally acceptable, and are consequently "the thing bargained for" in all sales, prices will be higher, that is, it will take more pieces to buy commodities, if the pieces are made lighter.

One ounce of silver is always equal to another ounce, no matter how it is stamped or named; and while money is coined without charge, coins can never have a value above that of bullion. Similar reasoning applies to the "price of bullion." If the melting and export of coin involved no risk or trouble, no one would give a greater weight of coined silver for bullion; but since melting coin is a crime, dealers are willing to pay a slight premium for bullion. Anything more than a slight premium, however, is due to the fact that payment is made in light coins, of which it obviously takes more to make even an equal amount of silver. The premium will not be in proportion to the lightness of the money, where the money is still current at full value. This reasoning is so far correct, but it overlooks the fact that, when another metal is legal tender at an overvalue, the competition of dealers will presently give the undervalued metal a "price" in terms of the numerary money unit — though of course not in full-weight coins of the same metal — which is higher than the mint price, that is, more shillings, etc., than the metal would make if coined. This influence, moreover, appears to have been the more important in Locke's time.[1]

Locke's discussion made a great impression upon his contemporaries, but they attached principal importance to aspects of it which to us seem rather secondary. It was some thirty years, for example, before even passing reference was made to his elaborate demonstration that the value of money is essentially a special case, being determined by quantity alone. His emphasis upon the influence of quantity was not without effect, to be sure; but the frequent references to this factor after this time offer no evidence, for the most part, that their authors had followed Locke in this reasoning. They sound more like Bodin, and some hold even simpler commodity theories. What appealed to them most, apparently, was his conclusions about debasement and similar practical questions, one writer declaring that his famous axiom that one ounce of silver is always equal to another ounce was "alone carefully attended to, sufficient to guide Mens Thoughts through all the seeming Intricacies that perplex this Matter." [2]

[1] Locke, *Works*, vol. v, pp. 22, 31, 34–49, 82, 83, 119–144, 158, 169–173, 199.

[2] *Review of the Universal Remedy for all Diseases Incident to Coin*, p. 5.

This emphasis is doubtless accounted for by the fact that these questions were really the occasion of most of their discussions.

The idea that bullion may be worth more than coin, discussed by Locke, was one of the principal arguments in favor of altering the coinage, on several occasions. For the most part this was not a theory, but a more or less erroneous interpretation of the quotations of the market — a fact, not a theory, in the minds of those who used the argument. It received theoretical support from North, however, who revived the theory long ago advanced by Copernicus. When money grows too plentiful for the needs of commerce, he says, it becomes of no more value than bullion, and indeed may occasionally fall below bullion and be melted.[1]

3. The Fiat Theory

The later canonists continued to discuss the question of the *valor impositus*, without clearing up the confusion between the legal and the economic aspects of the problem. Scaccia, following Aquinas, distinguishes two uses of money, primary and secondary. The primary use rests on the *valor impositus*, but not unconditionally; for the prince is bound to give money its "just price"; that is, money should be so coined that, if the stamp were lacking, it would represent the same value, minus at most the expense of coinage. Even in the primary use, however, the value fixed by the prince may be departed from under some circumstances, such as a change in the ratio between the metals, and other market changes.[2] These limitations and qualifications seem to leave nothing but the husk of the *valor impositus* in an economic sense; but Scaccia does not make clear in what sense it remained significant.

This almost complete surrender on the part of the canonists did not leave the royal prerogative without defenders. Le Bret, writing in 1632, declares it is only just that the manufacture, value, and currency of money should all depend on the will of the prince, who is the law of his state; and it will always be in his power to exercise this right as he thinks best.[3]

[1] North, *op. cit.*, p. 531. Locke was followed in the *Dialogue Between a Countrey Gentleman and a Merchant.*

[2] Endemann, *op. cit.*, vol. ii, pp. 207, 208.

[3] Bodin de Saint-Laurent, *op. cit.*, p. 79.

Conring's reasoning is more like the earlier canonists'. The value of money depends on the will of the state, he says, gold and silver having no natural price, but only one derived from "human opinion and imposition." The decision of the sovereign should not be wholly arbitrary, however, but according to "utilitas publica," and the convenience of commerce.[1]

Barbon was the only downright supporter of the fiat theory in these later years. He ingeniously develops many specious arguments in its favor, but they do not sound at all like those of the earlier writers. If the value of all things arises from their use, he reasons, it is but natural that money, "from the great use of it," should have a value above the price of the metal in it, and that the government should fix this value or price as merchants do on their goods and wares. The case is analogous to that of a medal or old coin. It is feasible, moreover, because the legal-tender quality of money insures the receiver of it against loss. Experience also supports this view. Were it not for the law which fixes its value, an English crown would be worth five shillings two pence, for that is its value melted or in a foreign country. Another evidence of the influence of law is seen in the effect that the Parliamentary debates concerning the calling in of clipped money have had on the circulation of such pieces.

Other theories rest on a mistaken idea as to the part played by the metal content of money in the making of prices and contracts. As a matter of fact, "it is the currancy of the Coin that all men regard more than the quantity of the Silver in it." Few, in fact, know anything about the weight and fineness of the coins they handle. The many bargains made in terms of copper money, and indeed the very coining of copper, show that Locke is mistaken in saying that what men contract for in sales is a certain amount of silver; the same conclusion follows from the custom of making contracts in terms of coins no longer used, or without regard to the loss of weight through wear, and from the lack of unanimity among the nations with respect to the weight and division of money. And finally, if the weight of the coins had any influence on prices, then all prices should rise or fall together when money

[1] Roscher, *op. cit.*, p. 260.

changes, and for no other reason, which is obviously not the case. Another source of error is the idea that prices depend on the greater or less plenty of gold or silver. This has no more influence on prices than the supply of lead has on the price of butter; for the plenty of one commodity does not alter the value of another, unless it be for the same use. The value of gold or silver may change, it is true, as a result of greater scarcity or plenty; but this is a different matter, and merely shows that these metals can never of themselves be the measure of other values.

If money, therefore, is the measure of commerce from the authority of government, we must take a different view of the "raising" of money, and conclude that such a procedure will have no more effect than splitting a yardstick — "so that the length be not alter'd." The ordinary cause of raising money is the rise in the price of bullion, and it is to make such changes less frequently necessary that princes usually fix the value of money considerably above that of bullion. On the other hand, they cannot place it too much above, because of the danger of counterfeiting; and hence Locke's fear of indefinite raising is vain.

This lengthy argument would seem to leave no doubt as to Barbon's position, but he drops some remarks which are not wholly consistent with his general reasoning. He says, for example, that the values of coins of different metals are made equal by "proportioning the quantities of the Metals in each piece of Money to their different Values," which hardly seems called for by anything in the foregoing discussion. He declares, moreover, that the lack of money in a country will lower prices, through the resulting decline in consumption. This eleventh-hour admission, brief and unskillful as it is, may perhaps be reconciled with his other reasoning, if by "fixing the value" he meant no more than determining how much silver shall be called a shilling, and if he believed prices to depend on the number of such shillings in circulation. This interpretation does not appear to be justified, however, and hence I have included Barbon among the supporters of the fiat theory.[1]

[1] Barbon, *Coining the New Money Lighter*, pp. 7–9, 15–31, 68–73, 80–93; Id., *Trade*, p. 17.

CHAPTER XX

THE THEORY OF PRICE CHANGES

1. Measurement of Price Changes

There was a considerable advance during this period in the discussion of general prices. Vaughan applies an entirely novel and ingenious analysis to the problem of measurement. There is only one thing, he declares, from which we can surely trace changes in prices, and which "carries with it a constant resultance of the Prices of all other things which are necessary for a Mans life," — though these may vary in different degrees, — and that is laborers' wages, "especially those of the meaner sort." He then undertakes a rather elaborate inquiry into the history of wage changes, which we need not consider here. The important point for us to note is that this principle amounts in effect to measuring the value of money by observing the changes in the price of a particular group of commodities, viz., the typical budget of the common laborer, which he evidently believes to be made up of substantially the same items at all times. Furthermore, it is clear that this basis of measurement is chosen because of the greater significance of the relatively stable value of the group; it gives us the "constant resultance" of things which separately may vary in different degrees. However his method of choosing and measuring a group of commodities may be criticized, Vaughan's discussion is the nearest approach to the modern theory of index numbers made by any author of the period we are studying.[1]

Several writers continued to rely upon the evidence afforded by the different prices of a commodity of stable value, as Bodin had done. Pufendorf follows Bodin in attaching peculiar significance to land prices;[2] while Locke suggests wheat as a basis for comparison, reasoning that, since farmers try to adjust production to demand, it "keeps the nearest proportion to its consumption" in

[1] Vaughan, *Discourse*, pp. 105 *ff.*

[2] Pufendorf, *Law of Nature*, p. 470.

the long run, and is therefore the "fittest measure to judge of the altered value of things, in any long tract of time." Over short periods, however, it fluctuates more in value than the precious metals.[1]

2. The Spread of Price Changes

Vaughan also gives an interesting analysis of the process by which a rise in prices comes to affect the whole range of commodities. The foreign merchant, he begins, will demand a price enough higher to give him an intrinsic value as great as before the coinage was "raised." Moreover, "there is then so much the more profit to return money into the Kingdom, instead of Forein Commodities," that these become scarce and consequently rise in price. The high prices lead to greater imports (that is, foreigners are encouraged to send more goods), and the imports, owing to the high price of money, will be paid for by sending domestic commodities, with the result that these in turn will become scarce and bring a higher price. This rise in prices must lead to increased wages, or production will be checked and other prices forced up in that way.[2] This is better than anything since Dubois, in the time of Philip the Fair. It introduces an additional link in the chain of causation — the influence of supply in raising the prices of foreign commodities. Although some exception may doubtless be taken to his application of this principle, the discussion is striking for so early a date.

In the writers thus far noted, it is only the process by which debasement leads to higher prices that has been studied. Montanari was the first to consider how an increased supply of the precious metals works out its effects. When the Spaniards came to Peru, he says, they opened up a host of new uses for gold and silver, and vast quantities of them flowed to Spain. In return a "torrent of merchandise" flowed out of Spain. The result of these two changes was that the scarcity of money and plenty of commodities caused prices to fall in Peru, while they rose in Spain for analogous reasons. This continued till equilibrium was established; and meanwhile the same process began to work itself out

[1] Locke, *Works*, vol. v, p. 47.

[2] Vaughan, *Discourse*, pp. 148, 149.

between Spain and France. In discussing the effects of debasement, he notes that merchants avoid raising wages as long as possible, since buyers long refuse to pay more than the price to which they have been accustomed.[1] This discussion tells us little about how the rise in prices takes place in a particular country, to be sure; but it is of the greatest interest for the view it takes with regard to the relation between the prices in one country and those in another. It is doubly notable in a period when so much importance was attached to money as national wealth.

Locke analyzes the effect on prices of changes both in the money-supply and in the metal content of the coins. His treatment of the first topic is more elaborate than Montanari's, in some respects. The landholder, he declares, is the first to feel the scarcity of money, for people necessarily bring less money to market, and prices therefore fall. The laborer feels it next; for, when rents fall, the landowners must reduce wages or dismiss the laborers. The merchant feels it last; for though he must sell lower, like the landowner, he also buys lower. No mention is made of the working out of higher prices. With regard to the effects of debasement, his treatment is not very satisfactory. When money is one fifth lighter, he writes, it will purchase one fifth less corn; and as this is the greatest item in laborers' expenses, they will have to have higher wages in order to live.[2]

A point similar to the last mentioned above is also made in the anonymous *Some Thoughts on the Interest of Money*, which appeared somewhat later. The author seeks not so much to show just how the rise of prices spreads, as to make it clear that a change in one price necessarily entails a change in the others. If the price of food rises, he argues, the wages of labor must also rise. If these rise, on the other hand, food must sell for more, or farmers cannot pay their rents.[3]

Pollexfen looks at the matter more like the earlier writers, and seems to imply that it is the high prices of foreign commodities which give the impetus to a general price change. The effect on the price of the produce of land of "raising" coin seems rather

[1] Montanari, *Della Moneta*, pp. 180, 292–294.

[2] Locke, *Works*, vol. v, pp. 70, 170.

[3] Kaulla, *Werttheorien*, pp. 91, 92.

doubtful, he says, for a rise in these prices would naturally come from an increase in rents, and rents are very slow to change. They are, in fact, the last to advance, since they have least immediate dependence on trade. All who furnish the markets have some need of foreign commodities, however, and the higher prices of the latter may soon cause them to raise the prices of their own products.[1]

3. The Effects of Price Changes

Although the great reputation of Bodin helped to spread the idea that creditors suffer when prices rise,[2] it cannot be said that this point became a commonplace till considerably later. References to it continued to be somewhat uncertain in expression. We find it mentioned in the remonstrances addressed to Henry III by the Cour des Monnaies, and in a work by Henri Poulain, written for the Duc de Sully;[3] and Grimaudet probably had it in mind when he declared that a recoinage was just if undertaken to relieve poor debtors.[4] Serra's only complaint, however, is that debasement reduces the citizens' purchasing power abroad.[5] Christian de Spaignart's elaborate denunciation of clippers, as robbers of widows, nobles, artisans, and so on, also appears to reflect a point of view not unlike that of Hales and Bodin. The same may be said of the protests of the Jena theologians against debasement.[6]

In 1621 an unknown official of the Cour des Monnaies gave a rather novel explanation of the trade disturbances caused by debasement, which may properly be considered here. A merchant owing debts to foreigners keeps on paying interest, in the hope that money will be restored; for to pay in debased money means a great loss to him; while his debtors hasten to pay him in the bad

[1] Pollexfen, *Discourse*, pp. 29, 37.

[2] Montchrétien, *Traicté*, p. 176; Faust, *Consilia pro Ærario*, p. 217; Klock, *Tractatus . . . de Ærario*, p. 511; and Pufendorf, *Law of Nature*, p. 468, clearly suggest the influence of Bodin.

[3] Cited in Melon's *Essai Politique sur le Commerce*, pp. 775, 776.

[4] *Revue d'Hist. des Doctr.*, vol. v, p. 355.

[5] Serra, *Breve Trattato*, p. 146.

[6] Roscher, *op. cit.*, pp. 178–180.

money. All this means such great losses to him that he gives up foreign trade.[1]

Among English writers there came to be pretty general recognition of the loss suffered by creditors through debasement. Malynes, Vaughan, Mun, and Petty all made this clear,[2] giving due emphasis to the fact that it is through the rise in prices that this loss makes itself felt — a point which had been largely left to inference since Hales's time. Only Vaughan's discussion deserves special mention. It is true, he says, that, when money is raised, the creditor who must receive it at the higher rate may also pay it out at that rate; but prices will be higher, and he can therefore buy less. All the following suffer in this case: receivers of rents, pensioners, wage-earners, military and civil officers of the state, artisans, and laborers. Some of these, however, will lose only temporarily, for they will be able, in time, to obtain higher incomes. On the other hand, the *lowering* of money works to the disadvantage of debtors; they receive less for what they sell, but must pay the number of pieces agreed upon. So important are these considerations that we can generally tell which faction in a state has the juster cause from the way they treat the coinage. Although Bodin had included wages among the items made uncertain by the alteration of money, Vaughan's more specific mention of this point deserves to be noted.

Montanari called attention more closely to the effect of debasement on the laboring classes and on industry. In the first place, when the landowners find prices rising on every hand, they have to curtail their expenses, with the result that there is less employment. Moreover, employers avoid increasing wages as long as possible, although the laborers' expenses are greater, for they wish to continue giving their customers the prices to which they are accustomed. In order to appease the resentment of the workers, on the other hand, they shut their eyes more and more to inferior workmanship, with the result that their goods become discredited and their trade, especially foreign, suffers. This decay of trade is

[1] *Revue d'Hist. des Doctr.*, vol. ii, pp. 30, 31.

[2] Malynes, *Lex Mercatoria*, p. 279; Vaughan, *Discourse*, pp. 53, 54, 146–151, 165, 166, 194–196; Mun, *op. cit.*, p. 150; Petty, *Economic Works*, pp. 84–86.

accentuated by the fact that the rich merchants, finding the traffic in money more profitable, devote themselves to it and forsake industry.[1]

Locke's discussion is not wholly satisfactory. He makes it plain enough that not only rents but all payments previously contracted for will be less valuable, as a result of "raising" money; but he attempts to draw some unjustifiable conclusions with regard to the gainers. Only those will profit, he declares, who have great sums of weighty money on hand, which they can then pay out at a higher rate than they paid for it. Holders of plate do not gain, for they lose more in the workmanship than they gain through the new rate. Nor do debtors gain, for they will both receive and pay the new coin at the same rate. This last argument must have been made in an excess of zeal, for it cannot be reconciled with his earlier statement with regard to the losses of creditors.[2]

Locke's reasoning did not wholly convince Lowndes and some others. The claim that raising silver will hurt the receivers of rents and other fixed sums may be met, Lowndes declares, by recalling that silver is now of greater value in England than formerly. A given sum in money at the new rate would have as much value as before.[3] The greater value of silver, on which this argument depends, may have been a fact, but it does not follow from Lowndes's reasoning, which we have considered elsewhere, that the price of silver bullion had risen.[4]

Barbon would not concede even so much of Locke's argument as Lowndes did. Landlords and creditors will not lose if money is raised, he insists; for the authority of the state makes the new money as valuable as the former.[5]

All the other contemporary writers, however, were in substantial agreement with Locke. Clement, Cary, and the anonymous "Lover of his Country" did not go into the matter at very great

[1] Montanari, *Della Moneta*, pp. 154, 177–183.

[2] Locke, vol. v, pp. 110, 166, 167. The anonymous *Dialogue Between a Countrey Gentleman and a Merchant* follows Locke on this question.

[3] Lowndes, *Report*, pp. 209–211.

[4] The same point is made by Sir Richard Temple. — Shaw, *Tracts*, p. 130.

[5] Barbon, *Coining the New Money Lighter*, p. 89.

length;[1] but the author of the *Considerations about the Raising of Coin* writes rather fully. After noting the loss to creditors which results from raising the coin, he remarks that rents will rise in time, but very slowly, for tenants will be slow to admit that the rise in prices is due to the alteration of the coin, and will protest that it is only an exceptional year. When the defrauded creditors are foreigners, they may instigate reprisals. With regard to the gains to be made, he follows Locke in claiming that only those who have money on hand will benefit.[2] Pollexfen also follows Locke on this point.[3]

Most of the above-mentioned writers noted the loss which the king suffered as creditor. Many of them, however, went no further into the financial aspects of the question, and we need not consider their discussions in detail. They are merely brief applications of the principles already set forth.[4]

Montchrétien revived the argument advanced by the champion of the Albertine faction in Saxony, and declares that everyone knows how the check to trade, which results from uncertain money, has caused the king's revenue to decrease.[5]

Montanari's discussion shows the influence of local conditions. When light money circulates along with better, he says, the treasury suffers if taxes are paid in light money, for prices rise because of the light money; while the tax-payer suffers if he pays heavy money. If tax-collectors have to make payments for salaries and the like, they can make a profit by paying in light money in every case. In order to avoid these evils, a prince who wishes to use base money in time of war should give it to his soldiers in the enemy's country, and take care that it does not get into his own country except at its bullion value. A special coin might well be used. Raising the value of money is even less advantageous for the prince. His revenues are fixed in terms of the small or imaginary

[1] Clement, *Discourse*, pp. 33, 34; Cary, *Coyn and Credit*, p. 22; *Regulating Silver Coin*, pp. 24, 25.

[2] *Some Considerations*, pp. 17–22.

[3] Pollexfen, *Discourse*, pp. 23, 24, 35, 36.

[4] Bornitz (Roscher, *op. cit.*, p. 190); Mun, *op. cit.*, p. 150; Vaughan, *Discourse*, p. 151; Locke, *Works*, vol. v, p. 89; Rowe, *Brasse Money*, pp. 354, 355.

[5] Montchrétien, *Traicté*, p. 180.

money of the country; and therefore, if gold and silver are given a higher value in this money, the real value of the public revenues paid in gold and silver will be so much less. This loss will probably outweigh any temporary gain. It is not true, moreover, that, when the prince farms out his revenues, he suffers no loss through debasement. Not only does he suffer indirectly through the impoverishing of his subjects and the decline of the arts in his country, but, if the tax-contractors find they lose through having to accept small base money and to pay the prince in gold, they will surely bid less for the tax-privileges.[1]

The author of the *Considerations about the Raising of Coin* appears to be the first to see the bearing of the loss suffered by creditors on the question of public credit. The nation's needs, he says, are so great that it must borrow, and if it does so great a wrong to those who have hitherto supported it, other lenders will be hard to find.[2]

4. Deferred Payments

There was no appreciable change in point of view on this question. The idea that justice demands the repayment of an equal weight of metal found favor, at least as a general principle, with most writers, but no new considerations were mentioned.

There was some tendency among the jurists to qualify their adherence to the legal value in questions of this kind. Thus Grimaudet declares that it conforms to "the ancient observation of the kingdom" to grant relief to the debtor, when the value of the money in which he pays has been lowered. If he had to follow the new legal value, he would be burdened with "double usure." [3] Whether he would reason similarly in the contrary case — the raising of money — does not appear. The law faculties of Leipzig in 1622 and of Wittenberg in 1623 laid down the principle that in debtor relations regard should always be had for the *valor intrinsecus*.[4] Grotius, however, held that, unless otherwise agreed, the legal value must be followed.[5]

[1] Montanari, *Della Moneta*, pp. 164, 165, 173–175, 183–185.

[2] *Some Considerations*, pp. 24–34.

[3] Quoted, but apparently misinterpreted, in *Revue d'Hist. des Doctr.*, vol. ii, pp. 35, 36.

[4] Roscher, *op. cit.*, p. 181.

[5] Grotius, *Rights of War and Peace*, p. 304.

Vaughan goes into the matter a little more fully. The receivers of fixed sums in money will suffer loss through the raising of money, he says, unless a law be passed that such payments must be made according to the old value of the money. Although such a law would be an "Innovation full of Danger and Confusion, and Impracticable in this State, yet it seemeth to have a foundation in Justice." He suggests no way out.[1] Pufendorf is more frankly an adherent of the Scholastic tradition. If any or all of the money in circulation has been raised or debased, due allowance must be made for this in repaying sums owed, in order to ensure the return of an equal intrinsic value.[2]

[1] Vaughan, *Discourse*, pp. 165, 166, 197, 198.
[2] Pufendorf, *Law of Nature*, pp. 512, 513.

CHAPTER XXI

THE PRINCIPLES OF CIRCULATION

The writers of this period had frequent object lessons in the disorders caused by various forms of currency overvaluation, and we find numerous and often penetrating discussions of these phenomena. Not long after Bodin's time there appeared in France a group of writers, who by profession studied these questions. They were the officials of the Cour des Monnaies, a body whose duty it was to rule on questions relating to the manufacture, weight, and fineness of coins, to decide disputes between money-changers and individuals, and to advise the prince on currency questions. In 1609 an anonymous writer complained that strangers who bought in France no longer attempted to pay for their purchases by bartering goods of their own, but paid in debased money, and took away their pay in good money, which they recoined elsewhere and brought back to work the same scheme. LeBlanc, a few years later, declared that foreign princes even debased their own money in order to make gains in this way.[1]

The complications presented by some cases in practice are suggested by Grimaudet's discussion. The lowering of a coin (*décri*) may result from unjust causes. Then a voluntary course establishes itself, and the good pieces alone remain in circulation.[2] This may refer to a case actually observed, in which the legal standards were voluntarily ignored, or it may be a mistaken attempt to minimize the effects of royal interference.

De Santis, whose discussion of foreign exchange called forth Serra's famous reply, is pretty hazy on this point. Although he held that an increase in the numerary value of gold would tend to drive silver away, he argued that a decrease in the value given to gold would drive away the gold with the silver, and believed that

[1] *Revue d'Hist. des Doctr.*, vol. ii, pp. 5, 12, 13 n.

[2] *Ibid.*, vol. v, p. 355.

lowering the value of silver would not help to retain gold.[1] Serra's discussion is much clearer. The overvaluing of foreign coins will cause ours to be exported, made into the overvalued coins, and so on over and over.[2] Turbolo follows him in this, and considers the relation between different domestic coins more carefully. Raising the gold scudo by two carlini (silver) is what has caused the plentifulness of gold which we now observe. It now pays to take out silver, for 137 ducats recoined elsewhere yield 100 scudi, and these at home are worth 150 ducats.[3] Bocchi's statement that gold and silver are converted to other uses when they are more esteemed there, also seems to be an explanation of the disappearance of undervalued money.[4]

The common suspicion of foreigners appears in Montchrétien. Debasement, he declares, is most prejudicial to the country, for it enables merchants to draw out all the good money — one might say it is their principal trade. Indeed, why should they bother with more difficult ways of acquiring our money, when they can get it so easily by sending us bad money, made perhaps out of our good money, which they obtained by a previous similar exchange.[5] Although this shows some idea of the cause of the difficulty, it exaggerates the influence of foreigners.

Malynes, the next Englishman to discuss the question after Hales and Gresham, was hardly as successful as they. He declares that base money "causeth much counterfeit money to be made to buy the commodities of the Realme, and to destroy the good monies"; but his theory that such money is more dangerous "in those Kingdomes where their monies are of a rich standard," because countries using several standards coin "according to the occasion," and his conclusion that, like all extremes, a complete ban on base money is also bad, leave us in considerable doubt as to just what he meant. As for the ratio between the metals, he asserts that England was formerly "a great loser of gold" by keeping the ratio 11:1 (the true ratio being 12:1); and later,

[1] Fornari, *op. cit.*, vol. i, pp. 202–204.
[2] Serra, *Breve Trattato*, pp. 142, 143.
[3] Turbolo, *Discorsi e Relazioni sulle monete*, pp. 195, 196.
[4] Gobbi, *op. cit.*, p. 172.
[5] Montchrétien, *Traicté*, pp. 171–173.

by keeping the ratio $13\frac{1}{5}:1$, was a greater loser of silver. He suggests in addition an interesting limitation on the working of the general principle by explaining that the reason why Spain can maintain the ratio 12:1 while Portugal keeps 10:1 is that there is no trade between them, so that export of silver for gold is but a permutation between them without any profit. This is left undeveloped.[1]

Vaughan's *Discourse* marked a great advance. He states the case from various angles. To the causes of disproportion in the coinage mentioned by earlier writers, he adds another: the irregularity due to careless or unskillful coinage will lead to the extracting of a part of the coins, the heavier or finer pieces being melted or exported. A new money of less value will tend to cause the disappearance of the old; and "raising" a part of the money, or overvaluing foreign money, will have a similar effect. He does not go into details, however, as to the methods adopted in carrying out these schemes.

His discussion of the influence of the coinage ratio is especially careful. It is from the proportion which gold bears to silver in England, he says, that we can discover why merchants bring gold thither in preference to silver, for they carry the metals where they receive most for them. For example, for the same quantity of silver they receive over four shillings two pence more in France than at the mint in England. Not only is gold brought rather than silver, but the silver coins are picked out, except those which are so light from wear that they really bear the correct proportion to gold. This will be done whenever the ratio is so incorrect that the merchant can make a profit by exporting the silver and "returning it in Commodities, or by Exchange, or . . . in gold." Thus the country's silver must inevitably be exhausted.[2] These explanations and qualifications make Vaughan's statement of the principle considerably the best up to his time.

Mun, like Vaughan,[3] qualifies the general statement by point-

[1] Malynes, *Lex Mercatoria*, pp. 206–208.

[2] Vaughan, *Discourse*, pp. 42–44, 65, 70, 71, 83–85, 145, 154, 176, 177.

[3] Vaughan's work, it should be remembered, was not published till after Mun's time, though written earlier.

ing out that, if the difference in the values in different countries be small, it will be without effect, for there will be more profit in ordinary trade. This seems to imply that the undervalued coins are carried out by certain traders, rather than in the payment of regular trade balances. He also refers to the loss of the heavier coins. This he attributes mostly to the country's "vigilant neighbors," who carry off the heavy pieces to recoin them; but he has no illusions about the superior rectitude of his countrymen, for he adds that even they might "turn Coiners and venter a hanging for this profit." [1]

Sir Richard Rowe, writing before either Mun's or Vaughan's work had been published, is much less effective. The heavier moneys (of a former coinage) "will be made of the most nereby Bullion and so transported." His reasoning on this point is obscure, but a little further on he makes himself clearer by asking "who will depart with any, when it is by seven more in the hundred in the masse, then the now moneys, and yet of no more value in the Market." He declares it is impossible to bring both gold and silver to the mint by raising their price, but possible to attract one of them by rating it higher in proportion.[2]

Saavedra, a little later, noted the dangers incident to the circulation of good money along with pieces of inferior weight or fineness, apparently without developing the point very fully. The amount of alloy in coins, he says, should be the same as other princes put in them, lest they be extracted from the kingdom. The circulation of old clipped pieces causes newer standard money to be exported. As for coins of different metals, he points out that, when Philip III doubled the value of his copper money, foreigners, realizing the profit to be gained, "made it a trading commodity, importing copper money into Spain and carrying away our gold, silver, and other merchandise." [3]

Petty's scattered references to this topic indicate that he understood the phenomena very well. Errors in fixing the ratio, he says, are "the cause of our having been pestred with too much

[1] Mun, *England's Treasure*, pp. 150–153.
[2] Rowe, *Brasse Money*, pp. 355–357.
[3] Quoted in Uztariz, *Theory and Practice of Commerce*, vol. ii, pp. 346–349.

Gold heretofore, and wanting it now." In another place he notes that in Ireland, where pieces weighing twelve pence pass for four shillings six pence, all the heavier pieces are picked out "to buy or make" lighter pieces, and also that English money, having a great reputation for goodness, is all carried out. He also points out the effect of overvaluing foreign money. If the French *quart d'escu* (really worth eighteen pence) were raised to three shillings, all the money of England would presently become *quart d'escu* pieces, while English money would be carried away.[1]

Montanari's discussion is notably clear and unprejudiced. The toleration of underweight coins is one of the principal causes of coinage disorder. It encourages two kinds of clipping, one subject to penalties, and one exempt from them. The second kind occurs when men collect full-weight money (especially gold, which is easy to transport), send it to places where full-weight money only is current, and exchange it for an equivalent weight in light pieces, which at home will pass for more than those exported. Or men send goods to those countries, and take their pay in light money. The overvaluing of foreign money is also productive of serious evils. Merchants and even princes from neighboring states will send all they can to exchange for our better money; and then the money of the country will probably be debased even below the foreign, to check the evil, and much confusion will result. The circulation of foreign base money of small denominations at an overvalue is still worse. An error in the valuation of standard gold and silver money can be easily corrected by an edict changing their price; but in the case of the small base money the differences in value are so small as to be hard to determine, and an edict is of less influence among the common people who make most use of such coins. The best thing is to forbid this money entirely. The only exception to the general rule of valuing foreign money strictly according to its metal content is in the case of certain very fine coins which may be allowed a premium for the refining.

With respect to the coinage ratio he develops interesting details. If in one place, he says, the ratio is fixed at $14\frac{1}{4}:1$, and in other

[1] Petty, *Economic Works*, vol. i, pp. 44, 87, 184.

places the common ratio is 14¾:1, merchants from the other places will send their silver to this place to get gold for it. On the other hand, merchants who wish to send out money from this place will find it to their advantage to send gold, and this will accordingly come to bear a slight premium because of the increased demand for it. The ratio need not be exactly the same, however, in all places; for silver, being expensive to transport because of its bulk, will not be exported unless there is sufficient profit to be made. This depends on the distance of the country from Spain, the great distributor of silver in Europe. His remark later that, in order to reap the gains from these money-changing operations, one needs occasions and go-betweens, or even trafficking in other wares, indicates that he was well aware that his first statement of the case was artificially simplified. And finally, on the basis of the above reasoning, he recommends that the proportion between the metals be varied a little according to the needs of the mint — not enough to make it profitable to send coins just to exchange them, but to make it preferable to send one metal rather than the other when a remittance must be made.[1]

It is notable that no such progress as we have seen in England, Italy, and France had been made in Germany. Faust laid down the principle that money should be coined in due weight and proportion; and declared that this alone would prevent its export.[2] Seckendorff demanded the elimination of all coinage practices which might lead to the displacement of the country's good money; but his discussion is rather vague and unsatisfactory.[3]

The discussion which preceded the great recoinage of 1696 in England occasioned many references to this topic. Locke devoted much attention to this phase of the problem. When current pieces of the same denomination are of unequal weight, he says, the heavier ones will tend to disappear from circulation, for various reasons. Traders in money pick them out and melt them with profit, and few who get weighty money will part with it, while clipped money of not half the value is current. In case the

[1] Montanari, *Della Moneta*, pp. 147, 148, 157–159, 190–194, 205–207, 251–265, 337, 338, 348–350.

[2] Faust, *Consilia pro Ærario*, pp. 605, 606.

[3] Zielenziger, *op. cit.*, pp. 346, 369.

inequality is due to debasement, it cannot be supposed that men will pay their heavy coins at the same rate as lighter new ones, when at the mint they will yield them more. As soon as debasement is ordered, all the heavy coins will be melted. This seems to be the first account of the effect of debasement on circulation under the simple conditions of free coinage, which Locke obviously assumes. In previous writers, the displacement of the older and better money is believed to be accomplished by roundabout and underhand transactions, mostly through the agency of foreigners; and this was largely true when neither free coinage nor complete liberty in trading in the precious metals existed. In Locke's description, however, it appears to involve nothing more criminal than melting the coin of the realm. He also notes the important point that, while the exchequer receives clipped money, its circulation, with the attendant evils, cannot be prevented.

He does not eliminate foreign transactions as an influence, however. If men find that a certain weight of silver with a certain stamp is equal to three pence here and two pence elsewhere, they will not fail to coin such pieces and bring them to exchange for our heavier pieces, to our loss, he declares in an earlier passage, only to contradict this later, when he maintains that coining heavy coins with light ones does not cause or encourage the exportation of our treasure, — which is wholly a matter of the balance of trade, — but simply causes one kind of coin to go rather than another, as long as they are current at the same rate. The former statement is, indeed, true under certain circumstances; but he does not discriminate, and it is to be feared that he was reasoning carelessly when he made it. At any rate he does not recur to it, as he does to the other in several passages. In these he gives a clear explanation of the reasons for this loss of the better coins. Since a weighty piece costs no more with us than a light one, but is worth more among foreigners who value it merely as bullion, it is sure to be used in paying foreign debts; and foreigners who wish to take away their pay in cash will seek to exchange for weighty money before they go.[1]

His discussion of the effects of the coinage ratio is not as notable

[1] Locke, *Works*, vol. v, pp. 85, 92, 96, 108, 127, 147, 159, 161.

as the foregoing. If gold is made current at less than the market rate, he says, people will refuse to part with their gold coins, or foreigners will reap the benefit by carrying away such gold as does get into circulation. Will they not, in fact, bring their silver to take away our gold? The reverse of this, indeed, is taking place as a result of the overvaluing of guineas, which foreigners are bringing in at a profit, to the great prejudice of the kingdom. This will in time drive away all the good silver. He adds the curious point that the overvaluing of gold is more readily felt than the overvaluing of silver, because in the former case silver disappears, and that is what accounts (in England) are kept in. He seems to have been the first to note that the undervalued coins may be hoarded till their true value has been recognized by a premium or otherwise.[1]

The clarity and discernment of Locke's discussion were not equalled by any of his contemporaries in England. Davenant merely remarks that the irregular form of hammered money caused the heavier pieces to be picked out and melted so that the same bullion might be coined over and over.[2] He may mean to imply the conditions of free coinage, but it is not so clear as in Locke. The anonymous author of the *Review of the Universal Remedy for all Diseases Incident to Coin*, a great admirer of Locke, also fails to equal the latter's discussion. When clipped money was made current, he says, the consequence was that men clipped still more, melted, or hoarded, till nothing was left but clipped money. And who that had a hoard of weighty money would refuse to sell it for a greater sum in tale, which he could immediately pay away again as if each piece were equal to those he had sold? No reference is made to Locke's discussion of the export of coin.[3]

The case of the overvalued guineas was, of course, frequently discussed. Clement declares bitterly that the neighbors will coin all their gold into guineas, if they can obtain five ounces of silver for them, while formerly they would have given them for four.[4] Lowndes, who was Locke's principal opponent on some points of

[1] Locke, *Works*, vol. v, pp. 97–101, 164, 194, 195, 198.
[2] Davenant, *Works*, vol. ii, p. 105.
[3] *Review*, pp. 12, 18. [4] Clement, *Discourse*, p. 24.

the coinage controversy, also refers to this. The distrust of the people for bad silver, he says, led to a price of thirty shillings, which was more than their value in other countries. This overvalue encouraged foreign merchants to import gold in order to take away silver, buy our commodities, or "draw back the aforesaid Value of their Gold by Bills of Exchange," making a large profit in any case. He does not elaborate this statement, however.[1]

This reasoning is developed further in the anonymous *Review of the Universal Remedy of all Diseases Incident to Coin*. The Dutch, we read, sent over gold, which they used to buy woolens and the like; and they were then able to undersell English merchants on these goods owing to the profit they made on the money. And money-changers soon discovered that by melting such heavy coins as fell into their hands and sending the silver to Holland for gold to be coined into guineas they could make a good profit. Such traffic depends on the amount of profit to be obtained from it.[2] The same limitation is noted in the *Considerations about the Raising of Coin*, where we are told that at twenty-two shillings the overvaluing of guineas is too slight to balance the risk of sending silver to Holland to exchange for gold to bring back to England.[3]

The anonymous "Lover of his Country," of whom we have heard before, remarks concisely that England must be as good a market for silver as other countries, or little will be imported; and in another place says that England's high price for gold may attract too much, and occasion a still greater rise of silver, for, "considering the present Balance of Trade, the more Gold is imported, the less there will be of Silver." [4] Pollexfen's statement of the principle is also pretty simple. Gold should be coined exactly in proportion to silver, or opportunity will be given to foreigners to carry away our gold and bring silver, or *vice versa*. Thus a price of twenty-six shillings on guineas would encourage the importation of gold, and allow foreigners a profit of four or five shillings per guinea, at the expense of the nation.[5]

[1] Lowndes, *Report*, pp. 230, 231.

[2] *Review*, pp. 6–8, 23, 24.

[3] *Some Considerations*, p. 40.

[4] *Regulating Silver Coin*, pp. 27, 28, 35.

[5] Pollexfen, *Discourse*, pp. 18, 21, 34.

Not all Locke's contemporaries, however, grasped the principle involved in these phenomena. Barbon, for example, supported his argument in favor of raising silver by pointing out that silver, which had not been raised, was very scarce, while gold, which had twice been raised, was very plentiful; and he says, truly enough, that, when bullion is more valuable in some other place, it ceases to be brought to the mint; but, on the other hand, he denies that lowering guineas will tend to keep silver in the kingdom. The merchant, he argues, may take silver for his goods and need not buy it with gold.[1] The source of this confusion is an erroneous idea of the value of bullion, which considers the numerary value of the metals an independent factor in the problem. Much the same mistake appears in the very confused discussion of Sir Richard Temple. Keeping a standard "below the value of bullion," he declares, carried away England's gold, then the broad money, and lastly the milled money, although the balance of trade was much in England's favor. A page or so later he falls into worse error, and maintains that "the plenty of silver money is the only thing that will reduce them [that is, the guineas] gradually."[2]

[1] Barbon, *Coining the New Money Lighter*, pp. 73–78, 95, 96.

[2] Shaw, *Tracts*, pp. 130–132.

CHAPTER XXII

THE VELOCITY OF CIRCULATION

EXCEPT for references to the need of maintaining a free circulation of money,[1] there had been no discussion of what is nowadays sometimes called the "efficiency of the currency." These early objections to hoarding, though interesting to the student of Mercantile thought,[2] have little direct bearing on monetary theory. In the seventeenth century, however, the beginnings of a much more significant analysis appear. This resulted from the discussion of another question, which had meanwhile been slowly coming to the fore — the amount of money needed for the successful carrying-on of a country's trade.

It is evident from the early discussions of "Gresham's Law" and from the references to hoarding just mentioned, that complaints about an insufficiency of money had already become familiar by the middle of the century; but apparently it did not occur to any one to ask just how much would suffice for a country's needs, until Sir William Petty turned his curious and ingenious mind to the question. His discussion is of the greatest importance, for in his computation he gave great weight to a factor which involved an entirely new idea of circulation — the frequency of payments. If these, he said, were "in such short Circles, *viz.*, weekly, as happens among poorer artizans and labourers, who receive and pay every *Saturday*," then one fifty-second of the annual expense would suffice; but if payments were quarterly, then one fourth of the annual expense would be required.[3] From this point of view, circulation is not simply the antithesis of hoarding, but a matter of the more or less frequent exchanging of money — a change of great significance.

In another respect, however, Petty's discussion only paved the way for much later confusion, since he quite ignored the influence

[1] Sir Thomas More (*Utopia*, p. 81) implied that this was pretty widely understood.

[2] This aspect of the matter is discussed more fully below (Chapter XXXVII).

[3] Petty, *Economic Works*, pp. 35, 36, 112, 113.

of circulation on prices. This attitude is not surprising, indeed, in view of his theory of the value of money. Holding that prices depend simply upon the respective costs of production of money and commodities, he not unnaturally went no further than the conclusion that circulation, an entirely independent factor, determines the volume of transactions, at these prices, which can be effected by a given supply of money in a given period of time, or, conversely, the amount of money needed for a given amount of trade.

As might be expected, the new idea of circulation was first taken up and elaborated by writers who were interested in the same problem that had engaged Petty's attention. About a generation later Locke worked out an elaborate analysis of it along similar lines. The amount of money needed for a country's trade, he says, is not merely a matter of its quantity, but also of the "quickness of its circulation"; for the very same shilling may at one time pay twenty men in twenty days, and at another time may remain a hundred days in the same hands. This seems to be the first use of the phrase now familiar in monetary theory. We cannot determine all this exactly, he goes on to say, but we can make an approximation by estimating how much money must constantly be in each man's hands; for every one must have "at least so much money, or so timely recruits, as may satisfy his creditor."

Taking up the different classes of society, now, he reasons that, since laborers are paid weekly, there is among them, or those who are to pay them, always about a week's wages; for it cannot be thought that most laborers pay out all their wages at once and live on credit till their next pay, and those who pay wages have to hold them a few days. Similarly a landowner's tenants must gather up their quarter's rent by degrees or borrow of those who have done so, and the landowners do not pay out their rents at once, so that there must be about a quarter's rent in the hands of these two classes at all times. Merchants may be supposed to keep at least one twentieth of their yearly receipts on hand; but in great towns, where bankers are ready to make loans, less may be necessary. The bankers in this case, however, must keep some money by them, so that it makes little difference. Although these estimates are, indeed, rough ones, they mark an obvious advance along the lines laid down by Petty.

This analysis of monetary needs, like Petty's, evidently assumes a certain level of prices. Here Locke's theory falls into serious difficulties, for, as we have seen, he believed that prices depend on the quantity of money, and thus they would have no independent determinant. It appears later, however, that other circumstances provide one; for in his further discussion, as we shall see in another chapter, he maintains that there must be enough money in a country to keep prices at about the same level as in other countries. Now this solution of the difficulty only raises another. If prices depend simply on the quantity of money, how can we say that the velocity of circulation is a factor in determining the money needs of a country, that is, in maintaining prices at a certain level? Must we not conclude that the velocity of circulation also affects prices? There is nothing in Locke's discussion to indicate that he had seen this point. The reference to foreign prices is made some twenty pages after the discussion of circulation, and the two do not seem to be connected in his mind. It is very interesting, nevertheless, to see these ideas brought so close together.

It also appears that he did not appreciate all the implications of the theory, even as he understood it; for he says in a later passage that, if a country has exchanges each day of two hundred pounds, and has only one hundred pounds in money, half the trade must be by barter or credit. It does not occur to him that the same shilling might not only pay "twenty men in twenty days," but several men in one day. Too much should not be made of this remark, however, for when he wrote it, he was trying to demonstrate the futility of altering the coinage as an aid to trade, and in this he was perhaps justified in omitting the due qualifications.[1]

This part of Locke's work did not appeal much to his immediate contemporaries, apparently, for we hear no more about it for some time, except in North's remark that more money is required for trade in war-time, because every one wishes to keep some on hand for emergencies.[2]

[1] Locke, *Works*, vol. v, pp. 23–29, 48, 49, 178.
[2] North, *op. cit.*, p. 539.

CHAPTER XXIII

THE PROBLEM OF REFORM

THE procedure to be adopted in effecting a reform of the currency was much more frequently discussed during this period than had been the case earlier. Biblia is of the opinion that a recoinage should not be at the expense of the holders of the old money — or, at least, not wholly so. If this were attempted, he argues, people would seek to hold goods rather than money, and this would cause prices to rise. A day should be set after which the old money should no longer be current, but could be exchanged — weight for weight — for new money at the mint. In case the supply of the latter should prove inadequate, interest-bearing certificates of deposit should be issued till the mint could catch up.[1]

Vaughan's ideas are much like those of Copernicus a century before. The new and better coins will not circulate at the same rate as the old, and the latter cannot be made current at their intrinsic value without using inconvenient fractions. Similar reasoning applies to the case of raising money. Here the small base money must be raised in due proportion; but since this would involve too many fractions, new coins of less intrinsic value have to be made. He also considers the case of an incorrect coinage ratio. If gold is lowered to restore the correct ratio, there will be, he says, "besides the general Objection against all Abasements, which is *Exportation*," the further disadvantage of having to recoin all the gold. It is therefore better to raise silver by coining it hereafter at the new ratio, that is, as the light silver coins are now.[2]

Petty considers the same question as Biblia. A recoinage is clearly necessary, he says, when the old money is worn and

[1] Fornari, *op. cit.*, vol. i, pp. 266, 267.

[2] Vaughan, *Discourse*, pp. 49, 50, 78–80, 192, 193.

clipped, for money, "the best Rule of Commerce," must be kept equal in all its parts. The expense of recoinage should be borne by the state, since it was not the owner's fault that the condition of the coinage became so bad. The loss of weight, however, must fall on the owners, because otherwise people might clip their coins in order to take advantage of the state's bounty. If any alteration of the standard seems necessary or advisable, it is better to raise the value of the coins rather than to increase the alloy, for if you ever want to use the metal, you lose both the value of the alloy and the cost of refining.[1]

Montanari's interest was in the coinage ratio, and his conclusions on this point are different from Vaughan's. When the generally accepted ratio between the metals changes, the government can follow, either by increasing the value of one metal or by lowering the value of the other. The second course is the more advantageous, for it will prevent the value of moneys from advancing, to the prejudice of base money, which rarely increases in value and hence yields less gain to the treasury according to the greater amount of it required to equal a pound of gold or silver.[2] The meaning of this will be clearer, if we recall that by lowering the value of money Montanari meant giving it a lower "price" in terms of the money of account, and that the profit on the base money was due to the fact that this money was overvalued. Now if the price of one of the metals were raised (the price of the base money remaining the same), it would take more base money to equal the "value" of a given amount of metal in the form of standard money, and hence the state would make less profit. The reverse would be true, if the price of one of the metals were lowered.

North does not agree with Petty as to the advisability of a general recoinage. The best way to deal with clipped money, he declares, is to have the government accept it in the public revenues by weight only. In a short time men would refuse it also, except in this way, and the evil would tend to right itself. There would be severe loss in very few cases, for people who have any

[1] Petty, *Economic Works*, pp. 439, 440, 445.

[2] Montanari, *Della Moneta*, pp. 355, 356.

considerable amount of money on hand have usually been careful to pick out good money.[1]

Clement's conclusions differ from those of both Petty and North. Like the former, he considers a general recoinage the only effectual remedy for a clipped currency, but he holds that the loss in weight should be made good at public expense. The use of clipped money should be prohibited after a certain date, and officers appointed in all market-places with whom such coins could be deposited in return for certificates to be used in making payments — a scheme which reminds us of Biblia's. The government need not be very solicitous about returning more of the new money to the owners than the weight of silver actually turned in by them. For the balance they may be given certificates whose currency can be assured by making them interest-bearing till the nation can redeem them. The objection that people might clip the money still more, if the government should undertake to make good the deficiencies in weight in this way, which Petty had shrewdly pointed out, did not occur to Clement, although he notes that even the rumor that such a course was to be adopted would make people save up the clipped pieces.[2]

A proposal something like Clement's was made the next year by the anonymous "Lover of his Country." The clipped and worn money should be called in and recoined with one fifth less weight than the old standard. Its value, however, should be kept up by paying interest to holders of one hundred pounds or more on the amount by which the extrinsic value of the coins exceeds the intrinsic. The exception of smaller sums will lessen the interest burden, but will not affect their value; for the possibility of combining them into larger, and hence interest-bearing, sums will be allowed for by those who receive them.[3]

Strangely enough, the coinage controversy of 1696 occasioned little direct discussion of the problem of reform from the point of view of the coinage ratio, the writers' views being generally implicit in their other arguments. Locke and a number of followers,

[1] North, *op. cit.*, pp. 533–535.
[2] Clement, *Discourse*, pp. 12, 20–23, 37, 38.
[3] *Regulating Silver Coin*, pp. 80–100.

for example, were opposed to any alteration in the standard of the silver coin, on the ground that it would be unfair and disturbing.[1] Although they must have seen, as Locke quite evidently did, that this involved changing the price of gold, either directly by law, or indirectly by leaving it to the valuation of commerce, they failed to make their position clear. As a result there was no little misunderstanding between those who favored lowering gold and those who wished to raise silver, as in the case of Sir Walter Raleigh's rejoinder that Locke might as well deny that raising gold had brought any guineas into England as to say that raising silver would not bring any of it in.[2]

The nearest thing to a direct expression of opinion is in Lowndes, who pointed out, as one of the advantages of raising silver, the fact that it would increase the sum in tale of the country's money supply, and hence meet the needs of trade better. His principal reason, however, for advocating this course was the erroneous idea that it was necessitated by the increased "price" of silver bullion[3] — an increase which was really caused by the overvaluing of gold. Barbon has somewhat similar ideas, and adds the further reason that lowering guineas would be a severe loss to those who have taken them at higher rates. Like Lowndes, however, he attaches more importance to a much less valid argument; for he considers it fundamental that princes must follow each other in fixing the price of bullion (which lies entirely in their hands), or they will lose all their money. Therefore he concludes that, if guineas were lowered, they too would be lost, and the country would have neither gold nor silver to carry on its trade.[4]

[1] Locke, *Works*, vol. v, pp. 110–175; *Some Considerations*, pp. 4, 5, 15–22; *Regulating Silver Coin*, pp. 39, 40; Clement, *Discourse*, pp. 31–39.

[2] Shaw, *Tracts*, p. 139.

[3] Lowndes, *Report*, pp. 206, 215.

[4] Barbon, *Coining the New Money Lighter*, pp. 95, 96.

CHAPTER XXIV

SUMMARY

MONETARY theory made notable, though uneven, advances during the seventeenth century, both in form and content. Although only one new topic was introduced into the discussion, many of those treated by earlier writers were more skillfully handled — in some cases greatly modified. There was a considerable shift in emphasis between the different parts of the theory, practical questions receiving much attention.

In general, there was little fundamental change during this period in the opinions held concerning the origin of money. The agreement concept continued to dominate this phase of the discussion, though there were hints of a different analysis. References to an earlier and happier "state of nature," to the use of pledges before the introduction of money, and to the various stages in the use of the precious metals as media of exchange, constitute the principal element of novelty here.

The functions of money also received comparatively little attention. Most of the references to the topic were along conventional lines, with the exception of some passages which distinguish money's service as a mere measure of value apart from its use in exchange. The idea of money as a store of value was hardly mentioned. The influence of money on mankind was held to have been rather unfortunate on the moral side; but with respect to economic interests, its effects were considered very stimulating.

On many questions of policy the writers of the seventeenth century did not follow their predecessors. Although there was general agreement with the opinion of Aristotle and the Schoolmen as to the material to be used for money, some writers believed that for a purely domestic trade money might be made of any convenient material. Bimetallism, which had been universally accepted hitherto, was rejected by a number of writers, and the comparative merits of the different money metals began to be discussed. In the later years of the period it came to be pretty clearly understood that the coinage ratio is really a problem in market value; but some crude ideas persisted. The liberal views of Bodin and Davanzati with regard to seigniorage made but slow progress during this century.

The growing interest in practical questions is seen in the numerous discussions of the problems of the coinage system. Although the proposals of Bodin and Scaruffi for a simpler and more uniform currency were generally ignored, there were many references to other aspects of the question. Much attention was devoted to the form of coins, especially the use of alloy; many important suggestions were made concerning the regulation of fractional currency, generally approving some limitation on the amount and legal-tender status of such coins, and recognizing their possibilities as a source of government revenue; and several writers discussed the treatment to be accorded foreign coins and clipped ones.

Both Bodin and Davanzati had many followers on the question of the value of money, but the former's ideas were more widely accepted. Many of these statements of the commodity theory are of a most elementary character, but some are of considerable interest. Among the latter Vaughan's deserves especial mention. Locke's famous principle that an ounce of silver is always equal to an ounce of silver occupies a major place in many of the discussions, while the causes determining the value of the precious metals themselves are often relatively neglected. In some cases the influence of supply and demand appears to be quite ignored. Petty's cost of production theory, assimilating the value of money to his general labor theory of value, is of unique interest.

Montanari, the first writer to adopt the analysis of Davanzati, developed many interesting qualifications of this theory, though he seems not to have realized their significance in some cases. He also attempted more than Davanzati in the way of proof, and noted the influence of utility on the value of the precious metals in the arts. Becher, the first writer outside of Italy to follow this line of reasoning, apparently drew his ideas from Davanzati rather than from Montanari. Locke, the first Englishman to adopt the "quantity theory," based his conclusion on a different line of reasoning, but like Montanari he stated the general principle with several important qualifications. He made explicit the proportional change in prices which may be expected to follow an increase in the money supply. It was his arguments against debasement, however, which made the deepest impression on his contemporaries.

Except for Barbon's ingenious and specious defense, the fiat theory received no real support during these years, although the tradition of the *valor impositus* was still discernible in the writings of the later canonists.

In some respects the theory of price changes made considerable advances. In particular, Vaughan's suggestions as to the method of measuring general price changes, and Montanari's analysis of the process by which an increase in the supply of the precious metals works out its effects may be noted. These writers also gave important accounts of the effects caused by price changes on various classes in the community, referring especially to the laboring classes. Many other writers pointed out the losses suffered by creditors, including the king, when prices rise. There was no appreciable change in point of view on the question of deferred payments, most writers favoring, at least as a general principle, the idea that the debtor should repay as great a weight of the precious metals as he received.

There were numerous and often penetrating analyses of the phenomena of circulation. Although the earlier writers of the period grasped the essential principles in many cases, Vaughan's discussion marks the first important advance. He states the case from various angles, his discussion of the influence of the coinage ratio being especially careful. From his time on we meet many important references to this topic. Montanari's treatment is notably clear, and free from the common prejudice against foreigners; and the recoinage of 1696 in England occasioned many discussions of this question, Locke's being the best. Some of Locke's contemporaries, however, failed to understand the principle at all.

The only new aspect of monetary theory considered by the writers of the seventeenth century was the velocity of circulation, to which they were brought in studying the question of a country's monetary needs. Petty's interesting discussion of this problem, though it ignored the influence of velocity on prices, had important results, being presently followed by Locke's elaborate analysis along the same lines. Locke also failed to see the bearing of this on prices.

The problems involved in making changes in the currency system were more fully discussed than in earlier periods. The principal question at issue in these discussions was whether the expense of a recoinage should be borne by the state or by the holders of the demonetized pieces. Next in interest was the policy to be adopted in correcting the coinage ratio. It cannot be said that there was a consensus of opinion on either of these questions.

PART V

THE EIGHTEENTH CENTURY

CHAPTER XXV

INTRODUCTORY

THE eighteenth century was a period of criticism and refinement. The continued dominance of Mercantile ideals ensured an active interest in monetary questions, and a large and able group of writers worked over the theories that had already been developed. Except for a greater interest in banking, — a phase of the discussion which is not taken up in the present study, — they did not greatly expand the scope of monetary discussion, and they did not work from a different point of view. They still, with few exceptions, assigned money and its services a high place as a factor in national prosperity; they still found it necessary to combat official tamperings with the currency; and they continued to discuss questions of administration with great interest.

Although practical questions continued to bulk large in all works on money, the theory profited considerably from the important developments in general economic science which were made during these years, and made significant advances. Clearer ideas regarding value and production led to changes in emphasis and more thorough analysis of monetary problems. The founding of several chairs of political economy encouraged systematic study of economic questions, and the published lectures of their incumbents generally contain significant chapters on monetary theory. Merchants, public officials, and pamphleteers, however, continued to take part in the discussion, sometimes with conspicuous success. In England, France, and Italy such studies are numerous.

In general, the writers of the eighteenth century built on the theories that had already been developed; but they found some of these crude or inadequate. Thus they took pains to reëxamine the doctrines that reflected an excessively mechanical view of social functions, and to study the working of general principles under actual conditions. This led them to restate many important propositions in a more careful and systematic way, and in some cases to modify the traditional theories. In both these respects the Italian writers did notable work.

In the opening years of the century we find discussions of widely varying character. In sharp contrast to most contemporary thought are the writings of Pierre de Boisguillebert, a forerunner of the Physiocrats, who wrote at length upon the depressing conditions in France. His *Traité de la Nature, Culture, Commerce, et Intérêt des Grains*, and his *Dissertation sur la Nature des Richesses, de l'Argent, et des Tributs*, though presenting no systematic theory of the subject, contain numerous references to money, all reflecting a singularly unfavorable view of its influence. John Law, on the other hand, famous as the originator of the famous "System" and the Mississippi Bubble, had exaggerated ideas concerning the utility of money. Despite these defects, however, his *Money and Trade Considered* (1705) contains much acute analysis. Of quite a different order from either of the foregoing were the reports of Sir Isaac Newton, warden of the English mint during the great recoinage, and later (1700–27) master.

The exploits of John Law aroused much discussion. Henri d'Aguesseau, Chancellor of France and a firm opponent of Law's projects, wrote an elaborate treatise on money, which contains some interesting analyses but no very original ideas. Jean François Melon, who had been Law's secretary, undertook his defense in an *Essai politique sur le Commerce* (1734). Several chapters of this were devoted to monetary questions, and the views expressed, especially concerning debasement, were widely debated both in France and abroad. Dutot, who had been a cashier in Law's *Compagnie des Indes*, combated Melon's arguments in his *Réflexions politiques sur les Finances et le Commerce* (1738), as did Joseph Pâris-Duverney in his *Examen du Livre Intitulé Réflexions Politiques sur les Finances et le Commerce* (1740). Most of the latter is an attack on Law's system, but there are some references to the theory of money.

During these same years discussion was active in other countries also. Isaac Gervaise's *The System or Theory of the Trade of the World* (1720), Erasmus Philips's *The State of the Nation in Respect of her Commerce, Debts, and Money* (1725), and Jéronimo de Uztariz's *Téorica y prâtica de Comercio y de Marina* (1724) treat monetary questions incidentally. Thomas Prior's *Observations on Coin in General* (1729) was largely influenced by Locke, but he does not always see the point of theories he is discussing and leaves some of his own conclusions hanging in the air. John Conduit, who succeeded Newton as director of the English mint, wrote some *Observations upon the Present State of our Gold and Silver Coins*, not published till many years later (1774), which have been supposed to reflect Newton's views. They contain nothing of importance on theoretical questions. Jacob Vanderlint's *Money Answers All Things* is not as bad as its title might indicate, but its reasoning is unsatisfactory in places and its value has been overestimated. Bishop Berkeley's *Querist*, and passages in his other works, contain analyses which display good judgment and considerable ingenuity, but they are unsystematized. William Douglass, a Boston (Massachusetts) physician, in *A Discourse Concerning the Currencies of the British Plantations in America* (1740), made a vigorous attack on the cheap money schemes of the American colonists.

More important than any of the foregoing is Richard Cantillon's *Essai sur le Commerce*, written about 1733 and circulated in manuscript, but not published till 1755. It was the ablest discussion of economic questions before the *Wealth of Nations*, and had great influence on the trend of economic thought. Parts II and III are devoted chiefly to monetary and banking questions. They are marked by a high degree of analytical skill, especially in the treatment of value, prices, and circulation.

Of equal importance, in some respects, was Montesquieu's *De l'Esprit des Lois* (1748), written and published while Cantillon's work was still in manuscript. Books 18, 20, and 22 are largely or wholly devoted to monetary questions. His observations on the influence of money on social development are often notable, but his statements of some points of theory are rigid and mechanical. The great prestige of the work gave these views an influence quite as great as that exercised by more specialized treatises, and for this reason it is of great significance.

In Italy there was a distinguished group of writers on money, some of the first importance. Salustio Bandini's *Discorso Economico* (written 1737) contains twelve or thirteen pages on this topic, but nothing of particular interest. The *Trattato delle Monete* (1743) of Antonio Broggia, a Neapolitan merchant, gives much attention to the practical aspects of monetary principles, especially with respect to Italian conditions. His reasoning is not always clear or convincing. The *Riflessioni Politiche* (1748?) of Trojano Spinelli, another Neapolitan, contains some liberal views on money. Girolamo Belloni, a Roman banker, won considerable reputation with his *Dissertazione sopra il Commercio* (1750). Like most of the Italian writers, he was much interested in practical questions, and his short chapter on money makes some interesting suggestions. Pompeo Neri, a public official in Tuscany and Milan, also deals with matters of policy in his *Osservazioni sopra il Prezzo Legale delle Monete* (1751), displaying much caution and insight.

None of these Italian writers compares in ability with Ferdinando Galiani. His *Della Moneta*, published anonymously in 1750, when the author was only twenty-two years old, and not acknowledged till thirty years later, when he had gained a great reputation as a wit and critic of the Physiocrats, is in many respects a brilliant performance. It contains much ingenious and original analysis, and though the author's fondness for dialectic sometimes warps his views, his conclusions are for the most part sound. Practical questions play a smaller part than is usual in the Italian writers. Besides the discussions of monetary problems, there are chapters on value and interest which are in advance of anything published earlier.

The next decade saw interesting developments in England. Hume's *Political Discourses* (1752) contained several essays on economic questions, including one on money, in which he criticized some of the fundamental principles of the Mercantile philosophy very effectively. He was particularly skillful in developing the qualifications to be made to certain general principles. Sir John Barnard's brief *Some Thoughts on the Scarcity of Silver Coin, with a Proposal for Remedy* (1759) made important suggestions for the regulation of subsidiary money. Malachy Postlethwayt's *Great Britain's True System* (1757) followed Cantillon very closely (without acknowledgment), and the author's own attempts at modification were rather unsuccessful. Massie, Magens, Tucker, and Wallace also touched upon money, but their work in this field was in no way distinguished. The most elaborate discussion of monetary questions during the decade was Joseph Harris's *Essay on Money and Coins* (1757–58). The author, who also published several works on navigation, trigonometry, and similar subjects, was appointed assay master of the mint in 1748. His views on some points are quite conventional and on others not fully developed, but some of his chapters, notably that on value, are of high quality. He devotes much space to the theory and history of debasement, arguing at length against the practice.

The most important German writers on economic subjects during this period were Johann von Justi and Joseph von Sonnenfels. The former, a professor of cameral sciences in Vienna and later a government official in Göttingen and Berlin, published numerous works on political, commercial, and financial subjects during the ten years following 1755. In general these do no more than present an effective combination of the best thought of the time, but there are some novel analyses. His point of view is liberal, and he is much impressed by English experience. Sonnenfels, also a professor in Vienna, followed Justi closely on many points. His *Grundsätze der Polizei, Handlungs- und Finanzwissenschaft* (1763–67) became an official textbook in Austrian and Hungarian universities, and was long used there. Though not an original thinker, he shows an intelligent and discriminating appreciation of contemporary thought in his field.

Some of the above-mentioned writers had made damaging criticisms of various points in the Mercantilist philosophy, but there had been no repudiation of the whole system. The Physiocrats, however, broke entirely away from these ideals. It is not surprising, therefore, to find them comparatively little interested in the monetary discussions which had seemed so important to the Mercantilists. The elder Mirabeau's *L'Ami des Hommes* (1756), written before he became attached to Quesnay's circle, contains some interesting references to money's influence on social development, and some of the chapters in Turgot's *Réflexions sur la Formation et la Distribution des Richesses* (1769) bear witness to his understanding of the basic principles of monetary theory; but Mercier de la Rivière's famous *L'Ordre Naturel et Essentiel des Sociétés Politiques* (1767) makes but brief reference to this traditional topic.

During these same years some writers were trying to defend the older doctrine and to restate its tenets in less vulnerable form. One of the most important of these attempts was Sir James Steuart's *An Inquiry into the Principles of Political Œconomy* (1767). Steuart was a writer of marked ability, and his elaborate discussion of money, though marred by certain curious prepossessions, is of great interest. Not so much can be said of Forbonnais, another defender of Mercantilism. The references to money in his *Principes et Observations Économiques* (1767) are not always clear and the reasoning is sometimes confused.

We continue to find much discussion in Italy during the later years of the period. Gian Rinaldo Carli's *Dell' Origine e del Commercio della Moneta* (1751–60) contains much valuable historical material and some interesting analyses, but its ponderous chapters occasionally miss the point of a controversy or fail to get anywhere. The *Lezioni di Commercio ossia di Economia Civile* (1765) of Antonio Genovesi, "most distinguished and moderate of all Italian Mercantilists," contains many able chapters on money, with special emphasis on the social aspects of the subject. Pietro Verri's *Meditazioni sull' economia politica* (1771), many times translated, displays keen analytical power. Giovan Battista Vasco, zealous advocate of freedom, combines ingenious and often subtle reasoning with many sensible practical suggestions in his *Della Moneta* (1772). The *Della Economia Nazionale* (1774) of Giammaria Ortes, an original genius, though highly artificial in some respects, is of considerable interest. The works of Pagnini, Beccaria, and Paradisi are not particularly notable.

There remain to be mentioned in this survey only three works — all of minor importance in the field of money. Joseph Accarias de Sérionne's *Les Intérêts des nations de l'Europe develop-*

pés relativement au commerce (1766) shows the influence of English writers, and points out some interesting qualifications of various points of theory. Isaac Pinto, a wealthy merchant of Holland, published in 1773 a *Traité de la Circulation et du Crédit*, which, though notable for its emphasis upon circulation, is not always clear or effective. And finally, in the same year with the *Wealth of Nations* appeared the Abbé Condillac's *Le Commerce et le Gouvernement*, remarkable for its discussion of value, but giving only a brief treatment of money.

CHAPTER XXVI

THE ORIGIN AND FUNCTIONS OF MONEY

1. The Origin of Money

Most eighteenth-century discussions of this topic appear to have taken the advantages of exchange for granted, and to have been more interested in other aspects of the question. Such references as there are, however, tend to emphasize the interdependence of men. Galiani refers to the "mutual needs which each man has"; [1] Justi declares that all men and all countries need help from each other, for no one is able to provide through his own efforts the things required for human needs; [2] and Turgot gives a Physiocratic twist to the idea by explaining that, since the products of earth require long and difficult preparation, before they are fit for consumption, there arises exchange between the cultivators and the other members of society, all gaining through the greater efficiency of production.[3] A few writers referred briefly to the advantages of the division of labor, without making any additions of interest.[4]

The inconveniences of barter were more frequently discussed. Law and Harris pointed out that differences in the values of goods of the same kind made barter uncertain.[5] Boisguillebert and Philips reasoned that the increasing complexity of needs, as society developed, had made barter more and more difficult.[6] Genovesi elaborates this idea in an interesting way. He distinguishes two stages in the development of barter: an earlier one, in which no evaluation takes place, but merely "a kind of mutual

[1] Galiani, *Della Moneta*, vol. i, p. 142.

[2] Justi, *Gesammelte Politische und Finanzschriften*, vol. ii, p. 414.

[3] Turgot, *Réflexions sur la Formation et la Distribution des Richesses*, pp. 244–246.

[4] Tucker (see Clark, *Josiah Tucker, Economist*, p. 167); Forbonnais, *Principes Économiques*, p. 181; Pinto, *Traité de la Circulation*, p. 230.

[5] Law, *Money and Trade Considered*, p. 6; Harris, *Essay upon Money and Coins*, p. 35.

[6] Boisguillebert, *Nature des Richesses*, p. 396; Philips, *State of the Nation*, pp. 39, 40.

donation"; and a later stage, in which men begin to put different values on different commodities, and in the course of time find their calculations too intricate.[1] Sonnenfels noted that not only are some goods indivisible, but some divisible goods lose value in the process.[2] These modifications, it is evident, add but little to the main outlines of theory as they had stood for nearly two hundred years.

During the early years of the century the introduction of money was still generally ascribed to an agreement.[3] Bishop Berkeley's treatment is the only one that deserves special mention. Starting with a shipwrecked crew on a desert island, he supposes that in time one man might procure more of some commodity than he could consume, and would exchange this surplus to supply his other wants. This would produce credit, and "to facilitate these conveyances, to record and circulate this credit, they would soon agree on certain tallies, tokens, tickets, or counters." [4] In other words, money originated as an aid to credit transactions. Though not very successful, this is rather interesting as an early venture in the field of "Crusoe Economics." The idea that money originated as a pledge or pawn is also met during these years.[5]

Criticism of the agreement theory presently developed. Although Cantillon does not go into this question very deeply, he clearly has no sympathy with the idea of an agreement. The use of money, he says, arose as a slow development from other uses of the precious metals. The latter, having come to be much sought for, because of their beauty, could easily be given as a pledge or sold by those who found themselves in need of other things; and thus arose their use as money.[6]

[1] Genovesi, *Lezioni di Commercio*, vol. ii, pp. 24, 25, 30.

[2] Sonnenfels, *Sätze aus der Polizei, Handlungs- und Finanzwissenschaft*, pt. ii, pp. 15, 16.

[3] Rohr (see Small, *The Cameralists*, p. 205); Doria (see Fornari, *op. cit.*, vol. i, p. 346); Böhmert, *Ein Lehrbuch über den Volkswohlstand*, p. 22; Philips, *op. cit.*, p. 40; Prior, *Observations on Coin in General*, p. 296; Melon, *Essai Politique sur le Commerce*, p. 780; Hutcheson, *Introduction to Moral Philosophy*, p. 226; Broggia, *Trattato delle Monete*, vol. i, pp. 303–305.

[4] Berkeley, *Complete Works*, vol. iv, p. 426.

[5] Dutot, *Réflexions Politiques*, pp. 907, 908.

[6] Cantillon, *Essai sur le Commerce*, pp. 130–135.

It was not, however, till some ten years after Hume's refutation of the contract theory of government that its counterpart in monetary theory was definitely attacked. Galiani declared that it is ridiculous to say that men all at one time agreed to use the precious metals as money and thus gave them value. Where and when was such an agreement made, and how did the makers represent all the nations of the world, even strangers and enemies to each other? His own explanation really consists of two parts. In the first he gives an ingenious but not very scientific account of how men became acquainted with metals. Iron and copper were doubtless the first to be known, being in large and not very deep veins, and often found in large masses pure. Curiosity and chance led men to bring them near fire and thus discover their nature. The metallurgical knowledge thus gained helped men discover the other metals. Gold was first found in streams, and then its existence in the mountains, from which the streams flow, was deduced. There they also found silver, which generally accompanies gold. In a later passage he considers the use of the precious metals as money, and concludes that this results from the nature of things, not from the deliberation of congresses held at the foot of the Tower of Babel.[1] The functions of money and the qualities of the precious metals are such that the latter are "naturally money." At first they passed simply by weight, alloying and the finer differences of quality being unknown.[2] Though the positive value of this is not great, its critical and analytical standards mark a real advance.

Although occasional references to the agreement theory occur after this time, they are mostly crude imitations of some earlier writer,[3] or careless expressions not to be taken literally.[4] It is rather strange that about the only exceptions were Carli and

[1] ". . . sono le disposizioni dell' animo nostro e le costituzioni intrinseche delle cose."

[2] Galiani, *Della Moneta*, vol. i, pp. 26–32, 110–137.

[3] Belloni (*Dissertazione sopra il Commercio*, p. 48) gives the words of Paulus almost verbatim.

[4] Hume's reference to the "agreement and convention of men" (*Essays*, vol. i, p. 321) is doubtless in this class. Also Harris, *Essay upon Money and Coins*, p. 36.

Ortes, who, being Italians, should have known Galiani's work.[1] Carli's account is not without interest, however, for he seems to have been the first to base the early esteem of the metals on their use as ornament, in which stage they were treated like other commodities. It was not until trade in them became extensive that they acquired a peculiar position, and then it was the merchants who agreed to deal in them by weight and use them as money. This agreement soon passed into law. The stamp on the earliest coins was merely an indication of value; the use of the figures of animals and so forth came later, and was perhaps due to the fact that these were the most common things. Some of the early signs, such as palms and grapes, may have been to show where the coins were made.

Galiani's analysis was soon modified. Justi considers foreign trade the immediate cause of the use of gold and silver as money, since in this trade an article of universal acceptability was necessary. Before the introduction of public coinage, it is probable that, in order to avoid the trouble of testing, those who paid out gold and silver put a sign on them to show fineness as well as weight, as is now done with bullion bars. Such signs found credit according to the good name of their makers.[2] Sonnenfels insists on the gradual character of the introduction of money.[3]

It was in Italy again, however, that the next important development took place. Starting with Galiani's idea that the use of money is a "necessary effect of nature and of time, like all the customs of mankind," Genovesi traces the evolution of money more elaborately. Among nomads certain animals in universal use gradually came to serve as a convenient means of expressing values and effecting exchanges. The memory of this primitive custom was preserved in the images of animals stamped on early coins. As agriculture developed, other common commodities also were used in this way; and after the discovery of copper and iron, these metals, being of prime importance for war and the arts of

[1] Carli, *Dell' Origine e del Commercio della Moneta*, vol. i, pp. 18–37; Ortes, *Della Economia Nazionale*, vol. ii, pp. 271–273.

[2] Justi, *Schriften*, vol. i, p. 359, vol. ii, p. 422.

[3] Sonnenfels, *op. cit.*, pt. ii, p. 18.

peace, gradually superseded all other representatives of things. In the course of time, however, the shining bits of gold which were found by various accidents acquired, through their use in luxury, a greater and more universal value than other commodities; men grew willing to exchange all other goods for them; and they became the only "eminent price of all valuable things." At first the metals were only arbitrary measures, which were given without weighing — by the eye; but as people began to know better the relations between things and needs, and gold and silver had become very valuable, men grew more diligent in guarding them, and thus weighing developed. As the value increased, fraud by means of alloying had to be guarded against, and sovereigns determined to certify both weight and fineness.[1]

Genovesi's treatment of this topic was not equalled by any later writer of the period. Beccaria shows clearly the influence of both Galiani and Genovesi. The adoption of the precious metals as money, he says, did not take place as the result of any actual agreement, but of a general "adhesion" to a convenient practice. The earliest money was cattle, as we can see from the stamps on early metallic money. In the course of time the sands of certain rivers, volcanic eruptions, fires, and men's natural curiosity led to the knowledge and use of metals. Religion, love, and ambition caused gold and silver to be widely demanded as ornaments and signs of distinction, and thus they gradually became the equivalent of all things. It was to guarantee their fineness that they were first stamped by public authority.[2] Turgot agrees with Galiani that gold and silver became money without any arbitrary agreement among men, but only from the nature of things;[3] while the ingenious author of an anonymous *Essay on the Theory of Money* published in 1771 maintains that chance and curiosity led to the use of money. Someone, having found a gem or piece of shining metal, took it to his village, where it excited the curiosity of all and tempted a person of means to give the finder something for it. By degrees gems and pieces of metal became an object of

[1] Genovesi, *Lezioni*, vol. ii, pp. 25 n., 30–35.

[2] Beccaria, *Elementi di Economia Pubblica*, vol. ii, pp. 13–22, 196, 197.

[3] Turgot, *Réflexions*, pp. 270, 271.

search to all.[1] Condillac says the use of money developed gradually, as people realized its convenience; and he gives an account much like Genovesi's of the evolution of coinage.[2]

The criticisms of the earlier theories did not cause them to lose all support. Harris, Pinto, and Bandini hold that money developed out of the use of pledges,[3] and Ortes has a simple agreement theory.[4]

2. The Functions of Money

Comparatively little attention was devoted to analyzing the functions of money during this century. The measuring of values is emphasized, as in earlier periods, generally as a phase of the process of exchange.[5] Galiani clearly distinguishes between these two functions. Money has two uses, he says, to value things and to buy them. The first is extremely important, because it helps us to grasp the relation between things much more readily; and, unlike the buying function, it is performed equally well by real or ideal money.[6] This is the clearest expression of the distinction during the period, but the point was noted by some later writers. Harris, for example, qualifies his insistence that money is both the measure and the thing bargained for, by admitting that, in the case of barter, where the goods exchanged are now often valued in money terms, money may be a measure only;[7] and Steuart explains clearly the use of a general measure of value.[8]

Money's service as a store of value is only implied in most dis-

[1] *An Essay on the Theory of Money*, pp. vi, vii.

[2] Condillac, *Le Commerce et le Gouvernement*, pp. 287, 288.

[3] Harris, *Essay*, p. 36; Pinto, *Traité de la Circulation*, p.231; Bandini, *Discorso Economico*, p. 143.

[4] Ortes, *Della Economia Nazionale*, vol. ii, pp. 271–273.

[5] Law, *Money and Trade*, pp. 11, 12; Rohr (see Small, *The Cameralists*, p. 205); Böhmert, *Ein Lehrbuch*, p. 22; Melon, *Essai Politique*, p. 761; Vanderlint, *Money Answers All Things*, p. 12; Berkeley, *Works*, vol. iv, p. 175; Broggia, *Trattato della Moneta*, vol. i, p. 305; Spinelli (see Fornari, *op. cit.*, vol. ii, p. 116); Neri, *Osservazioni*, p. 121; Hume, *Essays*, vol. i, p. 312; Tucker (see Clark, *Josiah Tucker*, p. 194); Turgot, *Réflexions*, p. 268; Pinto, *Traité de la Circulation*, p. 149; Ortes, *Della Economia Nazionale*, vol. ii, p. 273.

[6] Galiani, *Della Moneta*, vol. i, p. 112.

[7] Harris, *Essay*, pp. 37–39.

[8] Steuart, *Inquiry*, vol. i, p. 539.

cussions. Thus Law describes money as a value paid, with which the receiver may buy an equal value when he wishes;[1] and Broggia discusses the fitness of the precious metals for hoarding.[2] The idea also seems to underlie the references to money as a pledge, which appeared frequently after Vaughan's time,[3] and the related conception of money as a sign or certificate of commodities, which we meet in the second half of the century, probably as a reaction against the crude emphasis on money by earlier Mercantilists.[4] Some of these discussions contain interesting details. Galiani says money is the representation of a claim one has on society, like a ticket good at the communal warehouse; and Tucker similarly declares that money is "nothing more than a certificate of labor," probably implying a labor theory of value. Turgot brings the two ideas together by referring to money as a "representative pledge."

These are the only functions of money which were noted by any considerable number of writers during the period. Law's statement, that money is the "value in which contracts are made payable," seems to have been the first specific reference to money's use as a standard of deferred payments.[5] He was followed by Harris.[6] Forbonnais's attempt to distinguish a separate function in money's property of being a fictitious *immeuble*, that is, of being a source of income in the form of interest, has no scientific value.[7]

[1] Law, *Money and Trade*, p. 114.

[2] Broggia, *Trattato delle Monete*, vol. i, pp. 307, 308.

[3] Boisguillebert, *Nature des Richesses*, p. 397; Böhmert, *Ein Lehrbuch*, p. 22; Melon, *Essai Politique*, p. 761; Dutot, *Réflexions Politiques*, pp. 907, 908; Spinelli (see Fornari, *op. cit.*, vol. ii, p. 116); Turgot, *Réflexions*, pp. 267, 268; Neri, *Osservazioni*, p. 121; Harris, *Essay*, p. 36; Beccaria, *Elementi*, vol. ii, p. 8; Pinto, *Traité de la Circulation*, p. 231; Bandini, *Discorso Economico*, p. 143.

[4] Montesquieu, *Esprit des Lois*, pp. 376–379; Galiani, *Della Moneta*, vol. i, pp. 148–150; Hume, *Essays*, vol. i, p. 312; Tucker (see Clark, *Josiah Tucker*, p. 194); Justi, *Gesammelte Schriften*, vol. iii, pp. 29, 30; Sonnenfels, *Sätze aus der Polizei . . .*, pt. ii, p. 31.

[5] Law, *Money and Trade*, pp. 113, 114.

[6] Harris, *Essay*, p. 37.

[7] Forbonnais, *Principes Économiques*, p. 216.

3. The Reactions of Money on Man and on Society

Unfavorable views concerning the influence of money on human motives continued to be common during the eighteenth century. Boisguillebert held that theft and all crimes requiring secrecy are facilitated under a money régime, because money enables the criminal to conceal his unjust gains.[1] Montesquieu presents the same argument from a different angle. In a country where there is no money, a thief carries with him the evidence of his crime, for he takes away things, and things, being never alike, are easily identified.[2] Berkeley, Montesquieu, and Ortes point out the tendency to excessive accumulation. Ortes is the most effective. Men, he says, in their eagerness to assure their subsistence, naturally seek a durable means like money; and thus the check which they might feel from the limitation of natural needs and the perishability of commodities loses its effect, and their desire to accumulate becomes as unlimited as money is durable.[3]

Some writers discuss the matter in more general terms. Justi declares that money, by increasing the cravings and imaginary needs of men and extending their power more than is natural, has caused all injustice and oppression in the world;[4] and Genovesi enumerates new wants, false ideas of wealth, usury, and bad faith as due to the use of money.[5]

The influence of money on economic activity was more fully discussed. Law considers the question quite elaborately. Because of the difficulties of barter, there was little trade and few "artsmen" in that early stage, men working principally for themselves and trying to make their own lands supply all their needs, with the result that land was often not used to the best advantage; but as the use of money spread, more land was cultivated and its product was increased, the poor and idle were employed, trade and manufactures improved, and all lived in greater com-

[1] Boisguillebert, *Nature des Richesses*, pp. 399, 400.

[2] Montesquieu, *Esprit des Lois*, p. 330.

[3] Ortes, *Della Economia Nazionale*, vol. ii, pp. 339–341; Berkeley, *Works*, vol. iv, p. 450; Montesquieu, *Esprit des Lois*, p. 208.

[4] Justi, *Gesammelte Schriften*, vol. iii, pp. 39, 40.

[5] Genovesi, *Lezioni*, vol. ii, pp. 91, 111.

fort and independence. Although this reasoning marks a real advance, by making clear the connection between money and the division of labor, it hardly justifies all the important conclusions based upon it, and it soon led the author into more serious error. Not only does money facilitate greater and more efficient production, according to Law, but every addition to the money of a country will employ more people in proportion to the increase, and even though the employer loses, will add to the wealth of the nation.[1] The confusion of money with capital is obvious.

Though free from this error, the conclusions of Berkeley are in some ways inferior to those of Law. His statements that money is "only so far useful, as it stirreth up industry, enabling men mutually to participate the fruits of each other's labor," and that the zeal of the people for industry "depends principally on the means for counting, transferring, and preserving power," seem to show a grasp of the fact that the only influence of money on industry is through the aid it gives to exchange, but the argument needs clinching.[2] Even less can be said for Montesquieu's vague assertion that the cultivation of lands demands the use of money, since it supposes many arts and sciences, and all this leads to the establishment of a sign of values.[3]

In Genovesi's work the argument advanced by Law is handled with greater skill. In a nation having no money, men being obliged to provide for their own wants themselves or by barter, which is very inconvenient, will think only of necessaries, and arts will be few and slow; but introduce money, and each man, knowing he can exchange for what he wants, will engage in trade and thus increase commodities and industry.[4] Beccaria seems to have somewhat the same idea, but he is less definite. The introduction of the precious metals as money, he says, marked the age of commerce. Trade, which before this had been merely for the satisfaction of the momentary wants of individuals, now became more extensive, more rapid, easier, and more soundly directed.[5]

[1] Law, *Money and Trade*, pp. 7, 8, 18, 19, 20–23.
[2] Berkeley, *Works*, vol. iv, pp. 422–424.
[3] Montesquieu, *Esprit des Lois*, p. 329.
[4] Genovesi, *Lezioni*, vol. ii, pp. 93, 94.
[5] Beccaria, *Elementi di Economia Pubblica*, vol. ii, pp. 19, 20.

Some years before Genovesi's time Broggia pointed out an aspect of the problem which attracted little attention. According to his view, money has often caused industry to decay, for men need to know how to handle and manage goods, as all did in the days of barter or when domestic animals served as a medium of exchange.[1] Genovesi has the same idea.[2]

The Physiocrats' superior understanding of the factors of production is reflected in the ideas of Turgot on this point. The use of money, he says, enables every one to devote himself to a special task more readily, since he is assured of providing for his other wants by the money he receives. In this way money has greatly hastened the progress of mankind. To this consideration, which Law, it will be remembered, had already developed with some success, he adds another, of the greatest importance. Money has been of further aid to industry by facilitating the accumulation of capital and its advance to laborers. The meaning of this is made clearer by his statement later that money plays a large part in the formation of capital, since almost all savings are made in money, which is converted into supplies for various industries.[3]

Something like this may have been intended in Forbonnais's account of the influence of money on the cultivation of land; but he has such an erroneous idea of capital, that it is probably more accurate to say that Turgot was the only one to make this point during the period we are studying. Forbonnais also refers to the influence of money on the division of labor, and puts more emphasis on the changes in economic structure which this involves; but in general his work here is below the standard of his immediate predecessors. He makes one point not noted by other writers, arguing that the uncertainty of selling, under a system of barter, and the fact that dealings would have to be in commodities that are perishable or difficult to care for, tend to discourage any attempt at storage for speculation.[4]

Another example of the tendency to go too far in analyzing the influence of money on production is found in the anonymous

[1] Broggia, *Trattato delle Monete*, vol. i, pp. 308–311.

[2] Genovesi, *Lezioni*, vol. ii, p. 239.

[3] Turgot, *Réflexions*, pp. 273, 290, 316, 317.

[4] Forbonnais, *Principes Économiques*, pp. 179, 180, 215, 220.

Essay on the Theory of Money, to which we have already referred. Although the author sees that, by aiding exchange, money encourages the division of labor, which without money would be of only the simplest and most primitive kind, he confuses money in general with changes in the supply of money, and money with capital.[1]

There was at least one exception to this generally favorable view. Boisguillebert declared that money leads people to ignore the true relation between the members of a society, and thus often causes misery and ruin. Although his reasons are pretty obscure, the idea seems to be that the hoarding of money, or reckless attempts to obtain it for the satisfaction of immediate desires, may dislocate prices to such an extent that producers suffer great losses and are ruined.[2]

Our ideas of value are also affected by the use of money, according to some writers. Verri says that the idea of money leads to more uniform ideas of value,[3] while Condillac holds that it leads to erroneous ones. In the first place, he argues, the use of money in exchanges fosters the idea that values can be measured definitely; and in the second place, it leads to the error of thinking that in exchanges we give equal value for equal value. He also points out that, by facilitating exchange, money gives a value to things which before had none.[4]

A few writers noted a relationship between money and taxation. According to Boisguillebert, the practice of paying taxes in money allows inequalities to be perpetrated which would be all too obvious, if taxes were collected in kind, and serves to conceal taxation which is really ruinous to certain classes.[5] Hume, on the other hand, merely says that taxes in kind are inconvenient, and that consequently a state may be weak in this respect, though fertile and populous.[6] Möser also considers money a means of levying heavier taxes.[7]

[1] *An Essay*, pp. 29–40, 79.

[3] Verri, *Économie Politique*, p. 5.

[2] Boisguillebert, *Nature des Richesses*, pp. 399, 408–414, 419.

[4] Condillac, *Le Commerce et le Gouvernement*, pp. 286–292.

[5] Boisguillebert, *Nature des Richesses*, pp. 401–403.

[6] Hume, *Essays*, vol. i, p. 319.

[7] Roscher, *National-Oekonomik in Deutschland*, p. 525.

In political organization also the influence of money is traceable. Here, as in the case of human motives, we must not confuse the effect of money with that of wealth in general.[1] No significant treatment of this topic is found until the time of Montesquieu. If one should arrive among an unknown people, he says, and should see a piece of money, one could conclude he was in a "policed nation." For when a group does not use money, the only political arrangements are those of the weak, who combine for protection against violence, which is the only form of injustice known in such circumstances; but where money is established, good civil laws become indispensable as a check to the thousand forms of injustice through trickery to which the individual is then exposed. And since equality, moreover, is practically forced where men satisfy their simple needs themselves or by barter, rulers cannot be despotic.[2]

Mirabeau, a few years later, presented a different aspect of the matter. The easy transportability of money, he thought, had served more than anything else to bind together a great number of societies of men, and consequently to form great states.[3] Möser made a similar point about twenty years later.[4] Carli refers to the ideas of the classical philosophers concerning wealth and political organization, and connects money more specifically with the discussion. With the free field for the accumulation of wealth which money afforded, many private citizens became tyrants, he declares, and some law-givers were induced to take measures, such as ostracism and communism, against the tendency.[5]

Except for Genovesi's brief assertion that under a system of barter there would be no civil society or government,[6] there was only one other discussion of this aspect of the question during the period. The *Essay on the Theory of Money*, of 1771, elaborates several considerations which the author evidently developed un-

[1] It is the latter only which is meant in such discussions as those of Plato (*Republic*, bk. viii), Aristotle (*Politics*, bk. v), and Polybius (bk. vi; quoted in Carli, *op. cit.*, vol. i, p. 44).

[2] Montesquieu, *Esprit des Lois*, pp. 329, 330.

[3] Mirabeau, *L'Ami des Hommes*, pp. 183, 184.

[4] Roscher, *op. cit.*, p. 525.

[5] Carli, *op. cit.*, vol. i, pp. 42–45.

[6] Genovesi, *Lezioni*, vol. ii, p. 98.

der the influence of Montesquieu. Without money, he writes, there would be neither sovereign nor subject, because every individual could satisfy his wants by his own industry, and therefore could have no reason to submit to the will of another. Riches would be in the form of flocks, which could never give any man sufficient superiority to enable him to buy or force the submission of another. The world would be peopled with small and wandering societies, governed by the advice of their old men, and having no formal laws. Although the author impairs the value of this by later dubious references to the "introduction of circulation" in the disorderly kingdoms of western Europe, and to the wealth-concentrating tendencies of a "large circulation," I think we may call this discussion a significant example of the influence of Montesquieu.[1]

[1] *An Essay*, Introduction; also pp. 53, 65, 68.

CHAPTER XXVII

SOME QUESTIONS OF POLICY

1. The Qualities Desirable in Money

The writers of the eighteenth century made some interesting additions to the accepted ideas on this question. Law's discussion early in the period contains a number of important points. He agrees with some of his predecessors that money ought to be made of a material which is stable in value; but instead of basing this on the argument that all measures should be stable, as earlier writers had done, he says it is because money is a store of value. His inclusion of ease of delivery among the qualities which make silver suitable for money is reminiscent of Asgill a few years earlier. Some of his points, however, appear to be quite original. Thus his statement that one of silver's advantages as money lies in the fact that it is so much more "certain in quality" seems to be the first mention of homogeneity among the qualities desired; and he was also the first to specify, not merely divisibility, but divisibility without loss of value. He insists, moreover, that "goods given as a value," that is, money, ought to have a value for their other uses equal to that for which they are given. In this respect silver is defective, for it has a considerable additional value merely from its use as money, which would be lost, of course, if silver should be demonetized.[1]

Only two of the points made by Law were accepted by other writers, and practically nothing new was suggested. Prior, Cantillon, Montesquieu, Galiani, Turgot, Steuart, and Beccaria all agreed that the homogeneity of the precious metals was a distinct advantage for their use as money.[2] Galiani and Turgot explain

[1] Law, *op. cit.*, pp. 8, 9, 11, 114, 135–137, 157, 158.

[2] Prior, *Observations on Coin in General*, p. 296; Montesquieu, *op. cit.*, p. 378; Galiani, *op. cit.*, vol. i, pp. 126, 127; Cantillon, *Essai sur le Commerce*, p. 145; Turgot, *op. cit.*, p. 270; Steuart, *op. cit.*, vol. i, p. 532; Beccaria, *op. cit.*, vol. ii, pp. 11–14.

that this is because the value of such a material depends simply upon the easily ascertainable factor of quantity. Cantillon, Hutcheson, Neri, Harris, Sonnenfels, and Beccaria recognize the advantage of divisibility without loss of value.[1] A few writers mention stability of value, influenced more by Locke, apparently, than by Law, on this point.[2]

The only suggestions along new lines on this topic after Law's time are in Ortes, Prior, and the anonymous *Essay on the Theory of Money*. The first, with an obvious eye to his theory of prices, says the money material should be hard to find, for only thus can its total supply be determined and assigned.[3] The last two include a point mentioned by Barbon more than thirty years before and unnoticed since: difficulty of imitation makes a material more suitable for money.[4]

As in earlier periods, there were a few writers who held that the material to be used for money might, at least under certain circumstances, be a matter of indifference. Boisguillebert appears to be of this opinion, though he makes no specific statement,[5] and Ortes insists only on the requirement mentioned above: that the material be not too easy to find. Berkeley says that since money is only a "ticket or token," it is of no consequence what it is made of.[6] Pinto asserts that there is no physical reason why only gold and silver should be money.[7] A more moderate view, substantially the same as that advanced by Salmasius a century earlier, was held by Douglass, Pagnini, Justi, and Carli, who all agree that for purely domestic purposes money might be made of any convenient material, but for use in a state having trade with other peoples, a commodity generally acceptable must be em-

[1] Cantillon, *op. cit.*, p. 142; Hutcheson, *Introduction to Moral Philosophy*, vol. ii, p. 226; Neri, *op. cit.*, p. 133; Harris, *op. cit.*, p. 43; Sonnenfels, *op. cit.*, p. 18; Beccaria, vol. ii, pp. 13, 14.

[2] *An Inquiry into the Nature and Uses of Money*, pp. 25–27; Galiani, *op. cit.*, vol. i, pp. 136, 137; Steuart, *op. cit.*, vol. i, p. 541; Condillac, *op. cit.*, pp. 334–336.

[3] Ortes, *op. cit.*, vol. ii, pp. 277, 278.

[4] Prior, *op. cit.*, p. 296; *An Essay*, Introduction, p. ix.

[5] Boisguillebert, *Nature des Richesses*, p. 397.

[6] Berkeley, *Works*, vol. iv, p. 425.

[7] Pinto, *op. cit.*, p. 149.

ployed.[1] All these writers, it should be noted, were opposed to cheap money schemes in practice.

2. Problems of the Standard

Further opposition to bimetallism is met among eighteenth-century writers. Spinelli, Galiani, and Vasco reasoned much as Bocchi had done earlier: errors in the ratio established between the standard metals may lead to the loss of one of them, or necessitate the expense of recoinage.[2] Harris gives Locke's arguments for a single standard almost word for word.[3] Steuart's reasoning is quite unique. When the monetary unit, the pound, for example, is "attached to both species," creditors never can gain from variations in the ratio, for debtors will pay in the least valuable metal; hence it is better to attach the unit to one metal, in which case it is uncertain who will gain.[4] Prior completely misunderstood Locke's reasoning, and maintained that not only do we need more than one metal to provide convenient coins of different values, but there is no validity in the objection that the ratio between them varies, for that is equally true of one metal compared with goods.[5]

The question of choice between the money metals brought out some interesting opinions. Law, although recognizing that silver has many advantages as money, endeavored to make out a case against it. Silver, he claims, is open to the objection that it is more uncertain in value than other goods. Not only can the magistrates alter its denomination or fineness, but its very durability robs it of the power of adjusting its quantity to the demand, as perishable commodities do. Moreover, the practically uniform value of silver in all places makes it easier to export, and thus exposes a country to the grave danger of having too little money for the demand.[6]

[1] Pagnini, *Saggio sopra il Giusto Pregio delle Cose*, p. 210; Douglass, *Discourse Concerning the Currencies of the British Plantations in America*, p. 294; Justi, *Gesammelte Schriften*, vol. i, p. 359, vol. ii, pp. 436–438; Carli, *op. cit.*, vol. i, pp. 60–65.

[2] Fornari, *op. cit.*, vol. ii, p. 123; Galiani, *op. cit.*, vol. i, pp. 194, 195; Vasco, *Della Moneta*, pp. 111, 112.

[3] Harris, *op. cit.*, pp. 57, 58.

[4] Steuart, *op. cit.*, vol. i, p. 549.

[5] Prior, *op. cit.*, pp. 297–299.

[6] Law, *op. cit.*, pp. 114–116, 190, 191, 195, 196.

The Italian writers who now turned to this question came to conclusions very different from those of their English precursors. Broggia was strongly in favor of copper as the monetary standard. Copper circulates more than gold or silver, and is produced practically everywhere in apparently increasing abundance. It would therefore be a good idea to make it the money of accounts and contracts, though allowing payment to be made in other money according to the legal price. This would no more than recognize the existing situation, for copper evaluates, but is not valued, and is the basis of ideal money.[1]

Galiani was more discriminating in his support of copper. In the first place, it is the most useful of the money metals, for though some values are too small to express in gold or silver, none are too large to express in copper. The scheme of alloying the precious metals for the smaller coins is none the less an admission of the fundamental importance of copper. In the second place, copper is less subject to frauds. Not only are the gains to be made too small to be attractive, in view of the danger, but the sovereign and his agents have little opportunity to gain by adulterating copper. This, in fact, lessens concern so much that such coins become practically token money. It is not true, however, that the use of copper money is a panacea. There would still be some danger from erroneous values and official raisings, as long as the ratio between copper and the other metals was fixed by law; and not to fix the ratio would cause great inconvenience every time a payment was made in silver, as many large payments must be. Gold, at any rate, should not be used as money. It is so precious, and errors in it consequently so grave, that it would better pass by weight, though it may be coined to show its fineness.[2]

In England there was no longer unanimous support of silver. Magens held that, since gold had a greater value all over Europe, and was "more commodious for Dispersion," with all the advantages of silver besides, it would be preferable as the common measure of trade.[3] The anonymous author of the *Reflections on*

[1] Broggia, *op. cit.*, vol. ii, pp. 100, 101, 137, 138.

[2] Galiani, *op. cit.*, vol. i, pp. 196–204, 217.

[3] Magens, *The Universal Merchant*, p. 53.

Coin in General, published in 1762, though indifferent about the matter, considers it "*most rational* that the most scarce and precious Metal should be the *Unit* or *Standard*." [1]

Harris, however, favors silver. It is better for the coins of small value; it is less likely to vary in value, because it is so widely and abundantly spread over Europe that sudden additions or losses have comparatively little effect; its fitness for serving as the pricc of labor, gold being too valuable, makes it the natural standard; and finally, immemorial custom has linked the idea of pounds and shillings with silver.[2] Massie gives very similar reasons, and it is probable that he was influenced by Harris.[3]

Except for Genovesi's remark that the widespread use of silver was probably due to the fact that the quantity of silver available is "a kind of mean between the abundance of copper and the scarcity of gold," [4] which may imply approval, the Italian tradition in favor of copper was maintained. Vasco argues that great hoards are always of the precious metals; that their value is probably more affected by the whims of fashion; and that a recoinage of silver, being cheaper, is a better way of making the readjustments necessitated by the inevitable changes in the relative value of the metals. Copper, therefore, which affords a durable and hence cheaply maintained currency, should be made the stable element in the money supply — the standard.[5]

As for the ratio between the metals, the importance of market factors had become fairly well grasped by the eighteenth century,[6] and writers began to turn their attention to various refinements of the problem. Cantillon pointed out the fact, long ago hinted at by Bodin, that foreign markets have more influence on this ratio than on other values, because of the easy transportability of the metals; [7] and Broggia noted that, in addition to the general forces of supply and demand, certain special influences, such as the de-

[1] *Reflections on Coin in General*, p. 522.

[2] Harris, *op. cit.*, pt. i, pp. 60–63; pt. ii, pp. 92–94.

[3] Massie, *Observations Relating to the Coin of Great Britain*, pp. 11–14.

[4] Genovesi, *op. cit.*, vol. ii, p. 40.

[5] Vasco, *op. cit.*, pp. 113–119.

[6] It was not always adequately expounded. *E. g.*, Melon, *op. cit.*, p. 762; Dutot, *op. cit.*, p. 899.

[7] Cantillon, *op. cit.*, p. 369.

mand for particular coins for export, may cause temporary variations in the market ratio of moneys.[1]

Belloni and Neri discuss the principles to be followed in determining the ratio. The former objects to regulation according to the country's neighbors. If any neighbors have a wrong ratio, it is they, not we, who will suffer loss.[2] Neri holds the contrary opinion. Since it is the force of commerce that regulates the ratio, then the varying conditions of trade will lead to different ratios in different countries. Spain, for example, which has direct commerce with America and little with the Orient, will value gold more than other countries. It is the ratio in the nearer countries with which we trade that has most influence on ours. This acute qualification of the old idea of a world-wide ratio doubtless reflects the experience of the skillful Italian bankers. He also points out that temporary or uncertain premiums on particular coins should not be considered in determining their legal price, while the greater value of a given weight of gold when in the form of very fine coins should be recognized.[3]

At the same time Galiani revived Locke's plan of fixing a permissive ratio. Although a compulsory ratio is undesirable, because of the bad effects of an error in it, the proportion between the coins should by no means be left undefined, for there are several cases where an established standard is very useful. The easy valuation of moneys, the valuation of new moneys by the common people, the settlement of contracts in which no ratio was specified, and the protection of the young or incompetent are much aided by a public price. There are two reasons why peoples have generally regulated this matter by legal ratios. In the first place, men always think doing is better than not doing; and in the second place, they do not apply remedies to the ills of the body, and still less, of the state, unless these ills bring sharp pains, which the slow divergence of the true from the legal ratio cannot do.[4] Neri and Harris also favor a permissive ratio. Harris, a

[1] Broggia, *op. cit.*, vol. ii, p. 194.

[2] Belloni, *Dissertazione sopra il Commercio*, pp. 63–65.

[3] Neri, *op. cit.*, pp. 44, 45, 61–67, 98.

[4] Galiani, *op. cit.*, vol. ii, pp. 12–25. He does not mention the similar proposal of Locke, whose arguments against a compulsory ratio he, or Locke's Italian translator, seems to have slightly misunderstood.

strict monometallist, adds that in contracts gold should pass at the price fixed when payment is made.[1]

Although there was, in general, a clearer understanding of the factors determining the ratio during the remainder of the period,[2] there were few significant developments. Carli follows Neri in excluding the demand for particular pieces from the factors which should influence the legal ratio; [3] but only Vasco's discussion deserves any considerable mention. It is interesting less for its scientific value than as an example of the subtle analyses frequently found in Italian writings. There are several objections, he says, to basing the ratio on an average of the ratios of neighboring countries. These ratios may come from four sources: the official tariff of moneys, the popular prices, the values among bankers, and the value of bullion among merchants, of which the first, and least accurate, is usually chosen. The third is the best. Furthermore, if all nations, by successive readjustments, tried to conform to the average of the others, they would come to have practically the same ratio, which is "contrary to the physical laws of commerce." Such an average, moreover, makes no distinction between countries according to the volume of our trade with them. The difficulties in handling the foreign ratios make it seem desirable to depend simply on the bullion ratio among merchants at home. The ratio between copper and silver need not be fixed so accurately.

Among the influences which cause the ratio to change in particular countries he mentions the opening or closing of a "strong branch of commerce," probably having in mind a trade where balances are settled largely in a single metal. The possibility that the forces making for change may cause different ratios in the different provinces of a great state is largely neutralized, he says, by the levelling effects of continual circulation, cheaper expenses of

[1] Neri, *op. cit.*, p. 60; Harris, *op. cit.*, pp. 64, 65.

[2] Some erroneous ideas persisted. Robinson held that, since gold and silver are equally demanded, because equally available for the payment of debts, the ratio between them will be simply that between the physical quantities of them at hand in the country. (*An Essay on Coin*, p. 22); Beccaria (*op. cit.*, vol. ii, pp. 25–30), the author of the *Essay on the Theory of Money* (p. 95), and Ortes (*op. cit.*, vol. ii, p. 412) also considered the ratio purely a matter of quantities.

[3] Carli, *op. cit.*, vol. i, pp. 162, 163.

coinage near the mines, and full liberty for popular valuations. And, finally, when the ratio changes, it is only by comparing the metals with goods that we can tell in which metal the change has occurred.[1]

3. The Coinage Prerogatives

The sovereign's right of coinage, a tradition since Roman times, was supported by all who referred to the question during this period. Verri, however, thinks small states pay too dearly for their pride when they insist on exercising this right. Instead of having their own coinage, they should be content with an accurate "tariff of moneys." [2]

Some writers point out utilitarian as well as legal reasons for limiting coinage to public authority. Justi reasons that, since the private stamping of weight and fineness, which was an earlier stage in the use of the precious metals, as we have seen, inspired confidence only in proportion to the good repute of the individuals responsible, it was natural to transfer this function to the highest power in the state, as the one whose credit was greatest at home and abroad. Moreover, the duty of the ruler to care for commerce would naturally include the instrument thereof.[3] Sonnenfels's statement is very similar. To remove distrust between buyer and seller about the weight and fineness of the metal, a third party must intervene whom both parties can trust, because he has no reason to favor either. No one can do this better than the prince.[4] This idea is also implied in Vasco and Condillac.[5]

On the whole, opinion grew more favorable to gratuitous coinage than it had been during the preceding century. Leib does not definitely advocate it, but considers it entirely practicable. Since alloying of the coins tends to stimulate counterfeiting, seigniorage should not be sought in the coin itself; and if it be thought that this is an advantage only to dealers in silver, all charge for coinage may be dispensed with.[6] Wood argues that no owner of

[1] Vasco, *op. cit.*, pp. 91–110.
[2] Verri, *op. cit.*, pp. 95, 96.
[3] Justi, *Schriften*, vol. ii, pp. 325, 426.
[4] Sonnenfels, *op. cit.*, pt. ii, pp. 303, 304.
[5] Vasco, *op. cit.*, p. 15; Condillac, *op. cit.*, p. 398.
[6] Zielenziger, *op. cit.*, p. 388.

bullion will send it to be coined if it must cost him anything, for minting adds nothing to its value.[1] Vanderlint declares it is no less absurd for the government to fix the price it will give for gold and silver than it would be to fix prices for every other commodity; the mint should return as great a weight in coin as the bullion received.[2] Spinelli also advocates coinage at public expense. To diminish the intrinsic value of the money would be equivalent to imposing a perpetual tax on all revenues, credits, and salaries, because of the rise in prices which would result.[3]

Justi, especially, is a strong supporter of this practice. As the successful experience of the English shows, he says, the expenses of the mint are best paid out of other revenues. This removes all reluctance to bringing bullion to be coined; it accords with the practice of merchants, especially those engaged in foreign trade; and it does away with the confusing rise in the "price" of bullion, which is a principal cause of coinage disorders. It is an error to think that the *Münzregal* should be a source of profit: it is only a regulatory power. Since the expenses, moreover, can be paid out of the profit made on the subsidiary coins, the state bears no burden, and may even gain through the attraction offered to foreigners, who will doubtless spend something in the country. This discussion, though not presented in connected form, as I have given it, is one of the most interesting in the period.[4] Sonnenfels follows Justi here, as he often does.[5]

Beccaria differs with most Italian writers on this question. His reasons for preferring to have the cost of coinage borne by the state remind one strongly of certain ideas of Scaruffi. Attempts to deduct the expense from the coins themselves, he says, lead to the serious evil of disproportion between the different pieces of the same metal, or between the different metals.[6] Letrosne considers coinage a public service whose cost should be borne by the public revenues.[7]

[1] Wood, *Survey of Trade*, p. 372.
[2] Vanderlint, *op. cit.*, p. 54.
[3] Fornari, *op. cit.*, vol. ii, pp. 116, 117.
[4] Justi, *Schriften*, vol. ii, pp. 326, 442, 443, 487, 527, 530, 559, 569, 570.
[5] Sonnenfels, *op. cit.*, pt. ii, p. 318.
[6] Beccaria, *op. cit.*, vol. ii, pp. 209–211.
[7] *Revue d'Hist. des Doctr.*, vol. v, pp. 365, 366.

The other view, however, was still held by many. D'Aguesseau, although he objects to seigniorage deducted from the coins, on the ground that it places the nation in an inferior position compared to its neighbors by preventing its money from circulating outside at face value, thinks the expenses of coinage may well be collected from the owner of the bullion.[1] Uztariz agrees with Saavedra, whom he quotes, that the expenses should be deducted from the money.[2]

Galiani advances vigorous arguments against gratuitous coinage. It is impossible, he says, to find in so few words so many false things as in the passage where Davanzati advocates this practice and a return to casting instead of minting. It would not lessen the incentive to private coinage to make no charge at the mint, for, since private citizens are unlikely to be able to coin more cheaply than the prince, they have no opportunity to gain and hence no incentive. This seems unfair criticism. Davanzati favored gratuitous coinage principally as a protection against debasement, not against private coinage. Not only has this plan no advantage, Galiani continues, but it has the great disadvantage that goldsmiths would melt the coin whenever they needed bullion, thus greatly increasing the expenses of the mint, as the experience of England shows. If coinage, moreover, is a convenience added to money, it is only fair that the moneyed men, rather than the tradesmen and farmers, should pay for it.[3] This discussion does Galiani no credit, and does not show him at his best.

Neri also advocated a coinage charge, but held that it should be paid by those who have the coining done, and not deducted from the coins.[4] Carli justified a charge by the argument that, since coinage adds a value to the metal, the expense may properly be added to the bullion value.[5] Steuart thought a charge for coinage had the advantage of preventing melting, exporting, and unnecessary coinage, and that it tended to cause trade balances to be paid in such coin as had been exported, rather than in foreign coin.[6]

[1] *Revue d'Hist. des Doctr.*, vol. ii, pp. 278, 279.

[2] Uztariz, *Theory and Practice of Commerce*, vol. ii, p. 348.

[3] Galiani, *op. cit.*, vol. i, pp. 240–243.

[4] Neri, *op. cit.*, pp. 222, 223.

[5] Carli, *op. cit.*, vol. i, pp. 93, 94.

[6] Steuart, *op. cit.*, vol. ii, p. 75.

According to Vasco, the mint cannot be a source of revenue to the prince, because he is in competition with other princes in the manufacture of money, and therefore cannot make any monopoly profits; but it may be a means of investing capital with an ordinary profit. This depends on whether the prince can buy and coin bullion as cheaply as other princes can. Hence it is idle to discuss whether the expense of coinage should be borne by the money or the treasury. If the new money has a lower value in commerce than has been expended on it, the difference must fall on the treasury.[1] This curious argument, I need hardly add, is quite unique.

Some writers were interested in other aspects of the question of seigniorage, especially the effect of a coinage charge on the relative value of different coins. Dutot suggests that the charge be made proportionate to the value of the coins,[2] and Spinelli, Pagnini, and the *Essay on the Theory of Money* agree with him.[3] Neri and Vasco also consider this point, but with slightly different conclusions. Neri compromises by proposing to charge a little over one half as much on the gold as on the silver, which is more than in proportion to the actual expense, but less than in proportion to the value; [4] and Vasco thinks the greater diligence needed in manufacturing gold coins may justify a higher charge per coin, — that is, more nearly in proportion to the value of the piece, — and that commerce will not notice such slight differences as may remain.[5] Broggia maintains that the copper money of a country is least fit to be made a source of profit. The actual expense of coining it is relatively great anyway; through copper we strike at silver, which it values; and if we start reducing the weight of the copper coins, there will be no end to it. The last two arguments would seem to apply to other metals as well; but he apparently thinks that copper is peculiarly subject to these dangers.[6]

[1] Vasco, *op. cit.*, pp. 66–73.

[2] Dutot, *op. cit.*, pp. 894, 895.

[3] Fornari, *op. cit.*, vol. ii, pp. 122, 123; Pagnini, *Della Decima*, pp. 167, 168; *An Essay*, p. 109.

[4] Neri, *op. cit.*, pp. 122, 123.

[5] Vasco, *op. cit.*, p. 101.

[6] Broggia, *op. cit.*, vol. ii, pp. 141, 142.

CHAPTER XXVIII

THE COINAGE SYSTEM

1. General Considerations

The writers of the eighteenth century displayed relatively little interest in large schemes for an ideal currency system, but they discussed numerous details. Berkeley considers the need of small coins from a new angle. Plenty of small cash, he says, is absolutely necessary for "keeping up a circulation among the people"; four pounds in small cash can "circulate and enliven a market which many four-pound pieces would permit to stagnate." We may, therefore, say that copper is more necessary than gold. Moreover, in urging the need of a mint for Ireland, he declares that it is highly expedient that the money of a country be coined in values peculiarly suited to its trade conditions.[1]

Broggia holds that the standard silver should not be divided into more than quarters, but that smaller pieces, though of full value, should be heavily alloyed. This will reduce the loss from their rapid wearing, provide a greater variety of fractional coins, and save the mint the expense of refining the metal for these pieces. It will not encourage counterfeiting, for milling and careful workmanship will be effective checks, and it pays better, anyway, to imitate the larger pieces.[2]

Galiani takes direct issue with this view. It is true, since small pieces lose weight faster, being used more, and their wearing being in inverse ratio to their homologous sides, that the damage is less when they contain a large proportion of base metal; and such a practice enables the mint to make use of any silver of less than standard fineness, which may come to it, without the expense of refining; but the savings thus effected are small compared to the whole supply of money, and are probably balanced by the greater

[1] Berkeley, *Works*, vol. iv, pp. 442, 466, 474.

[2] Broggia, *op. cit.*, vol. ii, pp. 120–126.

expense of coining and by the loss of the value of copper. The greater facility of commerce afforded by such alloys was more important in ages past, when silver was much scarcer. Moreover, the dislike of the popular mind for money that appears false and adulterated, the censure to which the government is thereby exposed, and the greater facility of clipping and counterfeiting such money, more than outweigh any slight gains.[1]

Carli makes the suggestion — it can hardly be called a proposal — that the "equilibrium of moneys" would be better regulated, if all nations agreed upon the extrinsic value of money, as they do upon the intrinsic value. This would be an advantage principally to those nations which have to pay a balance of trade; they now lose when they make payments to countries which do not recognize the extrinsic value of their money. He does not appear, however, to have any hope that such an agreement will be made.[2]

Justi, however, is strongly in favor of doing away with all the subtleties of "numerary" and "extrinsic" values by stamping each piece of standard money with its weight and fineness only. This would probably prove an adequate protection against debasement; for, unless standards of public morality were much lower than now, no prince would allow a false weight to be printed with his image and arms. Subsidiary coins, however, which, as we shall see, are to receive special treatment, should be stamped with their extrinsic value. Like Galiani, he is opposed to mixing the metals for small coins, but recommends pure copper rather than silver for them. They must contain copper anyway, he argues, to make them wear longer; for they are the most used, and the proportion of copper must be large in order to make them of convenient size. What little silver might be put in would be as good as lost if one tried to recover it, so it would better be left out altogether.[3]

Steuart's interest in the general system of coinage reflects his peculiar ideas of money. "The unit in money," he says, "cannot

[1] Galiani, *op. cit.*, vol. i, pp. 255–258, vol. ii, pp. 35–37.

[2] Carli, *op. cit.*, vol. i, pp. 94, 95.

[3] Justi, *Schriften*, vol. i, pp. 358–364, vol. ii, pp. 519, 521.

be fixed to any particular quantity of gold, silver, or any commodity." The adjusting of the metals to the money of account is a matter of the greatest importance, for the slightest error destroys the usefulness of the whole; it requires "an exact and determinate proportion of both metals to the money unit" in all denominations.[1] The idea behind these rather cryptic sentences seems to be that the money unit is a fixed and absolute quantum, which is to be expressed in varying amounts of the money metal. When the unit is adjusted, its fractions must be expressed in exactly proportional amounts of metal. Further discussion of these ideas of Steuart's will be undertaken in another connection.

The *Essay on the Theory of Money*, of 1771, presents an idea that reminds us of Berkeley. If there is little circulation in a country, the coin must be divided into small parts to facilitate exchange among the people.[2] In other words, the denominations should be adapted to the conditions in the country.

The most elaborate and, in some respects, the most interesting discussion during the period is that of Vasco. In the first place, he declares that it is neither necessary nor advisable to fix the numerary value of all the current coins, that is, their value in the unit which is made the basis of the monetary system. Such tariffs, being frequently inaccurate, give rise to monopolistic practices on the part of merchants, great fluctuation in the value of certain moneys, unsteadiness in the value of bullion, and a general uncertainty about money matters. "There is no better system than to abandon the course of moneys to the fullest liberty of commerce." Merchants already ignore the legal values in their dealings; and the protection of people at a distance from commercial centres could be adequately secured by publishing an "instructive tariff," which, without any pretense of establishing compulsory values, would give such information regarding the weight and fineness of coins, market values in foreign countries, and so forth, as would enable people to form a satisfactory judgment in regard to values. This, to be sure, disregards the small losses which some individuals might suffer before a coin had acquired a definite value in the public esteem; but "such small

[1] Steuart, *op. cit.*, vol. i, pp. 527, 533.

[2] *An Essay*, p. 74.

considerations can never enter into the plans of public Economy." According to this reasoning, it would be a good plan for a country to coin only one metal, and for its other currency to depend on foreign moneys circulating at market value.

In the second place, he is in favor of reducing money to a decimal progression. Thus accounts would be simply and conveniently kept in four columns, — scudi, lire, soldi, and denari, — each from left to right being ten times the next. For further convenience, some of these units might be divided into halves and quarters. He argues at length that the difficulties of introducing the new system would not be as great as imagined. They would be no worse than those now met by travellers and those now presented by the practice of representing a given numerary value by different coins in different places; and, at any rate, they could be largely eliminated by having the mint buy all current coins at their just price, by requiring that, to be legally valid, all public and private accounts must be kept in the new terms, and by publishing a tariff of the equivalents of the new coins in terms of the old, as a standard for the payment of outstanding debts. He admits that twelve has a larger number of divisors than ten, but argues, rather lamely, that countries which use twelve as a basis rarely take advantage of this property.

Like Galiani, he is opposed to the use of "billon." It is not needed in order to provide coins of convenient size for the denominations "between copper and silver"; and even if copper pieces are somewhat bulky, this has the advantage of making them harder to hoard and traffic in.[1]

2. Ideal Money

Here we shall make a slight digression to consider certain discussions of "ideal" or "imaginary" money, a topic not wholly unrelated to that of the general coinage system. The fact that these discussions are all, with one exception, by Italian writers seems to indicate that the custom of reckoning in this kind of money was more widespread in that country than elsewhere. It was also of long standing. Thesaurus in 1607 referred to its origin

[1] Vasco, *op. cit.*, pp. 24–27, 62–65, 81, 123–131, 151–154.

as follows. "In many provinces there was introduced by exchangers and merchants the practice of estimating the prices of things in one kind of money, which is imaginary, but of making payments in another, which may be called real." The purpose of this device was to provide a certain basis for payments and to eliminate controversies about the alteration of money.[1] It is not till the eighteenth century, however, that we find active discussion of this topic.

Broggia declares that industrial nations since the Romans, having observed the inconvenience and disorder which arise from contracts in real money, because of the changes to which it is subject, resolved to avoid these troubles by agreeing upon a money which should be ideal only, and therefore stable. The use of such money is really necessary to a state. Besides the essential advantage of justice and security in contracts, which led to its adoption, it has others. It enables the government to alter the "price" of real money easily and safely when changes in the value of the metals require it (Broggia is strongly opposed to any alteration in the weight of the coins even for the purpose of this adjustment), and it permits the further use of coins which are considerably worn, by facilitating a readjustment in their price. Although the advantages of this money are due to the fact that its purely ideal character prevents its alteration, Broggia seems to think that it ought to correspond to something definite, it ought to have an "effective extrinsic" in some kind of money. This it has in its price, which is generally in copper money, but may also be in certain small silver coins "so made as not to be liable to alteration in price." This last provision seems to refer to heavily alloyed silver. Despite this rather elaborate discussion, the real nature of ideal money remains something of a mystery, the only clue being his remark that most ideal money was once "effective," which seems to identify the ideal unit with an unvarying weight of silver.[2]

Montesquieu remarks briefly that in the course of time bad faith or need causes the weight of the coins to be diminished without changing the names. Thus no piece weighing a pound may be

[1] Thesaurus, *Tractatus novus et utilis*, pp. 25, 28.

[2] Broggia, *op. cit.*, vol. ii, pp. 102–123.

made any longer, and the pound becomes purely ideal. It would be a good plan to have laws in all countries compelling the use of real money, and preventing operations which might render it ideal.[1]

Galiani deals with the subject briefly. Ideal money, he says, can be introduced only by means of real money, for men are not able at first to compute by abstract ideals. It probably developed as a result of alterations in money, the older forms being retained for convenience in counting.[2]

Belloni's explanation of the use of ideal money is more like Broggia's: it arose as a means of avoiding the confusion which results from debasement. He implies more clearly, however, that the basis of this money is the value of a definite amount of metal, saying that all imaginary money was once real, and that commerce, which considers only the intrinsic value, reduces all kinds of money to the same standard by means of ideal money.[3]

Neri's account is clearer. People, he says, often continue to use a unit of value that is no longer coined. Bank imaginary money is a further improvement. It is designed to restore certainty to contracts by taking as a standard a given weight of silver or a certain full-weight coin before debasement. Ordinary ideal money, however, does not, according to Neri, possess these advantages; it is exposed to all the variations of real money, of which it is but an uncoined equivalent part, and undebased coins come to be valued higher and higher in it.[4]

Pagnini's explanation is slightly different from the above. When silver money was altered, it could no longer equal the same fraction of the gold money. As a result, people presently began to use a new denomination, either for convenience in counting, or to hide the real reason (that is, the evasion of the new coinage regulation). This new denomination was once used to express a real weight of metal.[5]

Genovesi gives an account more like Galiani's. In former times it happened that certain old coins disappeared, and yet people did

[1] Montesquieu, *op. cit.*, p. 379.

[2] Galiani, *op. cit.*, vol. i, pp. 136, 153.

[3] Belloni, *op. cit.*, pp. 120–123.

[4] Neri, *op. cit.*, pp. 152–155.

[5] Pagnini, *Della Decima*, pp. 136, 137.

not cease to count by them, as they had become accustomed to do. These are called ideal money.[1]

According to Vasco, this money originated mostly from variations in the ratio between the metals. Thus, a soldo having come to equal not twelve but fifteen denari, the coin which was originally a soldo was valued at a soldo and a quarter, while the term soldo continued to mean twelve denari in reckoning. The convenience of these terms caused them to be preferred in counting.[2]

3. The Form of Coins

Galiani agrees with the arguments of English writers who had preceded him, that minting is the best system of making coins. The advantages of this method, as set forth by Locke, namely, greater uniformity of pieces, less danger of counterfeiting, cheaper and handsomer work, he considers decisive in its favor. He is unreasonably bitter toward Davanzati, however, who, nearly two centuries before, had suggested a return to an older method of coinage. Such an attempt to make a small saving would be niggardly and reactionary, he says; but he fails utterly to take into account the fact that Davanzati proposed this principally as a better alternative to the very defective and irregular coinage by the hammer which was used in his day. The most common fraud, according to Galiani, against which money must be protected, is clipping, to which silver is most subject, copper next, and gold least. The reason for this difference is that there is little gain from clipping copper, and gold is so commonly weighed that clipping would be of no avail. Moreover, the clipper of a gold piece runs the risk that it may be refused, in which case he will be left with a valuable article useless on his hands. Small coins are more likely to be clipped, since the little value involved causes men to accept them with less scrutiny. The best protection against this is to make the fraud easy to recognize, which is readily accomplished by minting.

He also considers the question of using alloy, and advocates it for two reasons: it is very expensive to purify the metals from all admixture, and the pure metals are not well adapted to coinage,

[1] Genovesi, *op. cit.*, vol. ii, p. 41.

[2] Vasco, *op. cit.*, pp. 14, 15.

gold being too soft and silver too fragile. It is an error to think the alloy can affect the money's value, for this depends simply on the quantity of fine metal which the money contains. The only reason why alloyed money is suspected is that fraud and legal compulsion have often tried to make it pass for more than it was worth. To reduce the wearing of coins, he recommends that they be made as flawless as possible and as thick as convenient.[1]

The arguments in favor of using alloy did not appear sound to Justi. It is not only useless, he declares, but, as long as it is continued, we can hope for no reform of the coinage. Mint-masters are responsible for it; they gave rulers the "unfounded opinion that pure gold and silver cannot be worked well," because the use of alloy made it harder to detect their own dishonesty; and the rulers adopted it all the more readily, because it concealed the overvaluing by which they sought to profit. It is "wholly contrary to the sensible purpose of the highest value of all things to make unnecessary additions and increase its weight without need." Alloying, moreover, adds a further complication to the mass of details which make it difficult for a ruler to grasp the whole situation and thus avoid detrimental coinage policies.[2]

Harris argues against a scheme, which he says had been recently proposed, of coining some pieces with the same weight of fine silver but more alloy. This, he says, would make the coins more brittle and easier to counterfeit, the people might discriminate against them, and, in general, unnecessary changes in the coinage are undesirable.[3]

Among other "palliatives" for the disadvantages of using the metals as money, Steuart recommends that the coins be made as large, solid, and smooth as possible, presumably to diminish the loss through wear.[4] Beccaria considers the use of alloy necessary in order to provide durable and accurate impressions on the coins.[5] The *Essay on the Theory of Money*, of 1771, also approves the use

[1] Galiani, *op. cit.*, vol. i, pp. 240–254, vol. ii, pp. 37–42.
[2] Justi, *Schriften*, vol. ii, pp. 327, 420, 501–505.
[3] Harris, *op. cit.*, pt. ii, pp. 117–119.
[4] Steuart, *op. cit.*, vol. i, p. 544.
[5] Beccaria, *op. cit.*, vol. ii, p. 22.

of alloy, but says no more should be added than is needed to harden the metal and cover the expenses of coinage.[1]

Vasco considers the question of alloy from a rather novel point of view. As the representative of goods, it would seem indifferent whether money were made of fine or mixed metal, he says, so long as the stamp is known and approved; but since some nations prefer finer coins, it may be better to make them so, in order that they may have wide currency. Moreover, goldsmiths prefer pure bullion to a mixture containing the same weight of fine metal, because they will be put to the expense of refining the latter. The same is true of money, and hence it passes for no more than the value of its fine metal content, and the alloy is wasted. A third reason against making base money is the danger of counterfeiting, which arises from the fact that in small trade money is commonly received "on the mere credit of its stamp," and hence excessively debased coin could get into circulation. From these considerations the fineness to be adopted can be determined; and he advises that the standard be that used in the finest articles of gold and silver. Copper bullion is consumed five per cent in melting, and the expense of coining it is relatively greater than that of other metals. We should, therefore, not increase the evil by such useless mint processes as adding a little silver to it, for the silver is lost, its recovery being impracticable owing to the excessive cost.

Besides these restrictions on the use of alloy, there should also be care that money be so stamped that the impression will not wear off easily, and that the pieces can be easily distinguished from each other. They should be milled to prevent clipping; and since this works better when the plates are of uniform density, thin plates, which are more apt to vary in density, should be avoided.[2]

4. Subsidiary Coins

Although there had been important discussions of subsidiary money in earlier writers, the ideas they worked out had apparently made no headway in official circles. Sir Isaac Newton, for example, director of the British mint, made no suggestions

[1] *An Essay*, p. 108.

[2] Vasco, *op. cit.*, pp. 75–83, 149.

with regard to this money except that it be made of baser alloy (though full value), to lessen the wear of the pieces.[1]

Cantillon seems to favor a limitation of the supply of debased small money, but suggests no other restrictions. Where there is not too much of it for the needs of small trade, he says, it passes without difficulty at its face value. Any slight loss through lack of intrinsic value is more than balanced by the convenience of the money. This seems to be the first attempt to discuss the question of the general acceptability of these coins.[2]

The canonist tradition, which favored some form of limited legal tender as well as limited coinage, was revived by Uztariz, who proposed these regulations as a means of keeping silver at home and preventing copper from taking its place. This would seem to imply a debasement of the copper coins, but he does not develop his reasoning further.[3]

Broggia's discussion gives little indication that he had ever heard of the proposals made by previous writers. Though he favors a heavy alloy for the smaller coins, as we have seen, he intends that they shall be on essentially the same footing as other money in their value and use. He would, however, make them not acceptable at the banks, in order to ensure their availability for the daily needs of trade; and in discussing their use as "effective extrinsic" of ideal money, he says they need not adapt themselves strictly to the standard silver, which may imply some overvaluation.[4]

Galiani is more satisfactory, but his ideas are not well coördinated. He favors some overvaluing of copper money to prevent its displacement, and assures us that such money will not fail to circulate readily as long as people believe that their neighbors will accept it. The danger of counterfeiting he holds to be slight, since the general refusal of large sums of such money makes the gains to be secured too small and slow in coming. And finally, he argues that overvalued copper cannot drive out the precious metals, apparently because of its limited quantity.[5]

[1] Shaw, *Select Tracts*, p. 157.

[2] Cantillon, *op. cit.*, pp. 359–361.

[3] Uztariz, *op. cit.*, vol. ii, pp. 353, 354.

[4] Broggia, *op. cit.*, vol. ii, pp. 119–121, 125.

[5] Galiani, *op. cit.*, vol. i, pp. 205–212.

The safeguards which had been suggested up to this time did not wholly satisfy Neri, and he was inclined not to take the risks involved in debased subsidiary money. He admitted that it could be tolerated, provided it was confined to domestic use and its quantity greatly limited; under these conditions the demand for it in daily trade would sustain its value, for holders could be sure of exchanging it for good money, if they wished. Such money is essentially a credit, and therefore its value depends on the ability of the holder to redeem his claim in full. In any event, no more than a certain part of large amounts should be payable in it. Since, therefore, the use of this money has to be so carefully restricted to prevent abuse, and full-value small coins would work perfectly well, why take the risk? The claim that the gain from it is a convenient means of making up the loss sustained in coining silver should be given no weight: if the state of trade does not permit the mint to coin without loss, it should not attempt to do so.[1] Though Neri had too little confidence in the restrictions which he mentioned, his discussion is important for its insistence on the credit character of subsidiary money.

Carli argues ponderously to refute those who favor debasing the small money, but unfortunately misses the point and discusses only the argument, which he says arose during the last century, that this money may be treated differently because it is intended only for use at home. Such money will be generally refused, he declares, because of its inferior value; and its effect on trade and prices will be as detrimental as that of any debasement; for prices depend on the small money, which is most used. When a nation having part of its money in this form pays a balance to foreigners, it loses a larger share of its real wealth than the nominal figures indicate. These arguments are obscure, at best, and seem to deserve no further discussion in this connection.[2]

Although Justi made no contributions of fundamental importance on this point, he combined very effectively the ideas developed by his predecessors. Subsidiary money, he declares, must never be current beyond the boundaries of the country

[1] Neri, *op. cit.*, pp. 107, 183–193, 229, 230.

[2] Carli, *op. cit.*, vol. i, pp. 273–281.

where it was coined. If a prince allows it, he suffers an invasion of his rights. Since its use is to be thus restricted, it need not be made of true intrinsic value, but must have a determined relation to the standard moneys, in order that those who receive it in retail trade may be able to use it readily when they come to buy their supplies at wholesale. This principle is subject to abuse, of course, for it opens the door to an easy way to profit. The prince must, therefore, limit himself in coining such money. The amount adapted to the needs of the country can be easily determined by beginning with what appears sufficient (he does not suggest any basis for such an estimate), and ceasing coinage in any year when it is seen to be increasing rapidly. Provision should be made for a moderate addition each year, which may be suspended if it seems advisable. Great care should be taken that no premium on standard money appears. This will depend on keeping the small money in due proportion to the other; for when this is done, those who receive rents and such large payments will have to have the larger pieces changed, and thus the merchant who receives small money will know that he will be able to obtain standard money for it, and will accept it at its face value. As a further precaution against the abuse of this money, it should be fixed by law how much a man must accept in business transactions. This amount should be no more than certain coins of higher denomination, that is, merely enough to allow the payment of fractional balances.[1]

That Justi was indebted to his Cameralist predecessors, and through them to the arguments of the canon lawyers, for his discussion of this topic seems clear. He has simply made a definite practical proposition of the ideas which Thesaurus expressed over a hundred years before. His discussion was so much better than that of his immediate predecessors, however, that it deserves considerable credit.

Similar conclusions were reached shortly after this by English writers. Harris asserts, somewhat vaguely, that copper coins are not properly money, but a kind of token passing in exchange instead of parts of the smallest silver coins, and their use should be strictly limited: they should be legal tender only for amounts

[1] Justi, *op. cit.*, vol. ii, pp. 327, 443–445, 505–526.

below the smallest silver pieces, and should pass only for the value of the copper and the necessary workmanship.[1] This last requirement seems hardly consistent with the concept of copper coins as a "token"; but it may be that by this phrase Harris merely wished to deny the fitness of copper for use as standard money, and was not considering the question of the value of the coins.

Shortly after this, John Barnard proposed a very interesting scheme as a means of remedying the scarcity of silver, which was then a subject of much complaint.[2] There should be coined two hundred thousand pounds in small coins, of standard weight but less than standard fineness. These should be marked to distinguish them from sterling, and should not be legal money but receivable at the creditor's option. Their value should be "guaranteed by law." If this supply proved insufficient, it could be increased as needed.[3] He does not undertake to prove the adequacy of his plan, or to enlighten us as to the nature of the proposed legal guaranties of value. As the first discussion, however, to treat this topic as a question of keeping certain coins in circulation, rather than of preventing the abuse of debasement (if we except Broggia's exclusion of such coins from the banks), and the first definite suggestion of a public guaranty of their value, Barnard's ideas are of great importance.

His scheme made little impression, apparently. Shirley replied that good money could not be made to circulate with bad money at the same price, and that the introduction of such silver would cause gold to be exported, missing entirely the significance of the safeguards that Barnard had included.[4]

Sonnenfels, a great admirer of Justi, adopted all his ideas on this point, and made slight refinements. The general rule that the extrinsic value of money should agree with the intrinsic value does not apply to subsidiary coins, for they are only for use at home in facilitating small sales. Their quantity should be limited, however, or they will displace the heavy money. It is hard to say just

[1] Harris, *op. cit.*, pp. 45, 65.

[2] *Some Thoughts on the Scarcity of Silver Coin, with a Proposal for Remedy.*

[3] Quoted in Sérionne, *op. cit.*, pp. 295, 296.

[4] *Ibid.*, *op. cit.*, p. 298.

how much should be provided, but we may venture as an estimate a sum equal to the amount of the daily consumption of the laboring classes as a maximum, for laborers are the principal users of these coins. To help ensure a proper restriction of the supply, foreign subsidiary money should be excluded, and it should be forbidden to pay more in small coins at one time than just enough to make up an odd fraction. This will prevent the secret purchase of heavy money at a premium, for there will be no way to make use of large amounts of small money.[1]

Vasco's discussion is interesting, but inferior to Justi's. The need of small coins in retail trade causes people not to notice closely whether they are full weight, every one being confident he can dispose of them without loss. They are regarded more as a sign than as money. Hence there are few nations in which princes have not debased these coins as a means of gain. If the quantity of such coins had never exceeded the needs of domestic trade, there would have been no harm in debasing them; for they would have preserved their credit as tokens representing standard coins, and people would have been deterred from paying them in taxes by the need for small change. Neither the people nor the state would have been embarrassed by them.[2]

5. Foreign Coins and Other Regulations

The question of foreign money was still of great importance in the little states of Italy. Broggia was in favor of allowing it to circulate freely. It should be declared acceptable in all payments, even in banks, at a price fixed by law, provided it is of full weight. In fixing this price, however, the domestic money should be favored; it should have "a certain greater dignity" in its price, to cover the cost of coinage, anyway.

Once the plentifulness of foreign money is assured by right legal prices, goldsmiths should be required to express the price of bullion in terms of the best-adapted foreign coin. In this way their price will merely express a weight-for-weight relation, and there will be no reason to raise the price of silver bullion in time of scar-

[1] Sonnenfels, *op. cit.*, pt. ii, pp. 317–322.

[2] Vasco, *op. cit.*, pp. 117, 118, 132–134.

city, as they do now when the price is in domestic money, which is underweight because of seigniorage and wear. Moreover, goldsmiths will then direct all their zeal to raising the price of foreign money, when there is scarcity of one of the metals, and this in turn will incite and oblige the legislator to do the same for domestic money. The meaning of this rather obscure last argument seems to be that the goldsmiths, charging weight for weight for their silver, will be anxious to have the foreign coins they receive in payment advance in value as justified by the scarcity of the metal, and thus will bring pressure indirectly upon the authorities to make the adjustments in the domestic ratio which the scarcity requires.[1]

Galiani considers the regulation of foreign money from a new angle. From large states, he says, foreign silver would better be excluded; but in the case of small states, such a policy would be too great a hindrance to commerce. Foreign silver should not be on a par in value with the national money, however, for it always carries some risk "that the changes and losses which it suffers in its own will be felt also in the country where it is received." [2]

Justi would allow the circulation of foreign money under certain conditions. It must not pass for more than its intrinsic value (lest it displace the full-weight domestic money), and this value should be stamped on it by public officials before it is allowed to circulate. Great merchants might be excused from this last regulation, and allowed to pay foreign coins in bags bearing the payer's name and the weight of the contents.[3] Sonnenfels agrees with Justi on this point.[4]

Massie takes middle ground on this question. As long as it is forbidden to export the money of the country, some kinds of foreign gold should be allowed to circulate (but not all); for otherwise coin will be melted for export, when there is a balance to pay, and this is to be avoided. Such restrictions on export, however, are unreasonable, for men do not export money except for good reasons.[5]

[1] Broggia, *op. cit.*, vol. ii, pp. 154–157.
[2] Galiani, *op. cit.*, vol. ii, p. 181.
[3] Justi, *Schriften*, vol. ii, pp. 326, 537–539.
[4] Sonnenfels, *op. cit.*, pt. ii, pp. 322–324.
[5] Massie, *Observations Relating to the Coin of Great Britain*, pp. 22, 23.

Italian opinion continued to favor the circulation of foreign coin. Some writers apparently took the advisability of this policy for granted, and did no more than discuss the problem of valuing the foreign coins.[1] Vasco, however, goes into the matter a little more fully. There is no advantage, he says, in forbidding the use of foreign money. The prince, by receiving and paying it according to his published tariff, can protect the treasury against loss, and its value in trade may be safely left to competition. All attempts to demonetize such coins in the hope of buying them cheap will be unsuccessful or unjust. Either they will be sent out of the country, or a loss will be forced on a part of the subjects, especially the poor.[2]

A number of writers were interested in regulations designed to ensure a plentiful supply of bullion for the mint. Law suggests that, if it is desired to coin plate, the law should allow the export of such plate as can be sold abroad for more than its weight because of the workmanship, the owners giving security to import money or bullion in its stead.[3] Uztariz approves a regulation already in force in some places (for example, certain German states), that all bullion should be brought to the mint rather than disposed of through the channels of trade.[4] Broggia, looking at the question from a different angle, remarks that it is not a good plan to depend on contracts with merchants; the matter is too important, and this method is likely to be expensive, though the expense might be reduced by granting the merchants some public distinction in lieu of other recompense. Elsewhere he declares that the banks can and ought to perform this service for the state. It would cost them only a little inconvenience and the loss of a few days' time, and they would benefit through the increase in deposits which always follows an increase in the supply of money.[5]

Justi also is interested in this question and favors the regulation mentioned by Uztariz. All uncoined silver and gold should be sold only to agents of the state, from whom the goldsmiths would

[1] Neri, *op. cit.*, pp. 119, 120; Belloni, *op. cit.*, pp. 51, 52.

[2] Vasco, *op. cit.*, pp. 43–45.

[3] Law, *op. cit.*, p. 102.

[4] Uztariz, *op. cit.*, vol. ii, p. 359.

[5] Broggia, *op. cit.*, vol. ii, pp. 233–235, vol. i, p. 375.

then obtain their supplies, which would be stamped and carefully accounted for. This work could be done in great part by the present underworked officials, and any expenses met by a slight fee. The purpose of this regulation is to protect the state from the loss which it suffers whenever bullion is sold for money which is really of less intrinsic value. It will thus help to keep bullion at home and provide the government with plenty for coinage. He takes the precaution to add that the government officials must not ask sellers of bullion to tell where they got it, lest pride induce those who sell because of reduced circumstances to go outside the country with their property.[1] Galiani opposes any artificial stimulation of the activities of the mint, and points out that the plentifulness of money in no way depends on the operations of the mint, but on the industry of the people.[2]

Except for a few references to the plan of having all money go by weight,[3] these were the only subjects of anything like general discussion. Some further interesting points, however, were worked out by individual writers. Broggia proposes a number of ingenious schemes to diminish loss through abrasion: stimulating the use of your money in other countries (that is, letting others bear the loss of its wearing), dividing standard silver no smaller than quarters, forbidding the transportation of money by wagon, and the free circulation of foreign money (which goes by weight).[4]

Vasco's discussion is more elaborate. The problem of clipped money can best be dealt with, he says, by refusing to accept it in payment of taxes. This will protect the treasury, and if the citizens are not required to accept such money, they will avoid loss by demanding that deficiencies in its weight be made good. No further regulation is useful. With regard to the melting of coin, he has equally liberal views. Since the value of money results from the value of the metal and that of the coinage, the principal part would be lost if melting were prohibited. Such a regulation is

[1] Justi, *Schriften*, vol. ii, pp. 528–535.

[2] Galiani, *op. cit.*, vol. ii, pp. 176–178.

[3] Galiani (*ibid.*, p. 182) approves such a regulation for gold money, but does not consider it of value for money in general. Steuart (*op. cit.*, vol. i, p. 544) favors it for large sums. Neri would make it optional (*op. cit.*, p. 137).

[4] Broggia, *op. cit.*, vol. ii, pp. 162–165.

therefore inadvisable. Moreover, the natural consequence of this prohibition, if enforced, would be the export of the moneys which could not be melted, and the departure of all the workers in the precious metals, whenever they needed to use coin for bullion. It is hardly necessary to refute the vain opinion that the prince is injured by putting his effigy into the melting-pot.

He concludes with some interesting suggestions for maintaining the efficiency of the currency. In the first place, since it takes probably fifty years to reduce the weight of the small silver by wearing, all inconvenience from this cause can be avoided by coining some additional supply at fairly frequent intervals and refusing in taxes those coined before a certain date, leaving them to the valuation of commerce. To prevent monopolies in certain coins, the prince should be ready to exchange one kind of money for another, not without limit, but in quantities "sufficient to conserve the proportion between the moneys." This regulation will, in addition, answer the question as to the relative quantities of the different denominations needed; the people will adjust it by exchange to suit themselves.[1]

[1] Vasco, *op. cit.*, pp. 46, 56, 57, 118 123.

CHAPTER XXIX

THE VALUE OF MONEY: COMMODITY THEORIES

1. Supply and Demand Theories

As in previous periods, there were a few discussions of prices which clearly implied that the value of coins was simply a matter of their fine metal content, but which did not go further into the question.[1] None of these deserves special mention at this stage of our study.

John Law's discussion is notable as the first, since Bodin focussed attention on the influence of supply, to give due importance to the demand. Silver as a metal, he says, had a value in barter, before it was used as money; and like other goods, it was subject to changes in value from changes in the demand for it or in the supply available. It is inconceivable that nations should have agreed to put an imaginary value on anything (as Locke says they put one on silver), much less in the case of silver, by which other goods are valued; or how such a value, if once agreed upon, could have been kept up. It is true, the additional use as money, to which silver was applied, would add to its value, because the greater convenience which it thus afforded would increase the demand for it; but this additional value is no more imaginary than other values. On the other hand, though the value of money is real, it is not the value for which goods are exchanged, as Locke says, but the value by which they are exchanged; for silver, while money, has no use but to buy goods.

In one respect, however, the value of silver differs from that of most commodities. The latter tend to bear about the same proportion to the demand at all times, production being checked in case of a surplus, and *vice versa;* but silver has increased more

[1] Leib (see Zielenziger, *op. cit.*, p. 388); Voltaire (see *Revue d'Hist. des Doctr.*, vol. v, p. 365); Douglass, *Currencies of the British Plantations in America*, pp. 337, 338; Broggia, *op. cit.*, vol. i, p. 376; Spinelli (see Fornari, *op. cit.*, vol. ii, p. 118).

than the demand for it, and hence its value has fallen. Despite this fall, nevertheless, money is worth "one half or two thirds more than its value as silver, abstract from its use as money," because the demand for silver is largely for use as money. It should be noted, moreover, that in speaking of the demand for and supply of money (as of goods), we refer to the situation in Europe as a whole, and not in any particular country. From these principles he concludes that the use of silver as money has certain undesirable consequences. Since it is liable to change in value from a change in either quantity or demand, the receiver of silver money suffers from a double uncertainty; and the evil is aggravated, if anything, by the fact that an ounce of silver, being always worth the same number of shillings, comes to be considered invariable in value. The only exception to this is the case of "raising" money, where the value may seem to be changed but is not.[1]

A view somewhat similar to Law's is presented by d'Aguesseau, a vigorous opponent of Law's projects. The value of money obeys the same laws as other goods, rising or falling in proportion to changes in supply and demand. This conclusion rests upon the principle, derived from the "droit des gens, auquel tout ce qui regarde les monnaies appartient," that the only true value of money is that of its material. From this principle it also follows that debasement of any kind will lead to higher prices.[2]

In the anonymous treatise of 1723 described by Böhmert, there are hints of several theories. The value given to the precious metals arises, we are told, from their scarcity, the difficulty of mining them, and "the number, will, and property of those who use money." No attempt is made, apparently, to analyze the relation between these factors.[3]

Melon, Law's secretary, also attached much importance to demand, and declared that the great amount of gold and silver brought into Europe from America would have raised prices, if the prodigious increase of commerce during the period had not

[1] Law, *op. cit.*, pp. 8, 14–16, 78–81, 117–140, 188.

[2] *Revue d'Hist. des Doctr.*, vol. ii, pp. 278, 279.

[3] Böhmert, *Ein Lehrbuch über den Volkswohlstand*, pp. 22, 23.

increased the need for money.[1] It cannot be said, however, that the influence of demand continued to be stressed after Law's time.

Vanderlint's discussion is lengthy but unsatisfactory.[2] To begin with, he unconsciously introduces a cost element. Money, he says, will be most plentiful, and hence least valuable, where the mines are; whence it follows that the prices of the products of every nation will be higher or lower as the quantity of cash circulating there is greater or less in proportion to the number of inhabitants. Ignoring the obvious *non sequitur* here, he goes on to apply this unique version of the supply-and-demand theory in various ways. If the people, for instance, increase and money does not, prices must fall, for each person has less to buy with. On the other hand, if gold and silver increase faster than the population, prices will advance. I need hardly point out that this reasoning either involves an erroneous notion of the nature of the demand for money, or, at best, assumes without proof or warrant that the volume of transactions in a country will change in proportion to the population. Furthermore, he says, this principle leads to the conclusion that removing taxes will not lower prices, since it does not affect the quantity of money in circulation; while, a page later, he argues that the cheapness of goods resulting from the elimination of taxes would so stimulate demand for them that rents would be raised — both of which clearly cannot be true. Equally puzzling is his statement that, although the seasons and like factors cause prices to vary, yet the increased prices so decrease consumption, or *vice versa*, "as in the event to make the Effect the same, as if they were strictly and invariably governed by the Quantity of Money circulating amongst the People." The same may be said of his assertion that in certain cases the demand for the fruits of earth will raise prices "higher than the Money circulating among them will well enable them to pay." [3]

Berkeley's only reference to the problem of money's value is his remark that the "discovery of a very rich gold mine in our midst" would cause all things to bear a high price. By a "rich" mine he

[1] Melon, *op. cit.*, p. 773.

[2] I pass over Philips's confused discussion — *State of the Nation*, pp. 41, 42.

[3] Vanderlint, *op. cit.*, pp. 13, 14, 19, 20, 110–113, 124.

apparently means one of large output, making this no more than another statement of the supply-and-demand theory.[1] Necker says that the increase of money is the *motif* of the increase of prices, without developing the argument; but he adds that, since the additional production of the mines is relative to the existing stock, there is reason to hope that the rise in prices will be less and less felt. He was apparently the first to note this point.[2]

It will not be necessary to consider in detail all the later versions of the supply-and-demand theory. Some of them go no further than a brief reference to the influence of quantity on the value of the precious metals,[3] while others add the conventional arguments about the effect of debasement on prices.[4]

In some cases, however, points of further interest were made. Belloni, for example, hints at the influence of cost of production in his statement that gold was given a higher value than silver because it was scarcer and the expenses of mining it were greater.[5] Justi gives a slightly different turn to the supply argument, saying that if a country has little money, prices must be low, for people simply cannot pay more, and sellers must take low prices or not sell. This argument is really closely akin to the "quantity theory," but he does not refer to the latter way of reasoning. Besides pointing out the effect of debasement on prices, he adds that, as soon as money is given a value above that of the metal, it becomes a mere commodity, and like other commodities may be raised in price by monopolistic practices.[6] This is one of the few recognitions in the period covered by this study of the possibility of a scarcity value for money as such.

Of Carli's lengthy discussion, only two points need be noted. The first is his statement that it is a "fatal mistake" for nations

[1] Berkeley, *Works*, vol. iv, p. 448.

[2] Bodin de Saint-Laurent, *op. cit.*, p. 55.

[3] Zinke's *Leipziger Sammlungen* (see Roscher, *op. cit.*, p. 438); Magens, *op. cit.*, pp. 69, 70; Mercier de la Rivière, *L'Ordre Naturel*, p. 583; Paradisi (see Graziani, *op. cit.*, p. 63).

[4] Hutcheson, *op. cit.*, vol. ii, p. 227; Massie, *Observations*, pp. 14, 15; *Causes of the Natural Rate of Interest*, pp. 37, 38; Neri, *op. cit.*, pp. 106, 136, 145, 166–169, 175, 216–219. The last-named supports his theory by appeal to natural law.

[5] Belloni, *op. cit.*, p. 49.

[6] Justi, *Schriften*, vol. i, pp. 289, 290, 295, 352, 353, vol. iii, pp. 31, 32.

to think that their small base money does not enter into "universal commerce"; for people adjust prices to the real value of the small money, of which they have most. Foreign exchange is also based on this money. This statement may have been true under the conditions then existing in the Italian states, but it would not hold in a country where the subsidiary money was properly regulated, according to principles already beginning to be understood in Carli's time. The second point is his conclusion that the high prices then prevailing in Italy were only apparent, and that there was really less money in the country than formerly. This is based on arguments and computations which I must confess are to me mysterious and unconvincing; but the idea seems to be that the decline of commerce and the heavy taxes required for the armies would have raised prices higher than they are, if the supply of money had remained the same.[1]

The influence of demand, though largely neglected, received some attention. Mirabeau concludes that, had it not been for the commerce of the Indies and the demand for jewelry and such uses, the flood of gold and silver from America would have made them too common for use as money;[2] and Turgot points out that the use of the precious metals as money increased their value.[3]

Before going on to what is in many respects the most interesting discussion in the period after that of Law — Sir James Steuart's — we may consider the work of a few authors who referred to the present theory, but who seem to have somewhat misunderstood it. The author of the anonymous *Inquiry into the Nature and Uses of Money*, published in Boston in 1740, states clearly enough that, although gold and silver have only an "accidental" value, this may change, like the value of other things, from a change in the proportion between the quantity to be sold and the demand for that quantity; but in applying the principle he falls into confusion. Thus he speaks of silver rising from eight shillings to nine per ounce, because of its scarcity in proportion to demand, with the result that the pound sterling was reduced in weight; yet on the next page he speaks of prices rising in proportion to the

[1] Carli, *op. cit.*, vol. i, pp. 100, 101, 126, 127, 276–281, 303, 358–363.

[2] Bodin de Saint-Laurent, *op. cit.*, pp. 52, 53.

[3] Turgot, *op. cit.*, p. 271.

raising of silver.[1] William Horsley, in his introduction to Magens's *Universal Merchant*, fails to grasp the concept of the general price-level, and argues stoutly that "Gold and Silver is as much balanced by the Plenty or Scarcity of other Things, as them by Gold and Silver," as is seen daily in the price of grain.[2] Tucker also appears to have inadequate ideas as to the effect of quantity on the value of money; for he reasons that, if England should receive suddenly a large sum of money, things would rise to a "most enormous price whilst the flush of money lasted." The people, not knowing the real value of money, would give any prices for commodities, and husbandry, moreover, would be neglected, with the result of decreased supplies of provisions.[3]

Of all the adherents of the supply-and-demand theory, only one saw fit to attack the variation of it which we have called the "quantity theory." Steuart opens an elaborate attack by declaring that he is "obliged to range this ingenious exposition of a most interesting subject, among those general and superficial maxims which never fail to lead to error." In the first place, he argues, if the increase of money leads neither to a "raising" nor "augmenting" of demand, the additional coin will simply be stored up in some form. If it be accompanied by "augmenting" of demand, it will circulate but not raise prices. Only in case it is accompanied by a "raising" of demand will it lead to a rise in prices. By "raising" the demand, he says, he means increasing competition merely, while by "augmenting" the demand, he implies a proportional increase in supply. To put this in a different way, we may say that an increase of money cannot raise prices unless people *spend* more, and even then the increased supply of goods called forth may bring prices back to the old level.

If a country, moreover, has trade with others, a rise in prices through an increase of money would be restrained by foreign competition. If all the produce of a country must be sold for what specie there is, there can be no foreign trade, or men will buy in the cheaper market. Another objection, of a very different sort, is

[1] *An Inquiry*, pp. 2, 3, 7, 13, 14, 23. [2] Magens, *op. cit.*, p. xvi.
[3] Clark, *op. cit.*, pp. 195, 196.

that many goods are not sold for money, and these have no influence on specie nor specie on them. Still another argument is the impossibility of keeping specie "in an equal repartition, so as to serve the occasions of everybody in proportion to their worth." Money comes into the hands of those who give the most for it, and any individual who thus acquires a large amount will raise prices in his neighborhood.

Behind this theory, to conclude, is the erroneous idea that money is the representative of all a country's commodities and labor. This clearly is not true, for other things may represent them as well. If there were no money, would things be had for nothing, or would there be no sales? Money is an equivalent merely, and "has no title to represent anything vendible."

These objections to the quantity theory, shrewd as they are in many cases, are themselves open to criticism. Not only are they aimed at a very crude version, which is hardly implied by the discussions of Locke and Hume, to whom he makes direct reference, but they ignore in some cases the concept of "other things being equal," and in others confuse particular prices with general prices. They are of considerable value, however, for emphasizing the fact that the other things often do vary, which was too frequently neglected even by writers who held views more like Steuart's.

Coming now to his own theory, we find some novel refinements. First, he points out that silver cannot be called a standard, since its own value may vary; and declares that a "florin banco" of Amsterdam has a "more determinate value" than a pound of gold or silver, admitting, however, that very few people can tell what this depends on. Where such an "ideal standard" is not used, the value of the money unit of account depends upon the "actual intrinsic value of that currency in which all obligations are acquitted and all accompts are kept," taking a mean proportion of the various coins in circulation. He who pays out money that is heavier than the average loses, and *vice versa*. A change in the market ratio between the metals, therefore, will debase the value of the standard, since this will always be a mean proportion between the values of the two weights of metal which by law are coined into pieces of equal denomination. If a charge is made for coinage, coin must be valued by that much more than bullion. If everyone considered coin only as a means of reckoning value, without regard to its value as metal, alterations in ratio or weight would make little difference; but in fact all do not do this, and there are those whose business it is to profit from such variations.

When bullion is sold in the market, payment is generally received in worn silver, overvalued gold, and the like, so that the price of bullion is always above the mint price. Goldsmiths may also pay more than the mint price, because they get it back in the price of the workmanship. If there is a coinage charge, the price even in full-weight coin may rise by the amount of the charge; but as long as the balance of trade is "even," the premium will be only half the cost of coinage.[1]

Beccaria holds that in fixing the value of money no weight should be given to the alloy it contains, or to the greater fineness of certain pieces, but only to the actual fine-metal content. The alloy has so little value that it is better to disregard it, for the sake of the greater simplicity. It is true that in a large sum of money the value of the alloy may be considerable; but the ignoring of this is largely balanced by the refusal to give additional value to coins of extreme fineness. To value these coins higher would simply be paying for foreign services.[2]

Vasco begins with the proposition that the value of coin, like the value of all other things, is simply the actual ratio in which it can be exchanged for other goods, what men will commonly give to have it. He seems to attach most importance to the influence of demand, but also mentions supply, and develops neither at any length. Bad money is merely that which is acquired at a greater price than its real value, which can never happen when the course of money is really free. This principle applies not only to the relation between money and commodities, but also to the relation between one kind of money and another. If copper money, for

[1] Steuart, *op. cit.*, vol. i, pp. 399–413, 528–538, 547–551, 561–571, 601, 620, vol. ii, pp. 3, 13, 17.

[2] Beccaria, *op. cit.*, vol. ii, pp. 208–212.

instance, becomes too plentiful, gold and silver rise in numerary value; while monopolists, on the other hand, can raise the value of certain pieces by restricting their circulation. As a result, the nominal values of coins tend always to increase; for after some kind of money has come to have a greater value because of special conditions, people do not like to go back to the lower value, and the nominal values of other pieces are raised instead, when the special conditions have passed.

From the above discussion it is evident how false and prejudicial is the opinion of those jurists who hold that the value of money is wholly a matter of the prince's will. To deny it is no attack on the "sacred rights of sovereignty," but simply to admit a physical limitation of power; the prince can no more fix the value of money than determine the quantity of rainfall and other "necessary relations of things."

It is likewise a mistake to say we should give our money the value it has as metal, or the value of the metal plus the cost of coinage. Since the value of money depends simply on public esteem, a coin may sometimes be worth more and sometimes less than its metal content. This does not mean, however, that the amount of metal in the coins makes no difference, for it has great influence on their values in relation to each other. Worn or clipped money, for instance, "cannot represent the same amount of commodities as before." In other words, unless special considerations intervene, a given amount of metal in one coin will exchange for the same amount in other coins.

From the above reasoning, it might appear that the prince could indirectly give his money any value he wished, by restricting the amount coined; but this is rendered impossible by the influence of foreign trade. You cannot separate the money of a country from the conditions in foreign commerce, and in this the weight of the coins is the only thing considered. The only course for the prince to follow is to calculate the expenses of coinage, including the cost of bullion, and not to undertake it unless the value of the money will be at least equal to the expense of making it. It will perhaps be advisable for only those nations to coin money which have the nearest and richest mines; but it is doubtful whether the cost of transporting bullion is greater than that for money, or whether the non-mining countries suffer any disadvantage from the laws of mining countries. It is probable, moreover, that copper can be coined without loss in every country of Europe, and hence none need be without its own currency. In any case, it would be worth while to bear some slight loss on it, for the advantages of controlling this basic part of the money-supply. As for the question whether money made in the mother country can be given the same value in the colonies, he says he has not enough data to decide.[1]

2. Equilibrium Theories

In the references to cost of production encountered in the foregoing discussions of the supply-and-demand theory it is clear that the authors were quite unconscious of the modification they had introduced, for none of them attempted to harmonize the two points of view. The first to do this for monetary theory, as well as for value in general, was Cantillon, whose work is of great importance.

The "real or intrinsic" value of the metals, as of all things, he writes, apparently under the influence of Petty, is in proportion to the land and labor necessary for their production. This value is no more imaginary than that of laces and fine linens; for although it is true, as Locke says, that the consent of men has given the precious metals their value, the same may be said of other articles of luxury. As in the case of other things, however, the market value of the metals fluctuates above and below this "intrinsic" value, varying "in proportion to their abundance or their scarcity, according to the consumption made of them"; for it is impossible exactly to proportion production to demand at all times. The influence of cost is fundamental, nevertheless; for if producers do not find their product in sufficient demand, they will discontinue their activities. There is thus a close relation between the different forces affecting value, and market values tend to correspond to intrinsic values. An ounce of silver tends to ex-

[1] Vasco, *op. cit.*, pp. 7–13, 18–20, 41, 45, 53, 54, 69–73, 104, 121, 122, 135, 136, 146.

change for a commodity whose production involved the same amount of land and labor.

Unlike Locke, Cantillon does not seem to regard even the market value of money as a special case, and does not subscribe to Locke's theory of the relation between money and goods in general. He is not at all clear about the nature of the demand for the money metals, and a careful reading of his discussion leaves the impression that he had not given this point any special attention. At times he seems to have only the arts use in mind, but at others he appears to give full weight to the monetary demand. He is much interested in describing how market prices are established by the rough "altercation" of buyers and sellers, but he does not generalize from this regarding the price level. This neglect is perhaps natural in view of the subordinate position which market value had in his mind.

With respect to the influence of supply on the market value of the money metals, he is more satisfactory. "Every one agrees," he says, "that the abundance of silver or its increase in trade raises the price of everything"; but it by no means follows that the increase in prices will be proportional to the increase of money. Much depends on how consumption is affected; and it appears from a study of the spread of price changes that a proportional change in prices is practically never to be expected. It is not that reasoning like Locke's is illogical, for there is a conceivable case where prices would rise proportionally, namely, where the additional money entered exactly the same channels as those which contained the old; but that it is not an accurate description of how the thing does work out. Moreover, there is likely to be less barter when money is plentiful. We cannot say there is even a tendency toward a proportional change in prices.

In the above discussion we have spoken as if coin and bullion were interchangeable so far as value goes. This is true, he points out, provided there is no charge for coinage. When there is a prohibition against the export of bullion, however, bankers will be led to pay a slight premium for bullion to pay foreign balances. This premium does not indicate how great a balance the country owes, but only that there is a balance. Debasement and raising cause proportional changes in prices.[1]

Galiani's application of the equilibrium idea was very different from Cantillon's. According to his view also, the value of money is simply a case of value in general, but this meant something very different from what it did to Cantillon. Value is a ratio compounded of two factors, utility and rarity, and it is because the precious metals have these qualities that they are used as money. Their value is not derived from their use as money, or from caprice, or from the consent of nations. As Locke says, a quality, however useful, does not increase value unless it increases demand;[2] and since gold and silver are used principally as metals, we may say that their value depends largely on this. It is probably ten times as important a factor as the money use.

These principles point to some interesting conclusions with regard to the precious metals. In the first place, their great durability causes their value to be less than it would be otherwise; for though they would be no less prized, if less durable, the supply would be less. Moreover, as the quantity of metal in the world increases, the number of mines fit to be worked decreases. The fall in the value of the metal increases the expenses of mining, till finally it no longer pays to operate the mine. After the discovery of the rich mines of America, the mines of Europe were largely abandoned. In fact, if additional uses had not been found for the vast new supplies, the new mines would also have soon ceased to be profitable. As it happened, India, "barren of silver," absorbed great quantities, and kept the value of the metals from falling in proportion to the increase in quantity. The greater cheapness of the metals also caused more to be used in plate, and this helped to counteract the increase in production. It is vain, however, to fear that gold and silver may sometime become as plentiful as copper; there are no mines rich enough for that. Nor need we fear that a decrease of luxury might cause the precious metals to lose value greatly; less would be mined in that case, and the same degree of rarity would be maintained. And finally, it is a mistake to put a

[1] Cantillon, *op. cit.*, pp. 127, 128, 148, 149, 154, 212, 232–239, 346, 347, 361, 396.

[2] Locke was talking about money's ability to earn interest.

value on money by law; this should be left to be regulated by the multitude, "misuratrice giustissima e fedele." [1]

Harris borrowed from Cantillon, and was also much influenced by the ideas of Locke. When the use of money became established, he begins, a greater or less quantity of the money material was given as the price for various things "in proportion to the respective values which before had been set upon them, as well in respect to that commodity now made money, as of one another." The use of silver as money, by increasing the demand for that metal, caused it to have a greater value. To be more specific, money, like other things, "will soon find a value, in proportion to the labor and skill, that are necessary to acquire it; or in a reciprocal proportion to its plenty."

Now these two determinants of value are plainly not the same thing, and their use in this alternative sense requires explanation. The reason for it seems to be that Harris believed there was a tendency for the quantity to adjust itself in such a way that the value would correspond fairly well to the cost of production. Later, however, he qualifies this very greatly, and declares that the value of bullion does not, like most things, "keep pace with the prime cost, at the mines." His reason for this opinion is not clear, but the point seems to be that since the precious metals are so durable, the production of the mines beyond the new needs is simply added to the existing mass, and serves to diminish the value of a given amount of the metal, regardless of what the new supplies cost. The owner of the mine must then take less profit or diminish his output. A similar fall in value occurs in the case of other goods, under like circumstances, but it is never so uniform.

The reason for this greater uniformity, he evidently means us to conclude, is to be found in the nature of the relation between money and goods, which he had just discussed. With regard to this, which we may call the market value of money, he is in full accord with the views of Locke. Since money exchanges for all commodities, the demand for it is without limit; and on the other hand, the demand cannot exceed, but must be satisfied with, the whole supply. Therefore, the value of the total money in circula-

[1] Galiani, *op. cit.*, vol. i, pp. 44–51, 58, 59, 95–107, 116–123, 254.

tion will be equal to the whole amount of commodities in traffic in that country. It appears, however, from a note on this passage, that it is not to be interpreted too narrowly. There is always a great part of the property in a country out of trade, he says; "but as things are continually shifting, and those commodities, and those sums of money, which are out of trade to-day, may be in trade to-morrow, the prices of things always fundamentally depend upon the above rule; that is on the proportion of the total of things to the total of money." This sounds so much like Montesquieu's argument on the same point,[1] that I am inclined to think Harris got his inspiration there; but it should be noted that he does not conclude, with Montesquieu, that the total of gold and silver is equal to the total of goods, but that all money is equal to all the goods exchangeable for money.

The foregoing theory of normal value, as we should call it, applies equally well to money and to the metals as used for other purposes; and there is no doubt that Harris considered them subject to the same laws in this respect. It is clear, however, that the "quantity theory" of the short-time or market value, which he held, applied only to money as such, and that it would not be a complete explanation of the market value of the precious metals. Just how this gap is to be bridged does not appear, but there are certain hints. He points out, for example, that coins made without charge must have the same value as their fine-metal content; and in the passage about the value of bullion, to which I have already referred, he says that additional production will cause the value of money to fall, unless the new supplies are consumed or hoarded or made into plate. It would appear, therefore, that he was aware of the relation between the monetary and non-monetary uses, and perhaps assumed some kind of an equalizing process between them, as Montanari had done earlier.

The principle that the value of a coin is simply that of the metal in it is subject to one qualification. In countries where coins pass by tale, "contracts and the prices of commodities" are measured by the amount of metal in the standard, and not by the actual content of the coins in circulation. If this standard be altered,

[1] See the next chapter below.

tradesmen will alter the nominal price of their goods in proportion, and workmen will demand higher wages. This qualification is more easily reconciled with the cost of production theory than with the "quantity theory"; but Harris does not undertake either.

With regard to the price of bullion, he offers some new refinements. This price, he points out, instead of "governing" the value of all other things, as many believe, is really "governed as well as measured" by the coin of the established standard. It may rise above the mint price when there is a demand for payments abroad and coin is not exportable, or when sufficient full-weight coins are not available for melting. In England a further cause has served to keep silver bullion above the mint price for over fifty years. This is the overvaluing of gold at the mint. The merchant always makes his standard of the metal which is highest valued, and will not part with the other metal except at the same rate it will bring elsewhere.[1]

Before closing this chapter, we should refer to an idea which found considerable support among the German Cameralists. Hornick, Schröder, Rohr, and Justi, for example, were so deeply impressed with the importance of money for a country's welfare that they declared explicitly that the mining of the precious metals should be continued by the public authorities, even though the returns were not sufficient to cover expenses.[2]

[1] Harris, *op. cit.*, pt. i, pp. 36–41, 67–79, 121; pt. ii, pp. 13 n., 37, 38, 55–64, 89, 94.

[2] Hornick, *Oesterreich über Alles*, pp. 173, 174; Small, *The Cameralists*, pp. 205, 361. Cf. what is said below (Chapter XXXVII) concerning Justi's views.

CHAPTER XXX

THE VALUE OF MONEY: THE QUANTITY THEORY

THE great prestige of Locke's work served to keep the quantity theory before the thinking world and to gain many followers for this line of reasoning. His influence is clear in Isaac Gervaise's *System or Theory of the Trade of the World*, which was published in 1720. Here we find the conclusion that the value of all things "is to Gold and Silver in proportion to the Quantity of Gold and Silver that is in the World." This is due to the steady demand for these metals, a demand which arises from the fact that they carry with them "a Right, or Demand at will on all things necessary," which otherwise would require the expenditure of labor and the sacrifice of our ease.[1] In this analysis there is no distinction between the forces which determine the value of money and those which influence the value of bullion in the arts.

In the anonymous *Some Thoughts on the Interest of Money* the influence of Locke is equally clear. Prices, we read, depend on the amount of money in circulation (not the total quantity of the precious metals), but it is important to note that an increase in the quantity of money will cause a proportionate change in prices only provided trade remains the same in volume. This, however, is likely not to be the case, for an increase in money tends to stimulate trade.[2] This important refinement had escaped Locke's attention.

Prior, like Gervaise, repeats Locke's argument about the stability of the demand for money, but he speaks of it as the demand for gold and silver. Their value, he says, is "proportional to their Scarcity and Demands for them or rather to their Scarcity alone, for since they are made Equivalents for all other Commodities, we may suppose the Demands for them to be everywhere much the same." Therefore a change in the legal value of money will

[1] Kaulla, *Moderne Wertltheorien*, pp. 86, 87. [2] *Ibid.*, p. 91.

cause a proportional change in prices, for prices depend on the metal content, not on the name.[1] He does not mention Locke, but the influence seems obvious. Locke, it will be remembered, had sometimes carelessly spoken as if it were all gold and silver that are equal to all commodities, and as if the arts use were negligible. This apparently was the impression which Prior got from him.

Although the influence of quantity on the value of the precious metals, and hence on the value of money, was recognized by numerous writters in France after Bodin's time, I have seen no instance of agreement with the reasoning on this point introduced by Davanzati before Montesquieu's *Esprit des Lois*. Here the quantity theory is developed in rigid form. If we compare the total of gold and silver in the world with the total of commodities, he says, we may say that each commodity can be compared with a certain portion of the entire mass of the precious metals. As the total of one is to the total of the other, so a part of one is to a part of the other. It is as if there were only one commodity to be sold, and it were divisible as gold and silver are.[2] As Zuckerkandl has pointed out,[3] this somewhat crude statement should be interpreted in the light of Montesquieu's later remarks about the ideal money, or "macutes," of certain African tribes. These are abstract units of value by which the people express the "degree of esteem" they have for each commodity. Now if such a custom were applied to our economy, we might say that the total of commodities was equal to a certain number of macutes, and the total of precious metals equal to the same number of macutes, from which it would obviously follow that, if the supply of the metals were increased, it would take more of them to equal one macute. The equivalence of money and goods is an equivalence of values, and presupposes exchange relations between the goods themselves.

Since neither all commodities nor all the precious metals are in commerce at once, however, prices will be fixed "according to a compound ratio of the total of things and the total of signs, and the total of things in commerce and the total of signs in

[1] Prior, *op. cit.*, pp. 297, 306. [2] Montesquieu, *op. cit.*, p. 380.
[3] Zuckerkandl, *Zur Theorie des Preises*, p. 135.

commerce." Nevertheless, the total of goods and of signs is fundamental, for what is not in the market to-day may come in tomorrow.[1] Increase the money metals twenty-fold, therefore, and double commodities, and prices may be expected to rise ten-fold. No reason for this peculiarity in the value of the precious metals is given directly by Montesquieu, but it seems reasonable to infer that it was much the same as that given by Locke — common consent has made them the only accepted equivalents for all goods.

This reasoning with respect to the value of the total of gold and silver is not always consistently followed. In a later chapter, for example, he says that silver as a metal has a value like all other commodities and also a value from its capacity to serve as money. This money use increases its value. This is true enough, but it does not agree with the idea that the value of the precious metals is merely a proportion between the supply of them and the total of goods; for the latter is strictly true, as Montanari pointed out, only if the metals are used for nothing but money. A little earlier another view is presented. As the supply of the metals in Europe increased, he says, the profit of Spain from working the American mines decreased. Not only was the silver they obtained of less value, but they had to pay out more of it for expenses as prices rose. He does not go on to the conclusion that the profit might eventually be wiped out, which would check further production, perhaps because such a possibility seemed too remote; but I think we may say that there is just a hint here of the influence of cost of production. And finally, it is hard to reconcile his general reasoning with his statement that the prince "establishes a proportion between a quantity of silver as metal and the same quantity as money." [2]

[1] Kaulla seems mistaken when he interprets Montesquieu as limiting the terms of the ratio to the goods and coin in circulation. (*Op. cit.*, p. 122.) The greater importance of the larger totals is made plain enough, and there is no mention of coin. The word "sign," which may give this impression, is used to mean simply gold and silver, in the same sense as in an earlier statement that the precious metals are "une richesse de fiction ou de signe." There is no attempt to distinguish the metals and money.

[2] Montesquieu, *op. cit.*, pp. 376, 377, 380, 381.

Hume had little interest in the logical basis of the quantity theory, but was principally concerned with its qualifications. "It seems a maxim almost self-evident," he writes, "that the prices of every thing depend on the proportion between commodities and money." The only hint as to his reasons for this opinion is his remark, in another connection, that the precious metals "are considered chiefly as representations." It is not the absolute quantity of money and commodities, however, which is meant in the above statement, he carefully points out, but the commodities "which come or may come to market," and the money which circulates. Coin locked up and goods not sold obviously have no effect on prices. Hence it is that prices are lower in France than in some countries not having half as much gold and silver: people are in the habit of keeping large sums in their coffers, because the use of credit instruments is undeveloped, and much of the metal is in use as plate.

Although he occasionally speaks as if changes in the quantity might be expected to cause proportional changes in prices, this is by no means the impression he means to convey. In the first place, changes in customs and manners may have caused a greater number of money contracts to be required, which means that the goods of the country "come more to market." This is one of the reasons why the great inflow of the money metals from America did not raise prices more. The supply of goods, moreover, may be greater, either because of greater population, or because of the stimulating effect of the transition to higher prices — a topic we shall consider later. This also helped reduce the effect of the American gold. Hence we may conclude that, if money does not increase, the necessary effect of advancing society is that everything becomes cheaper; for "the same national cash has a much greater task to perform."[1] These qualifications did not attract the attention they deserved, and it was Montesquieu's cruder statement that had the greater influence. In Germany, Italy, and even in England, we find writers referring to him as sponsor for the quantity theory; and it was his version that Steuart had in mind in his criticisms of this theory.

[1] Hume, *Essays*, vol. i, pp. 312, 313, 316–322, 333, 338.

At about the time that Hume's *Essays* were published, we meet the theory in Italy again. Pagnini quoted Davanzati with approval, and declared that no later writer had improved upon his analysis.[1] Pereira, however, writing a little later, does not refer to Davanzati, but follows Locke with respect to the value of the precious metals, and the necessary connection between this and the value of money.[2]

Postlethwayt does not refer directly to Locke and Hume in this connection, but appears to accept their conclusions, for he several times speaks of prices as varying in strict proportion to the quantity of money in the country. He is more interested in other factors affecting prices, however, and lays down the principle that the difference between prices at different times will be in proportion to the "effective Silver in the nominal Pound" and the rates of interest at these times, "Computation being made upon both those Heads." Thus, if there is one third as much silver in the pound, and the interest is one half as high, prices will be six times as much; for "six Times the Money must now be employed to produce the same Quantity of Silver or Gold." He fails to see that this applies only to capitalized values.[3]

Wallace introduces a curious qualification, of doubtful validity. It is not upon the quantity of current money alone that prices depend, he says, without attempting to demonstrate that they do so in any sense, but rather upon the proportion between the number of buyers and that of sellers. If there are more buyers than sellers, prices will rise, and *vice versa*. This proportion "depends on a thousand accidents," the manners of the people having great influence.[4] This is either a simple confusion of general prices with particular prices, or questionable logic. He may have in mind the varying tendency toward hoarding at different times, or perhaps the case where the soundness of the currency has been called in question, and sellers begin to hold off for better terms, or refuse to sell for money; but neither of these interpretations seems plainly called for.

[1] Pagnini, *op. cit.*, pp. 198–204. [2] Graziani, *op. cit.*, p. 71.

[3] Postlethwayt, *Great Britain's True System*, pp. 189–195, 204–206, 334.

[4] Wallace, *op. cit.*, pp. 38, 39.

Another novel analysis, somewhat more successful than the foregoing, and probably traceable to the influence of Locke, is found in Robinson's *Essay on Coin.* The value of commodities, including money, is determined by "quantity, goodness, scarcity, and demand." In the case of a coin, the first two items are simply a matter of its weight and fineness, the value of the alloy being disregarded. Scarcity and demand will be constant when the metals are equally scarce and demanded at all times, or when scarcity and demand are "reciprocally proportioned to each other," that is, when one increases as the other decreases. Now demand for the precious metals should be "proportional to the Debts contracted by Commodities purchased, that is, proportional to a Man's Expenses"; while scarcity varies as a man's riches. Expenses, however, should always be in proportion to riches, or gold and silver cannot be a just measure of the value of things; money will have a greater value to a poor man than to a rich man, unless each has proportionate expenses. The civil law assumes this, though it cannot enforce it. Then scarcity and demand will be constant, and each individual will value money simply according to its weight and fineness. From these principles it follows that the price of a commodity will be proportional to its scarcity and the plenty of money, taken together, understanding scarcity to imply not only absolute but relative scarcity. And finally, if coins are of constant weight and fineness, the weight of the price of a commodity will also be proportional to the scarcity of the commodity and the plenty of money.[1]

Genovesi draws his inspiration from Montesquieu, quite ignoring his countrymen, Davanzati and Montanari. Before money was coined, men had given gold and silver a value, which gradually became universal, and these metals had in consequence become the price of all things. The value of money is therefore inseparably based upon the value of the metals. As for this value we may accept Montesquieu's theory that, as the total of the precious metals is to the total of goods, so is a part of one to a part of the other. Like Montesquieu, he also falls into the inconsistency of reasoning about the value which gold and silver derive

[1] Robinson, *op. cit.*, pp. 3–16.

from their use as metals and the added value they have from their use as money.[1]

The tendency to enlarge upon the qualifications of the theory, which we noted in Hume, is seen also in Accarias de Sérionne, who was perhaps familiar with Hume's work, since he refers to other English writers. The rise in prices occasioned by an increased quantity of money may be neutralized in part by an increase in the number of transactions. We now have new wants, he points out, such as the desire for tea, chocolate, and tobacco, and hence gold and silver have more work to do as signs, more things to represent. Moreover, the increased use in the arts has helped to raise the value of the precious metals. Hoarding also contributes.[2]

The influence of Montesquieu appears again in Sonnenfels, who refers to him and gives his now familiar statement of the equivalence of the two masses, goods and money, and of their corresponding fractions. This relationship arises from the fact that money is simply the representative of goods. He does not make it clear whether he means to include all gold and silver in this ratio or only the coined pieces.[3]

Substantially the same view as the above is implied in certain remarks of Baudeau, who in one place says that money is "only the representation of the right to consume," and later notes that, if additional gold and silver are introduced into circulation, while the mass of commodities remains the same, proportionately more metal will be needed to represent each commodity.[4]

In Forbonnais's discussion, the exact nature of the influence of quantity is not made clear, but he seems to have in mind some such idea as Montesquieu's. As the discovery of mines, he says, multiplied the mass of money, each portion of commodities would have been represented by a greater amount of money, had it not been for the increase of industry which occurred at the same time. The phraseology here is distinctly reminiscent of Montesquieu. His failure to make more of the influence of quantity is probably

[1] Genovesi, *op. cit.*, vol. ii, pp. 17, 26, 27, 33–35, 42–45, 243.
[2] Sérionne, *op. cit.*, vol. i, pp. 284–287; Bodin de Saint-Laurent, *op. cit.*, p. 56.
[3] Sonnenfels, *op. cit.*, pt. ii, pp. 327, 338.
[4] Baudeau, *Science Morale et Politique*, pp. 8, 18.

due to his conviction that an increase in money was practically always followed by an increase in industry, at least great enough to counterbalance it. His discussion of the value of money contains one other point of interest. Besides the intrinsic value which the precious metals have from their use in the arts, they have another "of pure convention, solely relative to their fitness for money." This is the greater value, and absorbs the former. What he means by one value "absorbing" another, I do not know. The only case to which the term might be applied seems to be where one use supersedes another, but this is not true of the precious metals and money.[1]

Pinto's ideas as to the value of money are by no means clear, and it is even doubtful whether he should be classed with the group of writers considered in this chapter. On the whole, however, it seems best to take up his discussion here. In one passage he refers to the dependence of prices on "the quantity of current money," and in another he points out how the abundance of gold and silver has caused them to fall in value "in the quality of sign." These expressions seem to imply that the value of money depends in some degree on circumstances other than those which determine the value of the precious metals. It is not simply on the quantity of money that he makes prices depend, however, but rather on the proportion between the number of buyers and the number of sellers — an idea we have already considered in the work of Wallace. Moreover, he is obsessed with the idea, which we have met several times already, that an increase of money causes an increase of industry. Neither his explanation nor his application of the idea was very successful. The fall in the value of gold and silver, which resulted from their greater abundance, gave rise to many new wants, he reasons, and consequently to much new commerce. So great was this increase, indeed, that the available supply of money was not sufficient for the trade to be done, especially since it took more to represent each commodity, and it was necessary to eke out the currency by various paper representatives of money.[2]

[1] Forbonnais, *op. cit.*, pp. 214, 216, 225, 226.

[2] Pinto, *op. cit.*, pp. 23, 54–59.

The second of the above qualifications appears also in the work of Verri, who adopts the quantity theory without attempting any demonstration of its truth. He is convinced that, when an increase of money has been acquired by industry, it will be followed by increased production, so that prices will not rise, but will be lower, if anything. The more money people have, the more they feel able to spend, and hence new wants develop and production increases as the market increases. The larger output thus stimulated will be cheaper because of the smaller profit per unit which dealers find adequate. When the money has not been acquired by industry, it will cause higher prices. He is here definitely opposing Hume's argument that large imports of money tend to check a country's exports of goods.[1]

The influence of Montesquieu is seen again in the anonymous *Essay on the Theory of Money*, of 1771. The author first supposes that the whole mass of national productions is divided into a given number of parts and that the money of the country is likewise divided into a given number of equal parts. Then the number of parts of money which are given for any commodity is the price of it. "From this definition," he naïvely concludes, "it follows, that by increasing, or diminishing the quantity of money . . . or that of the commodities, the *price* or *ratio* between them will vary, in proportion to that increase or diminution." [2]

From the foregoing account it appears that there had been no improvement, and indeed some decline, in the quality of the presentations of this theory since the middle of the eighteenth century, a decline which fortunately was not paralleled in the case of the other value theories. Ortes, the next writer to hold the quantity theory, was no exception to the general tendency. The equivalence of all goods and all money, he says, is to be understood as referring to goods already in the hands of the consumers. In the hands of others, who possess them as capital, they are equal to less money. On the other hand, we cannot speak of an equivalence between all goods and all money in the technical sense. This would be true only in case the money material were restricted to this one use, as ideally it should be. Since gold and silver are not

[1] Verri, *op. cit.*, pp. 66–70.

[2] *An Essay*, pp. 82–87, 93.

so restricted, however, we must regard all gold and silver as money for the purpose of this equivalence. Given these principles, it follows that the value of a coin in no way depends on its stamp, but solely on its weight and purity; and also that an increase in the quantity of money, while goods remain the same, will cause proportionately higher prices.

This statement is subject, however, to a number of qualifications, for the true ratio between goods and money does not appear in prices at once, or under all conditions. The fact that neither money nor goods is a stable quantity, and that they change independently, leads to many variations from the real equivalence between them. Since goods are the less variable of the two, variations in price should, for the most part, be imputed to changes in money, which is just the opposite of the popular view. Moreover, the theory is true only when we can assume the free consent of all workers of all occupations.

A further impediment to the working out of true prices arises from avarice. This leads men to hoard money, which is so much more easily preserved than commodities, and thus goods are exchanged for less money than should be given for them. It is only gradually, as the greater need for goods than for money gives the advantage to the holders of goods, that prices advance toward the point of true equivalence between goods and money. Hence we observe a rise in prices which is more than in proportion to the increase in the supply of gold and silver in Europe. The chapter in which this qualification is developed is far from clear, but the above interpretation seems, on the whole, to be the most justifiable. In a later chapter a further consequence of this tendency is pointed out. Since goods tend to exchange for more and more money, while the quantity of money is limited, it is not always possible to exchange goods at the higher prices without increasing the numerary value of the existing money. Hence there is a tendency for numerary values to rise. This seems to refer to the depressing effect on prices of increased production. At best, however, all this part of Ortes's discussion is highly artificial, and of relatively little value.[1]

[1] Ortes, *op. cit.*, vol. ii, pp. 275–287, 334–384, 400–411.

The idea that the value of money presents an essentially peculiar case, which had not been emphasized much during these years, comes to the front again in Graslin. This seems to be the meaning of his flat declaration that the value of money as such has nothing in common with its value as metal. The total value of money, as "gage conventionnel de tous les objets de besoin qui sont dans la circulation," is necessarily equal to the total value of those goods. Now, the total value of all goods being always the same,[1] it follows that the value of all money is also constant, and that the value of a given piece depends simply upon the quantity of such pieces. This last argument not only confuses the value of all goods with that of the goods in circulation, as Kaulla points out, but it introduces an irrelevant time element into the total utility concept, which is of no value for the theory of prices. If the total of money is equal to the total of goods, as he says, the value of a given amount of money, that is, its purchasing power, will depend on the quantity of money, regardless of whether these goods mean a greater total of "riches" or not.[2]

Condillac's discussion of this phase of the question is very brief. If money became eight times as abundant, he says in one passage, "it would have eight times less value," and *vice versa*. By this he means not all money, as he tells us later, but only the money in circulation, and moreover the idea of proportional change is not to be taken too literally. The value of the money in circulation is not equal to that of all the goods in circulation, but only to a certain fraction of them. This is due to the influence of rapidity of circulation, which we shall consider later.[3]

[1] This conclusion is based on a curious bit of logical jugglery. A man whose wants are satisfied is as rich as another whose more numerous wants are also just satisfied. The same reasoning applies to the same man at different periods, and hence the above conclusion. (Kaulla, pp. 129, 130.)

[2] *Ibid.*, p. 131.

[3] Condillac, *op. cit.*, pp. 289, 295–297.

CHAPTER XXXI

PRICE CHANGES: ANALYSIS

1. Measurement

No suggestions of importance were made concerning the problem of measuring price changes. Prior agrees with Locke that wheat is the best measure of value over long periods, but that silver is better for short periods.[1] Cantillon, like Bodin, considers land the best indicator of changes in the value of money; but, more accurately than the earlier writer, he takes the rent rather than the selling price as evidence.[2]

In the anonymous *Inquiry into the Nature and Uses of Money*, of 1740, we find a curiously erroneous idea of general price changes. The best and clearest notion of a change in the value of money, says the author, is to be had from the influence it has on the "mode of living"; for when the supply of money is increased, people want more and finer commodities, so that their yearly expenses are increased.[3] Whatever may be said of family budgets as index numbers, it is evident that the above reasoning quite misses the point.

Galiani seems to have the idea of observing the prices of a group of commodities, but does not grasp the full significance of the method. When the rate at which a thing exchanges for all others changes proportionately, he says, it is a sign that the value of that thing has changed. If an ounce of gold, for instance, exchanges for twice as much grain, wine, and oil as formerly, we may conclude that the value of gold alone has changed; for it is very unlikely that all three of the other commodities have fallen in value. Though true enough, these propositions would, it is obvious, give little help in the actual study of price levels. He also suggests that the value of grain, being on the average very stable, is an indication of changes in the value of money over long periods.[4]

[1] Prior, *op. cit.*, p. 299.

[2] Cantillon, *op. cit.*, p. 247.

[3] *An Inquiry*, p. 10.

[4] Galiani, *op. cit.*, vol. i, pp. 154–157.

Carli introduces a new consideration which he considers very important — the ratio between the metals. To compare the prices in different times or places we must first consider the relation between goods and silver, that is, their prices in silver, and then the relation of silver to gold. If we find that goods cost as much silver now as formerly, but that silver is worth less gold, then goods are cheaper; if we find that goods cost more silver now, we must first consider how much gold this greater quantity of silver is worth, before we decide whether goods are dearer. All this amounts, after all, to nothing more than the abandonment of silver as the standard of value; but he is only partly conscious that this is the implication of his reasoning, and advances nothing in the way of argument in favor of it, except a ridiculous analogy to the effect that, just as one would not call a pound smaller because it was divided into a smaller number of ounces, so it would be incorrect to call an ounce of gold less valuable because it was worth fewer ounces of silver. This might mean something, if gold were stable in value; but he is plainly aware that such is not the case.[1]

Harris suggests nothing in regard to the methods to be followed, but hints at certain difficulties likely to be encountered. Over a short period of time the additions to the stock of money are so small, relatively, that changes in prices are hardly perceptible. They are obscured, moreover, by the more striking changes in the prices of particular commodities, which arise from other causes.[2]

Vasco merely indicates the nature of the problem. A change in the value of money can be determined only from its relation with "the universality of commodities." By this he apparently means some kind of an average of prices, for he explains that the value of money may be said to have fallen when all things exchange for a greater quantity of money, "making allowance for the particular circumstances of some." [3]

[1] Carli, *op. cit.*, vol. i, pp. 305–312, 329–340, 350–363.
[2] Harris, *op. cit.*, pt. i, pp. 76, 77.
[3] Vasco, *op. cit.*, pp. 10, 11.

2. The Spread of Price Changes

Of greater interest than the foregoing are the discussions concerning the process by which changes in the value of money spread through the economic structure. Law's reasoning reminds one somewhat of Vaughan's in the previous century, but his reference to the question is only indirect. In arguing that "raising" money will lead to higher prices, he makes the point that, if prices do not rise, then exported goods are sold for less value (that is, less "intrinsic" value), while imported goods are sold dearer. This would make trade in exports so profitable that competition among those anxious to take advantage of it would force prices up.[1]

Boisguillebert refers merely to the interdependence of prices. When things are in equilibrium, he writes, all trades are mutually indispensable, all get a living at normal prices. If, therefore, prices fall in any line, the trouble is sure to spread to all others.[2] This foreshadows much similar discussion among the Physiocrats.

Much of Law's reasoning was repeated by d'Aguesseau. The most interesting part of his discussion, however, is his ideas regarding the uniformity of a change in prices. Rents do not rise as much as other prices do when money is debased, since both tenants and owners consider the possibility of a return to good money. The principal obstacle to a uniform change in prices is the fact that the demand for commodities varies with their prices. To avoid a diminution in the power to consume, sellers often do not hesitate to bear a part of the loss caused by debasement. This point is not brought out clearly, but it appears to apply more to the period of transition than to the ultimate result. In the long run the "power to consume" would seem to be the same at any level of prices.[3]

Prior's discussion also attributes to foreign goods the first impetus toward higher prices, but gives no analysis of this beyond the implication that merchants ask more. With regard to

[1] Law, *op. cit.*, pp. 82–84.

[2] Boisguillebert, *Nature des Richesses*, pp. 404–406.

[3] *Revue d'Hist. des Doctr.*, vol. ii, pp. 282, 283; Landry, *op. cit.*, p. 207.

domestic commodities, his explanation is fairly naïve. Exporters of native goods, selling their goods for the same amount of money as before the coin was raised, can now afford to pay the producers of them higher (nominal) prices, and so the goods will rise. If they do not, foreigners will not fail to carry them off, when they can be had below their real value.[1] These arguments, if developed, might have been of some value; but as it is, they are left hanging in the air.

Practically all the above discussions are incidental to others. Cantillon, however, considered this attitude a great mistake, and believed the theory of prices could not be adequately presented without analyzing the process of change. This, he says, is the principal defect in Locke's treatment of the subject. The basic principle, according to Cantillon, is that an increase in prices is brought about by an increase in consumption. To take a simple example, suppose a new mine to be discovered. The owners of this mine will spend more on their living and so give work to more artisans; these in turn will increase their expenditures. Now this increased consumption must be at the expense of those not yet affected by the new supply of money, and prices will be forced up by the greater competition. The farmers, profiting by these higher prices, will spend more. Thus the increase of prices will spread throughout industry. The effect will not be the same, however, on all prices. It all depends, to repeat, on how consumption is affected. Bread, for example, will not rise as fast as meat, for the increase in the consumption of the latter will be greater in proportion to the previous consumption, and so competition for the available supply will be keener. An increase of money from a balance of trade works out its effects in a similar way; but, in this case, the increase of consumption starts among those benefited by the export business. It does not spread so rapidly, however; for people of this kind are likely to save their extra gains for a while.[2] I need hardly remark that this is the most important discussion of this topic we have yet encountered.

Although Cantillon's work was not published till considerably

[1] Prior, *op. cit.*, pp. 306, 307.

[2] Cantillon, *op. cit.*, pp. 215–229, 235, 236.

later, there seems to have been more interest in this subject after his time. There is just a hint of a similar point of view in Vanderlint's work, but it is undeveloped. The consumption of everything, he says, must lessen proportionally as the supply of cash decreases, if the prices of commodities are not lowered. He does not draw the rather obvious conclusion, however, that such a decrease in consumption would cause prices to fall, if nothing else would.[1] Dutot points out that all goods do not rise in price to the same degree; at least, not immediately.[2]

Galiani confines his account to the influence of debasement on prices. The first effect of this policy will be in the price of foreign exchange. Then suddenly the price of foreign goods will rise also, and the owners of domestic commodities will raise prices, in order to be able to buy the foreign supplies they want. People as yet unaffected will now begin to grumble, and thus the rise in prices will become general. The salaried classes will be the last to receive an increase.[3] In most respects, this is only a refinement of the old idea that merchants ask more.

Hume's analysis suggests Cantillon's[4] but the emphasis is different. When the money of a country increases, he reasons, the prices of commodities do not rise at once, and therefore manufacturers find they can employ more workers. This increase of employment probably does not lead to any rise in wages at first, for the workers are glad to obtain the steady work; but it does give them larger incomes. They will therefore be able to spend more, and from their greater expenditures the effect will spread all through the people. The increased supply of money must "quicken the diligence of every individual," before it will lead to higher wages.[5] Although he does not do as well as Cantillon in showing the relation between the increased consumption and the rise in prices, the discussion of the part played by wages is very significant.

[1] Vanderlint, *op. cit.*, p. 155.

[2] Dutot, *op. cit.*, p. 880.

[3] Galiani, *op. cit.*, vol. ii, pp. 84–87.

[4] There is no reason to suppose that he had seen the latter's manuscript, though it is known to have been circulated.

[5] Hume, *Essays*, vol. i, pp. 313, 314.

Massie's rather detailed discussion is not very successful. The first consequence of "raising" money, he says, quoting Locke, would be a proportional rise in the prices of foreign commodities. Our merchants would therefore sell them for more. This would affect the landholders principally, — for they consume the greatest amount of foreign goods, — and so they would try to raise their rents. The farmers, having to pay more rent, would in turn charge more for their products, and thus the change would spread to all classes.[1]

Carli barely refers to the influence of supply in the transition to higher prices. When money is raised, he writes, people, being unwilling to accept a smaller number of pieces than formerly, will either raise the prices of their goods or contrive to smuggle them out and sell them elsewhere. In the latter event, high prices will be brought about by scarcity. It is true that the money they received at home would buy as much as what they received before money was raised; but with the money they can still obtain abroad for their goods, they can buy even more at home than before.[2]

On this point, again, Postlethwayt is obviously indebted to Cantillon, but he does not mention him. Suppose the "undertakers" of a country to receive a sum of money equal to the present money supply, "for a Present from *Americans*," he says; then these dealers will seek to enlarge their business, and this will cause farmers' products to rise in price, through the "altercation of the market" (Cantillon's phrase). They will not double, however, till competition has had its full effect. The "undertakers" will also increase their consumption of wine and meat, causing these to rise, and this in turn will lead the farmers to turn to the production of these things rather than corn. The scarcity of this will raise its price also, and therefore laborers will have to have higher wages in order to live. Thus the rise of prices will spread to every industry, and the consumption of the different classes will return to what it was before. Similar effects would follow from the opening of rich new mines, but more quickly; for in this case, the new money would be spent more lavishly and hence

[1] Massie, *Observations*, pp. 7, 8.

[2] Carli, *op. cit.*, vol. i, p. 170.

would put more people in a position to increase their expenditures also.[1] If the new money first came into the hands of money lenders, interest would fall, and "undertakers" would be stimulated to enlarge their operations, with the results on prices as already described. It should be noted, moreover, that the increase of prices depends on the nature of the market for different commodities. Delicacies, for example, are consumed by relatively few; and therefore, if the new money supply fell into the possession of the wealthy, the prices of delicacies might, for a time, be raised considerably without affecting corn prices. Furthermore, the rise of prices tends to be checked, at first, by the fact that there is usually on hand in the country a stock of foods somewhat greater than the annual consumption.[2] Although he did not quite grasp the meaning of Cantillon's argument with regard to the more rapid rise in the price of meat, etc., Postlethwayt's discussion may fairly be regarded as an interesting elaboration of the ideas developed by the earlier writer.

There were no further discussions of much significance within the period we are studying. Sonnenfels touches upon the working out of both causes of price changes: debasement and changes in the supply of money. With regard to the former, he follows the traditional idea that prices rise because merchants ask more, and that the prices of foreign commodities are the first to show the effects. The native dealers raise their prices, when they see that they cannot spend money for foreign goods at the same rate at which they received it; other classes of sellers are compelled to follow them. His reference to the other aspect of the question occurs in connection with his discussion of the effect of a diminution in a country's money supply, and is not very successful. When the supply of money grows less, he says, those dealers who formerly had just enough to get along with must now restrict their activity or borrow funds. The interest they have to pay causes them to ask higher prices, or to take less profits, or both. In any case, production falls off. Further borrowing, due to the loss of foreign trade, causes interest to rise, and this encourages

[1] Elsewhere (pp. 342, 343) he seems to take just the opposite view on this point.

[2] Postlethwayt, *op. cit.*, pp. 204–209.

the "collecting of capitals," which only increases the scarcity of money.[1]

Steuart makes only brief reference to the matter. Price changes proceed very slowly, he says, and are influenced mostly by the commodities which enter into foreign trade. The home producers do not know anything about prices in the world-market, but this really determines what they receive. Thus foreign trade "regulates the value of the currency."[2]

Philippi's analysis is rather simple, and reminiscent of an earlier period. When money is debased, he writes, merchants find they must pay more for what they buy, or pay in foreign coin, which involves a like loss. Landowners, professional men, etc., seeing their expenses increase, raise their prices, and then the laborers have to have more wages. Thus all prices rise.[3]

[1] Sonnenfels, *op. cit.*, pt. ii, pp. 313, 314, 327, 328, 353–358.

[2] Steuart, *op. cit.*, vol. i, pp. 599, 600, vol. ii, pp. 8–10.

[3] Philippi, *Der Vergrösserte Staat*, p. 325.

CHAPTER XXXII

PRICE CHANGES: EFFECTS

1. General

Many writers referred to the effects of price changes on trade and industry in general. In contrast to earlier periods, most of these discussions have in mind the price fluctuations which result from changes in the value of the precious metals, rather than those which result from debasement.[1] Much of Cantillon's discussion of the effects of changes in the money supply bears on this question. The change in prices, as we saw in the last chapter, is brought about by a change in consumption, and this means an increase or decrease of industrial activity. He notes, moreover, that the higher prices which result from the increased demand stimulate production. On the whole, however, his discussion does not give one the impression that he attached any further importance to this effect on industry. The temporary character of it seems to be uppermost in his mind.[2]

The beneficial influence of an increase in the money supply is stated more explicitly, but less satisfactorily, by Montesquieu. After explaining the relation between the quantity of money and prices, and showing that changes in prices are the resultant of changes in the supply of both money and goods, he goes on to say that the quantity of commodities increases by the increase of commerce, while the latter results from the increase of money "which arrives successively," and by communication with new lands and seas.[3] The qualifying clause, "which arrives successively," seems to make it clear that it is the process of change which affects industry favorably, and not the mere possession of

[1] Among those which proceed from the older point of view we may mention Uztariz, *op. cit.*, p. 347; Broggia, *op. cit.*, vol. ii, pp. 18, 51; Justi, *Schriften*, vol. i, p. 356.

[2] Cantillon, *op. cit.*, pp. 215–229.

[3] Montesquieu, *op. cit.*, p. 381.

additional money; but the idea is not developed further. Nor is it expressly connected with the theory of prices, which it directly follows. I am inclined to think, however, that it should be regarded as the forerunner of the more definite discussions of later writers.

Galiani's point of view is wholly different. Four errors, he says, result from the insensible change in the value of money. In the first place, while the country is growing rich, complaints of dearness and misery are heard; in the second place, neighboring states and olden times are regarded with envy; the prince is charged with increasing taxes, when he is really only trying to make them equivalent to what they were; and finally, there is much complaint about luxury, idleness, and the like. These errors, it should be noted, are the reflection of various particular effects, which we shall consider more fully later; but the point of view seems more general than is usual in these discussions. He denies that the price changes caused by debasement tend to check commerce, reasoning that merchants have nothing to gain by waiting for prices to rise.[1]

The effect referred to by Montesquieu is directly analyzed for the first time by Hume. It is true, he says in the passage from which I quoted in the last chapter, that since the discovery of America, industry has increased all over Europe, except in the countries which possess the mines. The real reason for this is that the high prices of commodities do not follow at once upon the increase of money; it is only in the interval that this increase leads to greater demand, and is favorable to industry. After prices are readjusted, the quantity of money makes no difference. Similarly, the interval between a decrease in the money supply and the fall of prices is disadvantageous to industry. The workmen have less employment and so less to spend, with the result that the farmers find it harder to pay their rents, and so on.[2]

Harris, who was familiar with the work of both Cantillon and Hume, barely notes this point. The greatest effect of money, he says, is in its fluctuations. When money flows in, some branches

[1] Galiani, *op. cit.*, vol. i, p. 175, vol. ii, p. 99.

[2] Hume, *Essays*, vol. i, pp. 313–315, 321.

of trade will be enlivened, and many individuals will grow rich, since what they pay in taxes, rents, and so on, is of less value than formerly. It is not clear whether he meant to imply that these unusual gains would serve to stimulate industry, or whether he meant simply that a greater volume of business would result from the increased expenditures.[1]

Postlethwayt's discussion of this point shows the influence, not only of Cantillon, whom he followed so closely in many respects, but apparently of Montesquieu and Hume as well. It is not so much a great sum of money brought at once into a state that promotes industry, he says, as the gradual and continual bringing in of money. In fact, if the annual introduction of new money through trade should stop suddenly, the effect on industry would be the same as from a decrease in the money supply. Every increase of the mass of money, he explains, in language reminiscent of Montesquieu, "begins with multiplying it's Function as a Sign, before it encreases it's Bulk as such"; that is, it leads to increased production before it raises prices. At first, prices rise only enough to keep up the spirit of the workmen; but finally, they will rise "in composite Proportion to the old and new Masses, either of Commodities or of their Signs." Even then the sight of many buyers will encourage the workmen and prevent decline of industry to its former level. A diminution in the money supply has correspondingly unfavorable effects. There are fewer buyers, and production consequently falls off.[2]

The part played by prices in this industrial change, which is all too little brought out in Postlethwayt's discussion, is quite lost sight of in Wallace's. If a great sum of money should be brought into the country all at once, he says, the result would be (provided the laboring classes did not get so much of it as to make them idle) that people would spend more and therefore increase employment and stimulate industry.[3]

Genovesi, who was familiar with Hume's work, does not analyze the phenomena attending a change in prices, but merely asserts that, in a nation paying a balance of trade, agriculture and

[1] Harris, *op. cit.*, pt. i, pp. 83, 84.
[2] Postlethwayt, *op. cit.*, pp. 340–352.
[3] Wallace, *op. cit.*, pp. 21, 22.

the arts decline, while the reverse is true in a country receiving the balance of trade. As for debasement, he says that it checks "internal circulation" for a time, since many people withdraw from trade at first, because of the novelty of things, and many refuse to lend. All this is bad for industry.[1]

Forbonnais, however, makes clear the part played by prices. When the quantity of money in a country increases or diminishes, he says, all production will feel the effect. If the usual amount of money cannot be obtained for commodities, wages must be lowered or laborers must be dismissed; and since wages in many cases cannot be lowered, the latter is more apt to take place. Production therefore declines. If more than the usual amount can be obtained, on the other hand, production is stimulated and prices come back to their old level. This apparently explains his statement a little earlier that what nations envy is not so much the precious metals, as "the effects resulting from the continual increase of conventional riches in a society."[2] Beccaria also points out that it is the increase of money which is important, since during the period of increase activity is stimulated.[3]

Verri introduces a qualification with regard to the effects of an increase of money. If a nation acquires money without work, through mines or tribute, industry will not be stimulated, he says, for the money falls into the hands of a few, who give themselves up to luxury and disdain industry. It is quite different, however, when the money is gained through industry and a favorable balance of trade. On the other hand, in a nation paying a balance of trade, agriculture and the arts decline.[4]

2. Effects on Particular Classes

Prior to the eighteenth century the effects of price changes on debtors, creditors, and other special classes in the community were always discussed as a phase of the debasement question. The failure to apply similar reasoning to price fluctuations arising from changes in the value of the precious metals themselves is

[1] Genovesi, *op. cit.*, vol. ii, pp. 50, 51, 164.

[2] Forbonnais, *op. cit.*, pp. 220, 224, 225.

[3] Beccaria, *op. cit.*, vol. ii, p. 76.

[4] Verri, *op. cit.*, pp. 67–70.

very likely due to the feeling that, since debasement is subject to human control, the inequities which result from it are open to criticism on moral or ethical grounds, while the same cannot be said of other factors affecting the price-level. At any rate, it is significant that the first writer to point out the effects of price changes not caused by debasement was John Law, who had undertaken to demonstrate the unfitness of the precious metals for use as money, and who was therefore in just the mood to see the bearing on this problem of the old arguments against debasement.[1]

D'Aguesseau's discussion is worth noting, principally for the various useful classifications which he adopts. We must consider the effects of debasement, he says, both as to persons and as to periods. As to persons, we must distinguish individuals, the state, and the sovereign. As to time, we must consider the immediate effects, the effects while debasement lasts, and the effects of a return to good money. Individuals also are differently affected, according to their position as permanent, long-time, or short-time creditors, buyers or sellers, and so on.[2]

Cantillon, like Law, discusses the effect of price changes as resulting from other causes than debasement; and it is interesting to note that he too referred to the point in connection with a rather unfavorable analysis of the influence of money. When prices rise in a particular country as a result of an increase of money, he says, landowners, their domestics, and all workers at fixed wages suffer. The landlords will have to cut down expenses, dismissing some of their servants, and many laborers will have to seek work elsewhere. He then goes on to show that, if the rise continues, it will bring about the ruin of the country's industries.[3]

The effects of debasement on the relation between debtors and creditors, as pointed out by previous writers, did not seem to Melon to be as bad as painted. In the first place, he argues, the only ones injured are those who are buyers solely, such as *rentiers en argent* and soldiers. Rents rise along with other prices, and

[1] Law, *op. cit.*, pp. 79, 80, 119, 127, 128, 152, 153.

[2] *Revue d'Hist. des Doctr.*, vol. ii, pp. 280–282.

[3] Cantillon, *op. cit.*, pp. 216–218, 396.

therefore the landlords have no cause for complaint. Debtors, however, always benefit; and as they are more numerous than the creditors, their interests are more important. Indeed, it is a maxim of law that the debtor must always be favored. The reason why we may say debtors are more numerous is that he who is creditor to one and debtor to another will be only debtor in case his debtor becomes insolvent.[1]

Dutot took direct issue with Melon on these points. It is not true, he objects, that rents rise in proportion to other prices; there is plenty of evidence to the contrary. The real point to consider, moreover, is not whether there are more debtors than creditors, but whether there are more buyers than sellers. They are, in fact, much more numerous, and therefore their losses are not balanced by the gains of the sellers. (He evidently means sellers of commodities.) Even the sellers may lose, if they have large debts abroad. And, finally, there is nothing in the argument that the debtors should be favored. On the contrary, if this loss is inflicted on the creditors, they may try to recoup themselves by raising the interest rate.[2] This seems to be the first reference to the effect of debasement on the rate of interest.[3]

Voltaire and Paris-Duverney were inclined to agree with Melon that the benefit to debtors might justify debasement. According to the former, it is a natural law that oppressed debtors should be favored, and debasement is a much less crude method than the more obvious expedient of abolishing debts.[4] The latter was much impressed by the political dangers from suffering debtors, but he felt that the state should not go too far in relieving them.[5]

Dr. William Douglass, in discussing the paper-money schemes of the American colonies, again makes the point about the interest rate. After demonstrating the loss to creditors from a depreciat-

[1] Melon, *op. cit.*, pp. 773–779.

[2] Dutot, *op. cit.*, pp. 851, 882, 940–962.

[3] Picard is inclined to exaggerate the importance of Dutot's discussion in other respects, but fails to note this point. — *Revue d'Hist. des Doctr.*, vol. v, p. 363.

[4] *Ibid.*, p. 364.

[5] Paris-Duverney, *Examen du Livre Intitulé Réflexions Politiques*, vol. i, pp. 30–38.

ing currency, and declaring flatly that this explained the "infatuation" for paper-money in the colonies, he adds that these losses will naturally cause interest to rise, in order to "make good the sinking Principal." When money is depreciated ten per cent, for example, the lender must add that to the rate he would otherwise ask. He also refers to the effect of depreciation on laborers' wages, which had been somewhat neglected, though not ignored, and points out that wages do not rise in proportion to other prices.[1]

Melon's arguments in favor of debasement aroused a lively controversy among Italian writers. Broggia and Galiani were inclined to sympathize with his point of view, while Spinelli and Neri refused to accept his arguments. Broggia's opinion may be gathered from his argument that in his state there was no widespread oppression of debtors by usury, such as had justified the adoption of debasement in Rome.[2] Galiani is more outspoken. Melon alone, he declares, has recognized the truth about the raising of money, and had the courage to defend it. Merely to say that it takes from one and gives to the other does indeed make it out to be tyranny; but if those who lose are less in need than those who gain, it is really just, for the burdens of the state should be borne by those who are most able. Melon falls into error, however, in applying his reasoning; for he forgets that the poor are not debtors only, but creditors also — with respect to their labor. It is only in bad times, therefore, that raising helps them. The prince thereby avoids additional taxes, and the poor, being only very indirectly affected by the king's payments, bear least of the burden of the alteration.[3]

Spinelli disagrees with Melon's premise that debtors should be favored. Their obligation, he argues, receives its force from the law of Nature, and it is therefore not subject to the will of the civil power.[4] Neri criticizes the argument (of Galiani's still anonymous treatise) that debasement is to be defended on the ground of ex-

[1] Douglass, *op. cit.*, pp. 295–300, 321–325, 335, 336.

[2] Broggia, *op. cit.*, vol. ii, pp. 9–11, 16, 50–53. He also notes the loss suffered by wage-earners through the relatively slow rise in wages.

[3] Galiani, *op. cit.*, vol. ii, pp. 70, 71, 83, 84, 93–102.

[4] Fornari, *op. cit.*, vol. ii, p. 117.

pediency. The evil, he declares, outweighs the good. The poor especially suffer, for their wages do not rise as rapidly as their expenses.[1]

The influence of currency depreciation on the rate of interest, which Dutot had noted, now began to attract attention again. Magens remarks that men will lend readily when they can be sure of receiving money of equal value in repayment; and a little later says more specifically that nations which raise their money will have to pay more interest when they borrow again, to compensate for the risk.[2] Harris says that alteration is a "shock to credit"; but he fails to connect this definitely with the interest-rate.[3] Sonnenfels and Steuart also make this point.[4] Forbonnais, however, goes further, and concludes that the shock to credit causes interest to rise.[5] It seems quite likely that he was influenced by Dutot here.

Melon's arguments in favor of debasement continued to arouse discussion. Sonnenfels concedes that raising money will enable debtors to pay their debts more easily; but he objects that it is the rich, not the poor, who are the principal debtor class. The laborers are largely creditors.[6] Genovesi will not grant any of the argument. Debasement does not give relief on debts to foreigners, since exchange promptly rises; every debtor is also a creditor; what one loses, the other gains; at best the relief is only temporary — until prices are readjusted — and affects only those debtors who have money on hand.[7] Steuart also discusses the position of debtors, and points out that Locke was mistaken in thinking debtors would not gain through debasement, confining the gain to those who had hoards of money. The latter, in reality, would gain only if they were debtors.[8]

Vasco explains this evil of debasement along conventional lines, but emphasizes the effect on wage-earners. They may ob-

[1] Neri, *op. cit.*, pp. 366–372.
[2] Magens, *op. cit.*, pp. 9, 10.
[3] Harris, *op. cit.*, pt. i, pp. 91, 92, pt. ii, pp. 31, 32, 44, 79, 80.
[4] Sonnenfels, *op. cit.*, pt. ii, p. 331; Steuart, *op. cit.*, vol. ii, p. 67.
[5] *Revue d'Hist. des Doctr.*, vol. v, p. 360.
[6] Sonnenfels, *op. cit.*, pt. ii, pp. 329, 330.
[7] Genovesi, *op. cit.*, vol. ii, pp. 45–50.
[8] Steuart, *op. cit.*, vol. i, pp. 554–556, 590.

tain increased wages, he says, but the changes are likely to come slowly. Often there is no coin small enough to pay them the due increase, and they are unable to calculate just what it should be. This is bad for the state. There are more beggars and more crime, and the workmen try to make up their losses by slighting their work in various ways. It may be said, he concludes, that an increase in the quantity of money in circulation will bring the same evils as those just attributed to debasement. This is true, and we can only reply that the latter increases the evil.[1]

Condillac does not refer to the gains of debtors and creditors at any length, but he points out an interesting tendency, which clearly has this aspect of price changes as a basis. When kings wish to lower the value of money, in order to profit as creditors, they do it gradually. The result is that many shortsighted people, not realizing that there will probably be debasement later, hurry to pay their debts and to invest their money, before its value is lowered any more. It therefore becomes easy to borrow money, and many merchants are led to extend their undertakings excessively.[2]

3. Fiscal Effects

Many writers noted the king's position as creditor, in analyzing the effects of price changes; but their discussions are often only brief applications of the principles considered in the preceding section of this chapter, and need not be considered in detail here.[3] In some cases, however, they are of considerable interest.

Melon, impressed, no doubt, by Law's remark that raising the value of money is a tax which is sooner paid and less felt than any other,[4] declared that, when the king's debts were so large that they could not be paid without the levy of crushing taxes, "raising" should be resorted to. The creditors of the state should be glad to be made sure of their pay at some loss rather than run the

[1] Vasco, *op. cit.*, pp. 21–24, 128. [2] Condillac, *op. cit.*, p. 400.

[3] Belloni, *op. cit.*, p. 83; Carli, *op. cit.*, vol. i, p. 153; Justi, *Schriften*, vol. i, pp. 355, 356, vol. ii, pp. 480, 481; Sonnenfels, *op. cit.*, pp. 328, 329; Genovesi, *op. cit.*, p. 50; Harris, *op. cit.*, pt. ii, pp. 39–41; Le Trosne (see *Revue d'Hist. des Doctr.*, vol. v, p. 365).

[4] Law, *op. cit.*, p. 94.

risk of losing all. When the poor are overwhelmed with taxes, this course is the salvation of the state.[1]

Dutot, whose opposition to Melon we have already mentioned, rejoined that the gain from raising was only temporary at best, for prices would rise and the king's revenues would not go as far as before. Even for a temporary emergency, however, it would be better to use some other means — a temporary tax if necessary; for no tax that the people could conceivably bear would be so burdensome as currency alteration. A tax, moreover, gives more prompt aid.[2] This last argument was denied by Paris-Duverney.[3]

Broggia was inclined to agree with Melon as to the advisability of debasement in certain cases. The position of the prince, he pointed out, is different from that of the other creditors, for he can impose new taxes to make good his losses. The great harm which debasement causes through higher prices and shaken credit, however, makes it an undesirable expedient, except in one case. This is when the people cannot bear the taxes needed to meet the public obligations. The benefit would not be gained, it should be noted, unless the old taxes are raised in proportion to the debasement. (Melon, apparently, had failed to note this.) He adds the curious point that one way for the state to make a clear gain would be to assume bank deposits and pay them in the depreciated money.[4]

Galiani argues elaborately, and, it must be admitted, somewhat speciously, in favor of debasement as a fiscal device. The general dislike for the practice, he begins, is due to the fact that it has seldom been used because of real necessity, but generally through avarice or false counsels. Of course, the idea of growing rich in this way is as absurd as trying to increase the height of the soldiery by shortening the foot; what really happens is that expenses decrease, leaving the prince that much better off. Prices rise, it is true, but not immediately or all together, and he gains until the readjustment is completed.

Some of the arguments against debasement are ridiculous, in his opinion. The statement of Davanzati and most others that the

[1] Melon, *op. cit.*, pp. 774, 780–784. [2] Dutot, *op. cit.*, pp. 881, 882, 893.

[3] Paris-Duverney, *op. cit.*, vol. i, pp. 10–12.

[4] Broggia, *op. cit.*, vol. i, pp. 363, 364, 373, 374, vol. ii, pp. 12, 16, 48–63.

prince loses a great part of his revenues is an exaggeration, to say the least. It is absurd when coupled with the claim that the people also are impoverished, for what one loses the other must gain. In all probability they both come out about even. If the prince does lose, that means lower taxes, and it is hard to see what there is to complain about in that. As a matter of fact, however, the king's revenues do not decrease. A tax, it should be remembered, does not yield more as its weight becomes greater, but rather the contrary. The farmers, moreover, the greatest group of tax-payers, find themselves with larger incomes as a result of the higher prices, and so they will pay their taxes more readily. There is no basis for the claim that the people will become poorer because of the high prices, and therefore be unable to pay their taxes; the "dearness" is merely a matter of words.

He is equally unimpressed by another group of arguments. To say that raising is a tax, is not new, he replies; to call it therefore unjust, is foolish; to say it should not be employed except in case of need, is nothing rare and wonderful. It is improper to speak of it as a tax, however; it is rather a means of avoiding additional taxes, and of paying debts at the same time. How can it be a tax, moreover, if the revenues decrease, as is claimed? And if it be argued that the decrease comes only in time, we may ask what people would not bear a temporary evil in order to obtain permanent relief. To complain, on the other hand, that the prince does not pay what he agreed, is irrational, for either he will not pay or he cannot. In the first case, he will attain his ends somehow; and in the second, his subjects should not try to force him. Simple repudiation would be equally effective, no doubt, but it is politically much less advisable, being too sudden and too sharply felt.

Raising, he concludes, has three principal advantages: it helps to meet emergencies, to save expenses, and to pay debts. It is also a very just expedient; for, as its opponents complain, it puts the greatest burden on the receivers of fixed incomes, — the rich, — and they are the ones who should pay most. Melon, however, goes too far, when he says it must be used to relieve the poor of taxation; it is necessary only when no other way of lightening the burden is possible or advisable.[1] To judge from this conclusion, it seems that Galiani's fondness for dialectic led him to devote a disproportionate and misleading amount of space to his discussion of this question.

In the discussions considered up to this point, there has been little attempt to analyze the effect of a change in prices on the different parts of the public revenues; they were generally treated as part of the broad class of fixed incomes, and this was probably justified by the actual conditions. Toward the end of the century, however, Necker and d'Aguesseau noted that the various parts of the revenues were not all affected alike. Some increase in numerary value in proportion to the debasement, while others remain the same in numerary value, and therefore fall in real value. In the first category are those taxes which are based on the values (that is, the prices) of commodities, and the revenues from the directly managed parts of the royal domain, which rise with the selling price of the products.[2]

A scheme by which the prince, if daring enough, could escape the consequences of debasement, while gaining the benefits, is suggested in the *Essay on the Theory of Money*, of 1771. When the king of Prussia debased gold and silver during the last war, we read, he gained at the expense of those who had to receive the new money, but he avoided loss by refusing to receive his own coin.[3]

Pinto is rather sceptical about the king's losses. It is not true, he says, that Louis XV, with larger revenues in money terms, is in reality poorer than his predecessors. Many prices, to be sure, have risen as the money was debased; but others have not. The pay of soldiers, for example, is the same as in the time of Henry IV, and as much may be said of bread and several other important articles. To this extent, at least, the king's greater revenues will buy more.[4]

Vasco combats the idea that debasement may be adopted in order to lighten the burden of taxes. Only when the prince and his subjects are in a "stato di sorda guerra" can such an expedient

[1] Galiani, vol. ii, pp. 72–112.

[2] Landry, *Mutations des Monnaies dans l'Ancienne France*, pp. 119, 120.

[3] *An Essay*, pp. 105, 106.

[4] Pinto, *op. cit.*, p. 131.

be advisable. This was well recognized by some peoples. The Normans, for instance, paid their king a tax on condition that he should not alter the coinage. If the prince owes great debts, he can gain on the principal or interest by debasement; but this is simply paying less than was agreed, and will ruin his credit.[1]

4. The Standard of Deferred Payments

Although there had been a few hints at plans for providing a standard of deferred payments which should not be open to the objections against money, the first definite suggestion seems to have been made by Hutcheson. Perpetual salaries and such payments, he says, "should be constituted in certain quantities of such necessary goods as depend upon the plain inartificial labours of men, such as grain, or other necessaries in a plain simple way of living." [2] This seems to be the forerunner of the modern proposals for a multiple standard. It is also the first, apparently, which seeks to avoid the consequences of changes in the value of the money metals themselves.[3]

Harris also considers the need of providing for changes in the value of the precious metals, but he sees no feasible way of doing so. All that can be done is to limit contracts to a moderate term of years. Money changes value so slowly that for these shorter contracts it could be treated as invariable in value. He also hints at a modern proposal, when he declares that if any alteration of the coinage is called for, it must be to increase the weight of the coins, since creditors have a right to demand more of the metal than they lent, now that its value has fallen. Such a proposal, however, is quite impracticable, he says.[4]

The theory developed in the Middle Ages, that an equal amount of metal should be repaid by debtors, is directly criticized by Beccaria,[5] but he suggests no alternative. It does not seem to satisfy

[1] Vasco, *op. cit.*, pp. 17, 18, 30–40. [2] Hutcheson, *op. cit.*, vol. ii, p. 227.

[3] Locke had suggested that wheat was a better standard for comparing values at widely different times (vol. v, p. 47), but he had drawn no conclusions from this with regard to deferred payments.

[4] Harris, *op. cit.*, pt. i, pp. 40, 63, 64, pt. ii, pp. 65, 105.

[5] Steuart's brief references to the question contain nothing of special interest. — Vol. i, pp. 539, 603.

equity completely, he says; for if an ounce of silver will buy less now, we may say that the man who lent me an ounce a hundred years ago really lent me the right to more things.[1] Verri also attacks the old theory, and thinks we need not seek to provide any other basis of repayment. This loss must simply be regarded as one of the risks the capitalist takes. Some, he says, have suggested that an average of the prices of certain common commodities should be taken as the basis of comparison; but he does not enlighten us further as to the nature of these early proposals for a multiple standard.[2] Condillac remarks that the losses to landlords or farmers which arise from changes in prices would be avoided if rents were paid in commodities.[3]

[1] Quoted in Conigliani, *op. cit.*, p. 16 n.

[2] Verri, *op. cit.*, pp. 81, 82.

[3] Condillac, *op. cit.*, p. 336.

CHAPTER XXXIII

THE PRINCIPLES OF CIRCULATION

THE principles governing the circulation of different kinds of money, understood in some degree ever since the Middle Ages, were analyzed more fully during the eighteenth century, and some interesting refinements were pointed out. Uztariz quotes with approval the passage from Saavedra referred to in Part IV,[1] but he does not develop the point further.[2] Conduit's brief account may be mentioned because of an interesting refinement which he makes. The lightness of what silver there is left in England is what prevents it from being exported because of the overvaluing of guineas. Even light silver is not wholly secure, however, since foreigners, who take guineas by weight, may find some profit in picking out the lighter ones and exchanging them for the current light shillings at the legal rate.[3]

The great supplies of silver from America had so lowered its value with respect to gold, that the market ratio in Europe was very different from that in the Orient, where the influence of the American supply had not yet been felt. The first reference to this difference and the profit which it made possible seems to be in Prior, who says that this opportunity for profit causes so great a demand for silver bullion that it is often dearer than coin, and coin is therefore melted for export. The great flow of silver to the Orient may put an end to that trade, however; for silver will become so plentiful there that its value will fall and come to bear the same ratio to gold as in Europe.[4] Cantillon also considers this point, but his conclusion is different. At 15:1 in England and 8:1 in Japan there is over eighty-seven per cent to be gained in taking silver to Japan; but even this is not enough to pay for the long journey, and it is better to bring back commodities for silver than to bring back gold. The inference would seem to be that

[1] Chapter XXI, p. 129.

[2] Uztariz, *op. cit.*, vol. ii, pp. 346–349.

[3] Shaw, *Tracts*, p. 216.

[4] Prior, *op. cit.*, pp. 302–305.

the trade would not be undertaken simply for the profit on the money, but that silver would be sent in preference to gold for trading purposes.[1]

Vanderlint makes a curious application of the principle to the question of international trade. The export of gold to Spain, he declares, proves that England's trade is in a very bad way, unless it can be shown that gold is so much more valuable in Spain, with respect to silver, that its export thither will afford a profit over and above freight, insurance, and interest. This, however, cannot be the case, for the Portuguese would also be taking advantage of the opportunity and there would be none of their gold in England.[2]

Melon seems to think that foreign merchants are the chief agents in substituting poorer coin for good. When a certain coin is made of less intrinsic value, he says, all merchants will try to pay their debts in that, and to acquire the better coins to melt and make into the poorer pieces. The king will receive only the poor coins in his revenues. It would be bad, therefore, for the state to collect too heavy seigniorage, for this would make it profitable for foreigners to melt the old money. He also refers to the drain to the Orient, saying that a ratio of 13:1 would attract silver to France, just as 10:1 attracts it to China.[3]

Broggia's discussion is confused, but apparently sound.[4] A flourishing commerce, he says, will not help much to provide the state with the money it requires, unless the moneys are properly adjusted. Otherwise gold and silver will go out. This questionable statement is probably to be interpreted as referring to the danger of displacing the precious metals by overvaluing copper — a disturbance by which the Italians appear to have been much bothered, to judge from their writers. This interpretation is the more justified by his statements that the mint cannot manufacture when it is necessary to give more for a metal than its mint-price, because of its enhanced value, and that, when the price of

[1] Cantillon, *op. cit.*, pp. 370, 371.

[2] Vanderlint, *op. cit.*, pp. 132, 133.

[3] Melon, *op. cit.*, pp. 764, 765, 783.

[4] I pass over the brief references in Berkeley (*Works*, vol. iv, p. 424); Douglass (*op. cit.*, p. 339); and Hutcheson (*op. cit.*, vol. ii, p. 228).

money is raised too much, it pays to export the inferior (that is, copper) money, or melt it for other uses. He also refers to the profit afforded by the different ratio in the Orient, and like Prior thinks the value of silver may be lowered there as a result of its greater plenty, so that the traffic will no longer pay Europeans. "In that case," he continues, "we may expect that among us less copper will come to be given for silver and more silver for gold," [1] which seems to ignore the fact that this export of silver was raising its value in Europe more than the wiping out of the profit before gained could lower it.

Montesquieu's discussion hardly deserves special mention, except for an erroneous interpretation of his ideas by a recent writer. If silver is debased, he says, without debasing gold, the latter will suddenly disappear. There is nothing to justify Hoffmann's statement that, according to Montesquieu, the undervalued metal is hoarded.[2] A few pages earlier, it is true, we are told that people prefer to hoard gold rather than silver, and that, when silver is common, gold disappears, to reappear when people are obliged to spend it because of the scarcity of silver. This may be regarded as an interesting refinement of the theory of the velocity of circulation, but it hardly implies what Hoffmann says.[3]

The place of hoarding in this process is noted by Spinelli, however, who points out that, although the undervalued metal will ordinarily be exported, some may remain in the country in hiding.[4] Locke, it will be remembered, had mentioned this, also.

Galiani, who devotes considerable attention to this question, lays it down as an "invariable rule that weak money drives out strong of the same metal, as long as there is equilibrium of forces between the two." Everyone will try to pay with the poorer money, and so the better money will disappear, being melted for coining into cheaper money or for sale to goldsmiths and merchants having connections with foreign mints. If, however, the

[1] Broggia, *op. cit.*, vol. i, pp. 323–328, vol. ii, pp. 43, 166.

[2] Hoffmann, *op. cit.*, p. 53.

[3] Montesquieu, *op. cit.*, pp. 381, 387.

[4] Fornari, *op. cit.*, vol. ii, p. 120.

better money is more plentiful, the other loses currency, and comes to be taken unwillingly and refused. His treatment leaves something to be desired in its account of the use made of the coins which disappear. In one place we are told that they "leave the state"; in another that they are converted into baser coins; in a third that they may remain hidden; and in a fourth they are said to be melted for other uses or export. In this respect Galiani hardly does as well as Locke, whose work he criticized sharply for similar defects.

In discussing the effects of an incorrect ratio, he develops a number of refinements. The evil of a wrong proportion, he says, is the same as any error in valuation: people will be incited to acquire the one article and dispose of the other, and the holder of the undervalued article will profit by sending it where it will be truly valued. In the case of money there is a further evil; for after a considerable amount of gold has been lost because of a wrong ratio, it will not all come back when the ratio is corrected: it went at 13:1, but must be bought back at 15:1, and foreigners keep the difference. And if it is hoarded by citizens, there results injustice between individuals. Of the two precious metals, gold "is more agile to go and come." The disproportion between metals is not so bad as that between coins of the same metal, however; the former injures through the damage which neighbors are able to do, the latter enables both strangers and citizens to make harmful gains.[1] This last statement is not explained, and I am unable to surmise from the remainder of the discussion what his reasoning could have been.

The question of copper money bulks large in Galiani's treatment, as in the case of several other Italian writers. Such money, he holds, is not very subject to the forces just described. Unless the error in the ratio is considerable, it will have no effect, because "between copper and the precious metals there is no equality of forces." Copper, being much less in quantity and circulating much more rapidly, cannot drive out the other metals. On the other hand, it is not readily displaced because so necessary in every-day trade. It is better for being weak, how-

[1] Galiani, *op. cit.*, vol. i, pp. 164, 208, 209, 259, 260, vol. ii, pp. 12–15, 45, 57.

ever, for there is some danger that it may be displaced if made too good.[1] Although this reasoning is rather questionable, it is interesting as the earliest attempt to discuss the problem of subsidiary coinage along these lines.

Belloni, besides emphasizing the loss to the state from an incorrect ratio, makes one curious point which deserves to be noted. A country having an unfavorable trade balance and a wrong coinage ratio might continue to coin for a time. The export of the undervalued metal, because it found a greater price outside, would "hold commerce balanced" and keep exchange down, so that the other metal could be procured without loss to the mint.[2] It is true that foreign exchange, payable in the overvalued metal, might be offered more freely, because of the profit to be made through the ratio; but it is doubtful whether this would be enough to keep exchange at par, even for a time. The demand for foreign bills would more than offset this supply. At any rate, Belloni regards it as a strictly temporary case.

Neri does not discuss possible domestic channels into which the better money might disappear from circulation. Clipped and raised money, he says, not being acceptable to foreigners in exchange for goods or money, remains in the state, and such remittances of cash as may be necessary are made in good money.[3]

Justi makes his discussion of this topic the occasion for stern denunciation of money-dealers. When some coins have not their true face value, the skillful and unscrupulous seek to draw all the good money to themselves for the purpose of melting it, and they even have bad money come from outside, to flood the country with it. The ruler, of course, is to blame for this, for it is only when overvalued coins are allowed to circulate that such practices are possible. The most interesting part of his treatment, however, is his application of the principle here explained to the question of subsidiary money, to which, as we have seen, he gave much attention. In the present state of coinage, he says, subsidiary coins of full value would be culled out. They must there-

[1] Galiani, *op. cit.*, vol. i, pp. 205–207, 212, vol. ii, pp. 56, 57.

[2] Belloni, *op. cit.*, pp. 70–78.

[3] Neri, *op. cit.*, p. 172.

fore be made of less value. On the other hand, such debased coins will drive out the better unless their quantity is restricted.

He takes issue with the view that an incorrect coinage ratio causes a loss to the state. Nothing can come from an incorrect ratio except that foreigners will prefer to pay in one metal and our merchants in another, neither country having the least advantage. It is not till the undervalued metal has entirely disappeared and foreign payments have to be made in the overvalued metal that the state suffers damage.[1]

Harris's discussion presents no novelty. Upon the introduction of debasement, he points out, a new trade will be opened, namely, that of extracting and transporting the old coins, "perhaps to purchase others coined abroad in imitation of our new standard"; for those coins of a given metal upon which the state sets least value will always be drained away. Even the plan of debasing merely the small coins, in order to keep them in circulation, is open to this objection. "The mint at the Tower would soon be eased of its labor of making these base coins," for both citizens and foreigners would take a hand in so lucrative an operation. This seems to attach too much importance to the export of the undervalued coins, and, on the last point, ignores the safeguards which had already been suggested for the regulation of fractional currency.[2]

Carli's extended discussion did not advance the theory much, unless we except his invention of the term "sympathetic attraction" to denote the phenomenon of the displacement of the metals. Like the other Italians, he is much concerned about the danger from overvalued copper, but his method of treatment fails to make this clear at times, and is therefore confusing. He seems to imply that, when moneys are undervalued, gold will leave the country first, and then silver will begin to go. This reminds us of Galiani's remark that gold is "more agile" than silver. No reason is given for it, but the idea probably is that gold, being cheaper to transport, would offer somewhat greater opportunities for profit, and hence would be the first to be sent out, when all

[1] Justi, *Schriften*, vol. ii, pp. 466, 467, 470, 520–522, 568, 569.

[2] Harris, *op. cit.*, pt. ii, pp. 46, 59–62, 74, 81–83.

moneys were undervalued (in terms of copper). He adds that the greater demand for the undervalued metal for the purpose of export will lead to some premium on it.

Not only the confusion incident to the loss of the standard money, which indeed frequently leads to debasement, but also a loss to the nation, is brought about, in his opinion, for the precious metals are exchanged for less than they are worth. The effect on commerce is very bad. Merchants, finding that the money they receive for their goods abroad is worth less at home, will have to suffer a loss or raise prices, to the detriment of trade, both foreign and domestic. When people discover this, they are apt to raise money voluntarily, and, in fact, go too far and overvalue it, with the result that copper in turn seeks a better market. Moreover, another influence besides "sympathetic attraction" tends to rob the state of treasure, when money is undervalued. Merchants seek it to export it in payment of foreign debts, to make large purchases ahead, and to invest abroad.[1]

Several of the later writers referred to the influence of the ratio between the precious metals in the Orient. Sonnenfels noted that the traffic with the East was making gold more plentiful in Europe,[2] and Sérionne went a step further by pointing out that this change was raising the value of silver in Europe and lowering it in Asia.[3] Steuart explained that the European and Asiatic ratios continued to be different for several reasons: the lack of trade, the "high internal demand" for silver in China, the control of the India trade by certain companies, which limits the competition between sellers of silver, and finally, the expense of transportation, together with the loss of interest while the money is in transit. He agrees, however, that there is a tendency for such differences in ratio to be lessened.[4] None of these writers throws any light on the process by which the more valuable coins are extracted from circulation.[5] Sérionne, however, quotes an interesting point from Shirley, which I have not seen elsewhere.

[1] Carli, *op. cit.*, vol. i, pp. 119, 120, 158–187.

[2] Sonnenfels, *op. cit.*, pt. ii, pp. 309–315.

[3] Sérionne, *op. cit.*, pp. 294, 295.

[4] Steuart, *op. cit.*, vol. i, pp. 547–550, vol. ii, pp. 62–64.

[5] The same may be said of Genovesi (*op. cit.*, p. 51) and Pinto (*op. cit.*, p. 91).

The overvaluing of gold in England leads people of other countries who have balances due from Portugal to send them to England in gold and then withdraw them in silver.[1]

Beccaria endeavored to show that a country which maintains an incorrect ratio is always a loser. If fourteen ounces of silver will exchange for an ounce of gold in one country, while elsewhere fifteen ounces exchange for that much gold, a merchant from that country who receives fifteen ounces of silver from abroad will have given one and one fourteenth ounces of gold or the equivalent in goods of this gold. Therefore he had to give more things than a merchant from another country would. On the other hand, when he buys in a foreign country, he must give fifteen ounces of silver for what is worth only fourteen ounces at home. If sixteen ounces are given for one of gold in this country, the results will be equally bad. The merchant who sells to foreigners will receive only fifteen ounces of silver for a thing valued at sixteen ounces at home, and he who buys will obtain for fifteen ounces a thing which costs sixteen ounces at home. The industry of the country will therefore decline.[2]

In the anonymous *Essay on the Theory of Money* the very questionable assertion is made that "much of the adulteration in coins" is due to differences between the market and mint ratios; because when a man melts down metal for recoinage at a profit, he is "induced to add a few grains more alloy to increase his gain." The author also seems to be in error when he says that the Dutch, by sending gold in exchange for English silver, would raise its value with them and lower that of silver, while the reverse would take place in England, thus increasing the tendency to melt silver. This confuses the case where a metal is exported because it is undervalued at the mint with the case where the market ratios in two countries are different. In the second case, the change in values does tend to be in opposite directions in the two countries, as he says; but this is evidently not what is meant. If silver coins were being melted before the Dutch began to send gold, it must have been because they were worth more in the English bullion market, just as they were worth more in Holland.

[1] Sérionne, *op. cit.*, p. 299.

[2] Beccaria, *op. cit.*, vol. ii, pp. 36–46.

The market values were not different in the two countries. Not the reverse, therefore, would take place in the English bullion market, but the same thing, and it would lessen rather than aggravate the melting of silver.[1]

Verri, unlike most of the Italians, pays little attention to this question.[2] Vasco, however, considers the matter from several angles, and develops some refinements of the theory. The ratio will not necessarily be the same in all countries, he points out; for if one nation has more abundant mines of silver and the other of gold, some difference in their valuations of the metals will persist, because of the expense of transportation, which is more for silver than for gold of equal value. Moreover, since the metallic value enters so much less into the value of copper coins, small differences in the ratio with respect to them are of little consequence. Loss of weight through wear is to be noted as a cause of coinage disorders; it may result in a disproportion, not only between metals, but also between coins of the same metal. And finally, he shows the futility of seeking to avoid the consequences of a wrong ratio by prohibiting the export of national money; foreigners will simply take goods instead, and pay for them in the cheap money.[3]

[1] *An Essay*, pp. 97–102, 113–118. The author, it will be remembered, had the idea that the ratio was simply a matter of the physical quantities of the metals at hand in the country.

[2] Verri, *op. cit.*, pp. 94, 95.

[3] Vasco, *op. cit.*, pp. 51, 52, 93 n., 103, 117.

CHAPTER XXXIV

THE VELOCITY OF CIRCULATION

THE ideas worked out by Petty and Locke on the subject of circulation inspired much discussion during the following century. To a large extent, however, there was a change of emphasis, circulation being treated more and more as a matter of public concern. Thus the new theory was incorporated into the older protests against hoarding. This development, at which Locke had already hinted, is of great interest to the historian of Mercantilism, but it tended to breed confusion rather than light so far as velocity of circulation was concerned. It led many writers to identify monetary circulation with trade activity, and thus to neglect the analysis of it as an independent factor.[1]

References to the subject are to be noted early. Lau argues against the storing up of state treasures, on the ground that the value of money consists solely in circulation, and that the oftener it passes from one hand to another, the better for its owner.[2] The unknown writer whose work is described by Böhmert takes the same stand; the more frequently money circulates, he says, the more services it performs for society.[3] Berkeley, in a similar vein, points out that silver and small money circulate faster than pieces of greater value, and are therefore a better form of currency.[4]

Cantillon, like Locke, developed his ideas of circulation in considering the question of the amount of money needed by a nation. This varies, in the first place, he says, according to the frequency with which payments are made: the longer the interval between payments, the larger are the sums which have to be accumulated in the payers' hands, and the more money is required in the country. Commerce with foreign countries also may retard circula-

[1] This point is discussed more fully in Chapter XXXVII below.
[2] Zielenziger, *op. cit.*, pp. 397, 398.
[3] Böhmert, *op. cit.*, p. 23.
[4] Berkeley, *Works*, vol. iv, p. 465.

tion to some extent, even when the balance of trade is even: it makes it necessary for money to pass through more hands. The amount is not increased as much as one might think by the paying of rents in large sums, for the landlords generally deposit their rents at once, instead of paying them out gradually, and the money is therefore put into circulation again. All the thrifty classes, however, save various sums, which they hold out of circulation till they have enough to invest; and many through avarice or fear keep money locked up for considerable periods. On the other hand, the rapidity of circulation is increased by the practice of offsetting accounts between merchants, and by the use of bankers' and goldsmiths' notes, for these men do not keep an equivalent amount of money on hand. In view of these conflicting tendencies, it is difficult to estimate the money requirements of a country, but we may perhaps venture to say that it is about one third of the annual rentals.

Up to this point there is nothing in his discussion to indicate that he saw the influence of all this on the price-level, any more than Locke had; but somewhat later, in discussing the rise in prices caused by an increase in the money supply, he says, pointedly enough, that an increase in the rapidity of circulation "vaut autant qu'une augmentation d'argent effectif," up to a certain degree. This would seem to leave no doubt that he considered it a factor in the determination of the price-level, and I think we may say that this is the first unmistakable expression of such a view. The point about the influence of offsetting accounts and the use of bankers' notes does not seem well taken, so far as velocity of circulation is concerned; but, on the whole, the discussion is very important.[1]

Galiani's analysis also shows the influence of Locke, but his point of view is rather different. With him it is not so much a question of how much money a country needs, given a certain velocity of circulation, but how rapid the circulation must be to

[1] Cantillon, *op. cit.*, pp. 168–193, 213. Cantillon also uses the term circulation to denote the process of paying and receiving money by which the exchange of commodities is continuously effected; and although he does not seem to confuse the two ideas, he may have contributed to the later confusion on this point.

enable a given supply of money to suffice. In the case of Naples he computes that the existing monetary stock must circulate about eight times a year if it is to do the work required of it; and concludes that, since this seems a very moderate rate, there is every reason to believe that the country has money enough for its trade. He suggests a number of remedies for an "insufficient" circulation, among which the most important are payments at shorter intervals, large fairs and markets leading to many exchanges in a short time with less money, shortness of lawsuits, security of contracts, and freedom of trade.[1] Bandini appears to have the same point of view when he says that a single scudo passing from hand to hand a hundred times a month maintains commerce as well as a hundred scudi which change hands only once a month.[2]

Postlethwayt adopted Cantillon's analysis, without improving it in any way. He borrows whole passages almost word for word, but does not acknowledge the debt, and, on the contrary, implies that he is something of a pioneer in the field. The full significance of Cantillon's discussion seems to have escaped him, however; for he mentions velocity and prices in the same paragraph, without quite seeing the connection between them. It makes no difference, he says, whether the total money of a country be much or little, the money requirement will be about one third the annual rents in any case; for if there is much money, the landlord will receive large rents, and *vice versa*. On the other hand, if circulation is slow, it will take more money to effect the exchanges.[3]

Sonnenfels appears to be acquainted with such ideas as Locke's on this point, but his application of them is pretty unskillful and marks a further step toward the confusion to which we referred at the beginning of this chapter. A rapid circulation, he holds, is of great importance to the state, not only because it enables trade to maintain its usual round, but also because it leads to increased activity. In his mind, apparently, these are merely different state-

[1] Galiani, *op. cit.*, vol. ii, pp. 135–153.
[2] Bandini, *op. cit.*, p. 142.
[3] Postlethwayt, *op. cit.*, pp. 60–66.

ments of the same thing. He explains that the circulation is decreased by infrequency of payments, by the unequal distribution of property with respect to place, and by whatever tends to remove money from circulation.[1]

The value aspect of circulation, which seemed to have been quite forgotten, now appeared again in the work of Accarias de Sérionne. The reason why prices are not higher in the Orient, in view of the great treasures of gold and silver there, is that the metals do not circulate as they do in Europe. Riches are more concentrated in the hands of the great, much is hidden in the ground, and the standard of living is very low.[2] This discussion has little in common with the ideas about velocity of circulation developed by Petty and Locke. It is simply the question of hoarding. For this reason I am inclined to be skeptical about the significance of the reference to circulation which Bodin de Saint-Laurent cites from a later work by Sérionne.[3] It is very interesting, at any rate, to see the question of value again brought into the discussion.

This reference remained a solitary instance, however, and discussion continued along the lines already observed. To Forbonnais, the first French writer to show the influence of the new point of view, the significance of circulation lay in its relation to the amount of money needed by a nation, the same aspect that had interested Petty, Locke, and Cantillon. Since money may fulfill its function several times a day, he writes, the sum necessary for a country's trade is much less than the sum of the transactions into which money enters. This circulation may be retarded by unsatisfactory adjustments in the mechanism of collecting and distributing the public revenues, by avarice or fear, by great distances between landlords and their estates, and the like.[4]

Genovesi, Beccaria, and Pinto discuss circulation in terms which clearly show that they considered it merely another aspect of the movement of goods, an index or reflection of trade activity.

[1] Sonnenfels, *op. cit.*, pt. ii, pp. 335–352.

[2] Sérionne, *op. cit.*, p. 289.

[3] Bodin de Saint-Laurent, *op. cit.*, p. 56.

[4] Forbonnais, *op. cit.*, p. 217.

Since money is the sign of commodities, and cannot move without them, they reasoned, its circulation may be taken as an indication of the circulation of goods themselves. This, of course, ignores prices, or at any rate assumes them to be constant.[1]

Verri's analysis is rather novel. When money is rare, he says, individuals tend to hold on to it; but when it is plentiful, they are not so careful, and its circulation increases. Gold circulates more rapidly than silver, and banknotes more than gold. He does not mention prices in this connection.[2]

Condillac, according to his own statement, borrowed largely from Cantillon on this point, but his application of the ideas is somewhat different. He begins by describing circulation in terms which leave no doubt that he meant simply the process of paying, receiving, and paying out again, by which the different members of society exchange their products and satisfy their wants. He says nothing to imply that this should, or even could, be more or less rapid. The important point is that it be free. It is in another connection that the idea of circulation developed in Cantillon's work is brought in. To refute the common error about the importance of a country's money supply, he points out that more or less money simply means higher prices, and that, furthermore, the amount of money needed depends on the frequency with which payments are made. If all bills are paid together once a year, and amount to, say, a thousand ounces of silver, then there must be a thousand ounces in circulation; but if they are paid twice a year, only half as many ounces are necessary. The importance of driving home this point filled his mind, apparently; for although he brought prices and circulation into this close connection, he failed to note the relation between them.[3]

Another reference to circulation is cited in Paradisi by Graziani. Like many of the preceding, it is concerned with the amount of money required by trade. This will be greater when

[1] Genovesi, *op. cit.*, vol. ii, pp. 95–114; Beccaria, *op. cit.*, vol. ii, pp. 69–71; Pinto, *Traité de la Circulation et du Crédit*, pp. 33, 34, 47–60. The same point of view is found in the anonymous *Essay on the Theory of Money*, pp. 27–39.

[2] Verri, *op. cit.*, pp. 89–93.

[3] Condillac, *op. cit.*, pp. 294–298.

circulation is less rapid. Graziani's quotation from Paradisi does not bear out his statement that the latter recognized the influence of circulation on value;[1] and in view of the practically complete failure of other writers to see the connection, I am inclined to think he has read this interpretation into Paradisi's work.[2]

[1] "Tanto maggior denaro esige la circolazione, quanto è più lenta."

[2] Graziani, *op. cit.*, p. 63.

CHAPTER XXXV

THE PROBLEM OF REFORM

THE question of ways and means in effecting a reform of the coinage continued to attract much attention. Law refers to only one aspect of the matter — that of expense. The cost of recoinage itself should be borne by the state, he advises, but the state should not make good the loss in weight of the old coins.[1]

Sir Isaac Newton, who managed the English mint during the great recoinage, considered a different aspect of the problem — the changing of the coinage ratio. He agreed with Locke that this should not be effected by raising the value of silver.[2] In a report to the Lords of the Treasury he recommends lowering gold; and it appears from Cantillon's reference to his opinions that he opposed the raising of silver on the ground that it was the legal standard of the country and hence could not justly be changed.[3]

Newton's reasoning did not seem convincing to Cantillon. In the circumstances then existing in England, the better course, he thought, was to coin silver lighter, for this was more nearly what the public had already done by valuing silver higher and leaving only the clipped silver in circulation, thus virtually abandoning the old legal standard. Moreover, lowering gold is less favorable to England with respect to debts owed to foreigners.[4]

Berkeley's ideas as to the proper policy in such a case are very novel. If the overvalued metal is lowered, it will be necessary to provide some substitute, such as banknotes, for the amount thus wiped out, or great difficulty will be experienced in paying rents and other fixed charges. If such an expedient is not practicable, the best way is to raise silver some and lower gold a little also, in

[1] Law, *op. cit.*, p. 165.

[2] Even after the recoinage, gold proved to be somewhat overvalued.

[3] Shaw, *Select Tracts*, p. 154; Cantillon, *op. cit.*, p. 377.

[4] *Ibid.*, pp. 374–381. Quoted with approval by Pagnini (*Della Decima*, vol. i, pp. 151–155).

such a way that the sum total in denomination of the country's money supply will remain the same.[1]

Broggia's rather elaborate discussion, based principally on Italian conditions, did not advance the theory very much. It is impracticable, he says, to lay a tax to restore the coinage, and the king cannot do it from his treasury. It is therefore necessary to resort to an expedient by which the burden to individuals can be rendered more tolerable by causing it to appear gradually. But, he adds mysteriously, it cannot be divulged, for it would no longer have its good effect.

With regard to errors in the coinage ratio, he first lays down the principle that changes in the ratio should never be carried out by changing the weight or fineness of the coins of either metal, because such a course would alter money's "intrinsic," which should be "come sacrosanto." If the weight were altered, the people, being accustomed to consider the weight only of the pieces, would tend to ignore the increased value of the metal, and to raise the prices of all things, so that conditions would be worse than before. On the other hand, if the fineness only were changed, though the people might not notice it, goldsmiths and foreigners would, and the older finer money would tend to be melted or exported. To avoid the evils of disproportion by a general recoinage is, moreover, inexpedient; for, owing to the loss of the expense of the previous coinage, the expense of the new coinage, and the loss through wear of the old coins, it is necessary to lower the weight of the new money by more than the difference in the ratios (to recompense the state), and the country will again suffer from the effects of an incorrect ratio. The proper way to make the readjustment is to vary the "prices" of the different moneys. Thus, when gold is scarce and silver plentiful, more silver money should be given for gold money; if silver is scarce, more copper money should be given for silver. We might, it is true, give less silver money for gold, thus lowering the price of gold, but it is no less advantageous to have gold also abundant, and hence it is better to lower copper, which is sure to be plentiful anyway. If copper should become scarce, however, it would be necessary to lower

[1] Berkeley, *Works*, vol. iv, pp. 592–594.

the weight of that money, since there is no inferior money in which its value can be expressed and hence raised.[1] Neri follows Broggia very closely on this question.[2]

Galiani discusses some aspects of the problem pretty fully, but is not always as clear as one might wish. Taking one statement with another, his conclusions seem to be about as follows. The course to be taken in restoring a worn or mutilated currency depends on circumstances. In general, it is best to carry out recoinage plans all at once, rather than gradually, for the latter method leads to disproportion between the different kinds of money, with all its attendant evils. When such a general recoinage is undertaken, the government should prepare a considerable supply of the new money beforehand from silver obtained from other sources, and then issue it all at once in exchange for the old money. This advance provision should be about two thirds of the money in circulation; more will not be needed, for it will be impossible for all holders of old money to exchange it immediately, and the old money already paid in can be recoined in the meantime; less would not suffice, on the other hand, for the percentage of old money might prove large enough to drive out the new, or if its course were forbidden, there would not be enough money for the needs of trade. There are some cases, however, where a general recoinage need not be undertaken. When the money is not all in bad condition, and only a part of it needs to be replaced, it will suffice to retire the worst pieces gradually, and issue new ones in their stead. Only a few should be changed at a time, lest the people become aware that the old money is inferior and refuse to accept it at the same value. No recoinage scheme, however, should be undertaken until the state has completely eradicated clippers.

The question of meeting the expense of a recoinage also depends on circumstances. Where the replacement takes place gradually, it is out of the question to put the charge on the money itself, that is, by reducing the weight or fineness of the coins, for that would give rise to disproportion. The deficiency in weight and the ex-

[1] Broggia, *op. cit.*, vol. i, pp. 328–336, vol. ii, pp. 22, 23, 69, 144.
[2] Neri, *op. cit.*, p. 43.

penses of coinage should be paid out of taxes, and be regarded as just as legitimate a burden on the public finances as such public functions as the repair of roads and bridges. If all money is to be recoined, either method of meeting the expense may be followed, and a compromise of some taxation and some burdening of the money itself is probably best. This is because taxes once levied are likely to become permanent, and those required for such a considerable undertaking would have to be large. No statements should be given out beforehand regarding the state's intention to bear all or part of the burden, for this would encourage clipping.

On the question of the ratio his discussion is brief. If it is necessary to change the ratio, he says, it is better to change the value of copper and gold rather than silver; for changing copper causes less disturbance in prices, and gold, being wholly strange in the country (that is, in Italy), can be changed without arousing any public uneasiness.[1]

Magens is inclined to give weight to considerations similar to those introduced by Berkeley and Cantillon. Since a great part of England's cash is now in guineas, he reasons, the lowering of these to correct the ratio might cause much inconvenience. Moreover, England received them from foreigners at the higher rate and would lose by paying them back at a lower rate. Every alteration of money, however, he concludes uncertainly, will cause some injustice.[2]

Justi, like Berkeley, is for a compromise in changing the ratio, but for different reasons. If the value of silver is raised, he says, loss is caused to the prince in his revenues, to debtors, and to the citizens through high prices. These statements would seem to require some explanation, but none is given. If the value of gold is lowered, those who possess gold lose, as do those creditors who have made their bargains in gold. Hence the best way is to change the value of both metals a little.

He also considers another problem — the case where a country is suffering from a flood of overvalued foreign subsidiary coins. In such a situation the government should demonetize all this

[1] Galiani, *op. cit.*, vol. i, pp. 212–215, vol. ii, pp. 38, 43–55.

[2] Magens, *op. cit.*, p. 60.

foreign money, and after making sure that its edict is effective, issue a previously prepared supply of its own standard and subsidiary money. This course entails loss to those who hold the foreign money, it is true, but it is the lesser of two evils.[1]

Harris brushes aside the argument that the relations of debtors and creditors should be considered in determining how to correct the ratio. The fact that many loans were made in overvalued gold has nothing to do with the question, he declares, for they were made with the understanding on both sides that silver was "the true and only measure of the contracts."[2] Massie also insists that silver, being the standard, should never be the money to be altered when the ratio is incorrect. Since gold and copper are "only auxiliaries," it is they which should be changed.[3]

Barnard, who, it will be remembered, had made his important proposals regarding subsidiary money as a remedy for the scarcity of silver, understood fully that this scarcity was due to the incorrect coinage ratio between gold and silver; but he considered neither raising silver nor lowering gold a good plan for correcting the error. Either course, he objected, would cause the extraction of the heavier pieces for melting or export. Moreover, the raising of silver would be an act of public bad faith toward foreign creditors; while the lowering of gold would cause the nation to lose on its debts to foreigners, and would cause an embarrassing diminution in the sum of current money in the kingdom. Hence he advocated the scheme just mentioned for a limited supply of overvalued silver coins.[4] Shirley, who opposed Barnard's scheme, agreed with him, however, as to the undesirability of altering silver. This, he declares, is England's "natural money," but gold is only a merchandise, and therefore the country should take care not to buy it at too high a price.[5]

Sérionne, from whose account I quote these last two opinions, agrees with neither of them. Shirley's argument about silver being the natural money of the country he regards as a mere un-

[1] Justi, *Schriften*, vol. ii, pp. 515–519, 546, 547, 553, 555, 556.
[2] Harris, *op. cit.*, pt. ii, p. 107.
[3] Massie, *Observations*, pp. 14, 20, 21.
[4] Sérionne, *op. cit.*, p. 297. [5] *Ibid.*, p. 299.

founded prejudice; while Barnard's objection that raising silver would defraud foreign debtors is answered by the argument that, though less silver is returned to foreigners, that silver is worth more per ounce than formerly. The price of silver in the market is as subject to variations as the price of gold, and the numerary values of the metals must be changed to conform to changes in their market values. In this particular case in England silver was below the market price, and hence silver should have been raised.[1] By the market price of silver he apparently means the numerary value of a given weight of the metal in the market; and in this sense, as we have before noted, the market price of the undervalued metal will always be higher than the mint price. Hence a "raising" will always be in order when the mint ratio is incorrect, according to this reasoning, and his principle is really of no significance.

The anonymous *Essay on the Theory of Money*, of 1771, points out that there are three possible ways to correct the overvaluation of gold: by lowering the rate at which the existing gold coins shall pass, by lowering the amount of silver in a given denomination, and by increasing the weight of a given denomination in gold. The first of these is the best, because of its greater cheapness and convenience, no new coinage being required. The second method, however, has the advantage of increasing the supply of silver coins, which are much wanted in England. Whichever method is adopted, the previously overvalued metal will suffer a loss, and this ought to be indemnified by the public. The simplest way to do this would be to allow that metal to be received at the bank at its former value for a stated time.[2] This last point would seem to be incorrect so far as the second method of making the change is concerned. There is no question of loss or indemnification for holders of gold when the amount of silver in the shilling is diminished.

An entirely unique scheme is proposed by Philippi. When a country is full of bad money, one way to remedy the trouble, he says, is for the prince to turn his bad money into idle treasure, — which every prince keeps by him, — and from his treasure issue

[1] Sérionne, *op. cit.*, pp. 301–304.

[2] *An Essay*, pp. 121–123.

good coin in preference to bad. When the army of such a prince is abroad, this store of bad money can be used to good advantage, provided care be taken to compel all payments from this foreign country to be made in good money.[1]

Vasco, like Justi, discusses the reform of subsidiary money. When such money becomes so badly worn that its value begins to fall, — at first among foreigners, later among all the people, — it should be left to the market, that is, no longer be legal tender at a fixed value, and new coins should be issued. The old ones will then fall until they are valued practically as metal only, and will eventually be exported or melted.

When it is a question of correcting the coinage ratio, it is equally bad to raise the precious metals or to lower copper. The only thing to do, therefore, is to reform the old money by retiring it and distributing new, coined on the correct basis. This operation has the disadvantage, it is true, of being an expense to the treasury, which must make good the excess of value which the overvalued money now bears; but this is not so great as is often believed; for the riches of the prince are the riches of the nation, and the expense of recoinage may therefore be paid, as in the case of other public needs, either out of funds on hand or from the proceeds of new taxes. If the second course should prove necessary, it may be undertaken without hesitation; for, when the coinage is changed, there will have to be a readjustment of the tax regulations to the new denominations anyway, and the people, between satisfaction at receiving good money in exchange for bad and the confusion of the new tax laws, will not know whether they are worse off or better, till they begin to see the good effect of the new coinage on trade, and then they will be glad of it.[2]

[1] Philippi, *op. cit.*, pp. 328, 329.

[2] Vasco, *op. cit.*, pp. 118, 141–143.

CHAPTER XXXVI

SUMMARY

The length of the chapters in this part of the present study is evidence of the great interest shown by the writers of the eighteenth century in monetary questions. On most of the topics discussed in earlier periods they had something interesting to say, often in the way of judicious qualification and sometimes as a more substantial contribution. In general, it was a period of progress, though in uneven degree in the different divisions of the theory.

The most notable development in the analysis of the origin of money was the attack on the older theory that the use of money had arisen as the result of an agreement, and the development in its place of a theory of gradual and evolutionary change. On this point the work of Galiani and Genovesi was the most important. There was also a tendency to place greater emphasis on the interdependence of men.

The functions of money had now come to be a fairly conventional topic, and few writers devoted much attention to it. The measuring of values was distinguished from the effecting of exchanges by some writers, and there were a few references to money's use as a standard of deferred payments. Opinion continued unfavorable concerning the influence of money on human motives, and decidedly favorable as to its other social effects. Of the latter, in particular, there were some very interesting discussions.

On questions of policy numerous developments are to be noted. Following John Law, several writers included homogeneity and divisibility without loss of value among the qualities desirable in the money material; and some continued to hold that, under certain conditions at least, money might be made of any convenient material. There was further opposition to bimetallism, especially among English and Italian writers, but little agreement as to the relative advantages of the different metals, except among the Italians, who generally favored copper. In discussing the ratio between the metals many refinements were developed, particularly by the Italian writers. On the whole, opinion grew more favorable to gratuitous coinage, the example of the English practice having much weight, but many still advocated a charge to cover expenses. Among the latter there was considerable discussion as to the distribution of the burden among the various kinds of coins.

As in the previous century, the practical interests of the Mercantilists caused them to devote much time to technical coinage problems. Few suggestions of importance were made concerning the coinage system as a whole; but such special topics as foreign money, ideal money, the form of coins, and subsidiary money, were discussed at length. On the last point the ideas which had been developing since the later Middle Ages were brought together in several more or less definite proposals, notably by Justi and Barnard; but some writers appeared not to grasp the significance of these proposals.

What we have called the commodity theory of the value of money continued to have more adherents than the quantity theory. John Law, for the first time in over a hundred years, emphasized the influence of supply, but this lead was followed by few later writers. The most notable development was the introduction of a cost concept into these discussions — vaguely in some cases, but with clearer grasp in others. Conspicuous among these is the work of Cantillon, who held that the value of the precious metals tended to conform to cost of production, temporary variations therefrom leading to readjustments in supply. Galiani held that the value of the vast and growing supply of the precious metals determined which mines could be worked profitably. Steuart made a vigorous attack on the quantity theory.

Locke's prestige won many adherents to the quantity theory, though few appreciated the full significance of his reasoning. Hume and several other writers pointed out important qualifications, especially the influence of changes in the volume of trade, but many crude versions are found throughout the period. To a considerable extent this was due to the influence of Montesquieu's rigidly mechanical theory, Italian, German, and even English writers citing his authority. There was considerable confusion as to the exact scope of the theory.

No important suggestions were made concerning the measurement of price changes, but several writers gave interesting analyses of the spread of such changes through the economic structure. Notable among these were Cantillon and Hume, the former considering this topic of the first importance for an understanding of the value of money. These discussions led to a clearer understanding of the effects of price changes on industry. Hume is especially effective in showing the temporary and transitional character of the stimulus derived from new supplies of money.

The effects of price changes on debtors, creditors, and other special classes now began to be studied as aspects of the changing value of the precious metals, whereas they had formerly been treated in connection with the debasement evil. Melon's defense of debasement aroused much discussion, and Dutot brought out the point that such practices would lead to an increase in the rate of interest. The losses sustained by wage-earners were emphasized. Some writers considered in detail the effects of price changes on the state finances, generally with reference to debasement, and there was a great difference of opinion. Except for Hutcheson's suggestion that fixed incomes should be made payable in articles of common necessity, there was little of interest on the subject of deferred payments.

The principles of circulation were analyzed more fully, and some interesting refinements were pointed out. Domestic agencies were given greater weight among the factors causing the disappearance of the better coins, the peculiar position of copper and subsidiary money was discussed, and the influence of the ratio between the precious metals in the Orient was frequently referred to. Italian writers were especially interested in these questions.

The concept of circulation developed by Petty and Locke inspired much discussion. Although several writers brought their discussions of velocity into close connection with their ideas on prices, Cantillon was apparently the only one to see the relation between them. The newer idea of circulation was incorporated into the older theory opposed to hoarding, and much confusion resulted, many writers identifying velocity with trade activity while reasoning about it in terms applicable only to the technical efficiency of the currency.

The problems involved in reforming a disordered currency continued to attract much attention. There was much difference of opinion as to the question of expense, especially the cost of making good the deficiency in weight of worn or clipped coins. Opinion differed also on the question of correcting the coinage ratio: whether one metal should be "lowered" or the other "raised." English writers generally objected to changing silver in any way, regarding it as the immemorial standard; the Italians favored making the adjustment through the copper money; and some argued in favor of a compromise, changing both gold and silver.

CHAPTER XXXVII

CONCLUSION: MONEY IN MERCANTILE THOUGHT

The very bulk of the foregoing chapters is evidence of the great interest shown by the Mercantilists in monetary questions. No aspect of economic theory was more fully discussed, and in none were there such steady and consistent advances. We cannot, of course, conclude from this that these writers accepted the crude monetary fallacies which were long associated with their name; the numerous currency disorders for which these times are notorious would alone have served to keep this topic in the foreground. The question does arise, however, whether it may not be worth while to reëxamine this phase of Mercantile theory, and to inquire whether money has been given its proper place in later interpretations of that system.

Such interpretations, I need hardly point out, have appeared in great variety, especially since the advent of the Historical School with its doctrine of relativity.[1] The logic of Smith and the scorn of Mill have been met by counter-arguments and flat denials; the field of controversy has been shifted by subordinating the economic to the political and social implications of the doctrine, or by passing over its theoretical aspects to debate the practical soundness of its proposals; the propriety of treating Mercantilism as a unit has been questioned from various angles, some writers denying that it ever existed as a system either of thought or of practice, and others pointing out the great divergences with respect to both which we discover when we compare different periods or different countries. Amid so much difference of opinion it is difficult to generalize; but on the whole we may say that the tendency has been to temper criticism and to give greater emphasis to non-economic considerations.

On the point in which we are now interested, however, there

[1] For a summary of the more important of these, see Zielenziger, *Die Alten Deutschen Kameralisten*, pp. 18–42; also Bidermann, *Über den Merkantilismus*, pp. 4–17.

has been little progress. Indeed, the question has received diminishing attention as the new lines referred to above were developed. Most writers were content to refute Mill by citing passages in which the distinction between wealth and money is clearly recognized — not a difficult thing to do after reading the later exponents of the doctrine. This method of dealing with the question is entirely inadequate. It leaves unexplained the relatively large space devoted to monetary questions by Mercantile writers; it ignores the modifications of doctrine and policy normally incident to time and experience; and it fails to discriminate between the cruder and the more subtle manifestations of the monetary fallacy. It will therefore repay us to consider this question at some length.

First, however, we should mention a few writers who have not dismissed the question of money so briefly in their analyses of Mercantilism. Chief among these is Bidermann. According to his interpretation the basic theory of all the doctrines of this school is a realization of the vital importance in the normal round of economic life of a regular, dependable, and adequate circulation of the accepted medium of exchange. Only thus, they reasoned, could an efficient division of labor be maintained and developed, for only thus could every craftsman be sure of a sale for his product at a remunerative price. To ensure such a circulation of money the intervention of the state is often advisable or even necessary. This reasoning, he maintains, though not to be found in Mercantile writers in so many words, underlies their treatment of particular problems.[1] At about the same time Dühring pointed out that the error of the Mercantilists consisted, not in confusing gold and silver with wealth, but in overemphasizing the importance of possessing them as signs of wealth, making money both cause and effect of economic activity.[2] Von Heyking follows Bidermann in stressing the importance of providing an adequate medium of exchange and seeing in this a fundamental principle of Mercantilism.[3] Wirminghaus gives a similar interpretation.[4]

[1] Bidermann, *Über den Merkantilismus*, pp. 18–23.
[2] Dühring, *Kritische Geschichte der Nationalökonomie*, pp. 30–33.
[3] Zielenziger, *op. cit.*, pp. 33, 34.
[4] Wirminghaus, *Zwei Spanische Merkantilisten*, p. 4.

Bunge distinguishes between the practical and the scientific aspects of Mercantile doctrine, and finds in the latter a tendency to ascribe a value to money as such, and to believe that its increase is necessary in order to stimulate economic life.[1]

The ancient philosophers, being contemptuous of wealth in general, developed no theory of the public importance of money. Aristotle recognizes the necessity of providing funds for the purposes of the state,[2] and Xenophon remarks that when communities are in distress from scarcity of grain or from the effects of war, they are still more in want of money; [3] but these references led to no general conclusions concerning the wealth of nations. The Romans' proverbial description of money as *nervi rerum*, and Cato's advice to farmers to "sell, not buy," [4] both of which were often quoted by the Mercantilists, can hardly be said to reflect a reasoned theory of the social rôle of money, though they come nearer to generalizing than anything we find among the Greeks. The Schoolmen, following Aristotle, noted the financial needs of the state; [5] and Antonine of Florence says that it is bad for a state not to have an adequate supply of money, because this makes it necessary to resort to much barter, which is very inconvenient; [6] but here again no general theory was developed.

With the extension of the money economy, however, and the development of strong centralized states, the commercial and fiscal importance of money began to attract more attention. In 1381 the English Parliament complained that gold and silver in money, plate, and ornaments, and through exchange, were leaving the country, so that none was left, and declared that, if this were allowed to continue, it must lead to the ruin of the kingdom. To this Richard Leyc of the Mint replied that the principal reason

[1] Zielenziger, *op. cit.*, p. 424.

[2] "For a state is often as much in want of money and of such devices for obtaining it as a household; hence some public men devote themselves entirely to finance." *Politics*, bk. i, chap. 11.

[3] Xenophon, *Minor Works*, p. 255.

[4] Quoted in Haney, *History of Economic Thought*, p. 66.

[5] St. Thomas, in the *De Regimine Principum*, recommends that the prince keep a store of treasure always available, so that he may not be reduced to the necessity of borrowing. Rambaud, *Histoire des Doctrines Economiques*, p. 97 n.

[6] Ilgner, *Die Volkswirtschaftliche Anschauungen Antonins von Florenz*, p. 97.

was the buying of foreign luxuries.[1] In a similar vein Louis XI begins his edict (1466) establishing the "fabrique de Lyon": "Comme nous considerans la grant vuidange dor et dargent que chacun an se fait de nostre royaume es moyen et occasion des draps dor et de soye, qui sont debitez et exploictez en nostre dict royaume en diverses manieres. . . ."[2] These quotations, which were doubtless typical of the best opinion of their period, have a much more definite tone than anything hitherto, and plainly show that the nation's money supply had now become a matter of serious concern. The loss of money is feared as a real loss of wealth. Here we have the beginnings of Mercantilism as an effective doctrine.

This conception dominated economic thinking for more than a hundred and fifty years longer. In Hales's *Discourse of the Common Weal*, the Doctor declares that, just as a good husbandman will buy no more than he sells, so England should save treasure by purchasing fewer foreign trifles, "that we might ether clene spare, or els make them with in oure owne Realme, for the which we paie enestimable treasure euerie yeare, or els exchange substanciall wares and necessarie for them, for the which we might receiue great treasure." He also emphasizes the need of state treasure. It is not enough, he says, for a prince to live from hand to mouth — he must have "some store for sodeyne eventes ether of warres or of dearth"; and he fears that England's present stock of coin would be quite inadequate to provide for such an emergency.[3]

Similar expressions are found in the writers of other countries. Osse complains in vigorous language of the loss which the country suffers through the purchase of luxuries from abroad: "denn gleich wie die Eigeln das Blut aussaugen, also saugt solcher unnützer Pracht und ander vergeblicher Kosten."[4] Bodin, in his reply to Malestroit, declares that "l'abondance d'or et d'argent est richesse d'un pays";[5] and Serra's treatise *On the Causes which*

[1] *Handwörterbuch der Staatswissenschaften*, vol. vi, p. 652.
[2] Rambaud, *op. cit.*, p. 96 n.
[3] *A Discourse of the Common Weal*, pp. 63, 113.
[4] Bidermann, *op. cit.*, p. 39.
[5] Rambaud, *op. cit.*, p. 97 n.

can make Gold and Silver abound in Kingdoms where there are no Mines shows that the Italians were no less concerned than their neighbors about the money supply. Even as late as the middle of the seventeenth century we find Klock reasoning along the same lines.[1]

Further evidence of the importance attached to money from the national point of view is afforded by the analogies used in describing its functions. The comparison with the blood in the quotation from Osse in the foregoing paragraph was a favorite one. Davanzati calls money "the second blood" of society; from the poorer it returns to the richer purses, and "thus circulating it preserves alive the civil body of the commonwealth."[2] Hobbes later developed the same idea more elaborately, his description plainly showing the influence of Harvey's work on the circulation of the blood.[3] An even more important rôle is credited to money by an unknown French writer of 1621, who seems to consider it a kind of physiological factotum. Money, he says, is the meat which nourishes the state, the sinews by which it moves, and the blood which gives it life and causes it to function in all its parts.[4] Malynes likens money to the soul in the body.[5]

These expressions are more than the reasonings of closet philosophers. The Mercantilists were, above all, believers in the principle of state intervention and the efficacy of public regulations; their belief in the importance of the money supply was therefore bound to beget active measures to safeguard so vital a resource. Hence they developed a mass of cumbrous restrictions, regulations, and manipulations, whose avowed purpose was the preservation and increase of their respective countries' treasure. Prohibition of specie exports, statutes of employments, alteration of the currency, control of the foreign exchanges, and the like, despite the development of insight which they reveal, are all inspired by the same fear and defended by the same arguments.

1 "Pecuniæ studiosissimus quisque publicæ utilitatis minister debet esse solers et diligens." Held, *Carey's Socialwissenschaft und das Merkantilsystem*, p. 21 n.

2 Davanzati, *Lezione*, pp. 37, 38.

3 Hobbes, *Leviathan*, pp. 193, 194.

4 *Rev. d'Hist. des Doctr.*, vol. ii, p. 23.

5 Malynes, *Lex Mercatoria*, p. 44.

Mun's attack on these policies in his *England's Treasure by Forraign Trade* (written about 1638), shows that they and the ideas they reflect were an effective force until well on into the seventeenth century.

Although the whole of this long period was dominated by the theory of the basic importance of treasure, it was not devoid of significant developments. During the sixteenth century we meet indications that another matter was beginning to give concern — the problem of circulation. Thus in Sir Thomas More's *Utopia* we read that the king of the Maccarians kept little treasure by him, in order to promote "that free circulation of money, so necessary for the course of commerce and exchange." [1] Probably the same point of view underlies Davanzati's remark that, just as the stopping of the blood in the head or other parts of the body causes consumption, dropsy, and other diseases, so, if all money be in a few hands, the state falls into serious disorders.[2] These expressions involve no essential modification of the fundamental ideas of this stage of Mercantilism, but they seem to imply that men were beginning to value money, not only as treasure, but also for the services it renders to society. They are the beginning of a development which eventually transformed this phase of Mercantile thought.

In the seventeenth century we find more frequent references to this point; the Cameralists in particular made much of it. Faust declares in a tone of protest that there is plenty of money, just as in former times, but a large part of it lies idle and useless. This hoarding should be vigorously checked. Becher and Schröder also complain of this evil; and one of Hornick's nine rules of financial management is that gold and silver must in no case be allowed to lie idle, but must be kept in circulation.[3] Montanari seems to disapprove hoarding, but is not very explicit.[4] It is hard to say what reasoning underlies these objections to hoarding. Probably it was little more than a vague feeling that no agent so useful as money should be allowed to lie unused.

[1] More, *Utopia*, p. 81.

[2] Davanzati, *Lezione*, p. 38.

[3] Zielenziger, *op. cit.*, pp. 126, 127, 252, 283, 310.

[4] Montanari, *Della Moneta*, pp. 98, 99.

Up to this point we have encountered no hint that the indefinite acquisition of specie might be in any sense unimportant, let alone undesirable. Vaughan, however, believed that, from a philosophical point of view, at least, it was possible to have too much money; "for if Money were invented for the Exchange of things useful to man's life, there is a certain Proportion for that use, and there is as well a too much as a too little." Want of money makes men penurious, while too much makes them luxurious and wanton.[1] Mun's point of view is more practical. He realized that "plenty of money in a Kingdom doth make the native commodities dearer," and feared the effects of high prices on the country's trade. On the other hand, he declared that, if the prince should lay by in treasure more than was gained by the balance of trade, he would ruin his subjects by causing industry and the arts to decline.[2] This plainly implies that a country has certain fairly definite monetary needs; but Mun did not develop the point further.

Schröder also held that the state treasure must not be built up at the expense of the money needed for trade, but he subscribed to the conventional doctrine that "ein Land wird nur reicher, je nachdem entweder aus der Erde aber aus andern Ländern mehr Gold und Silber hineingebracht wird." [3] Petty is more explicit. "There is," he says, "a certain measure, and proportion of money requisite to drive the trade of a Nation, more or less then which would prejudice the same"; and he describes money as "the Fat of the Body-Politick, wherof too much doth as often hinder its Agility, as too little makes it sick." He advocates storing up any surplus in state treasure.[4] Davenant follows Petty closely on this point.[5]

At first glance it might seem that these conclusions leave the older doctrine substantially intact; but in reality they are of great significance. Although they still hold to the ideal of accumulating treasure, and fear its loss, they make the important

[1] Vaughan, *Discourse*, p. 58.

[2] Mun, *England's Treasure*, pp. 138, 188–190.

[3] Zielenziger, *op. cit.*, p. 302.

[4] Petty, *Works*, pp. 35, 36, 113.

[5] Davenant, *Works*, vol. i, p. 382.

step of distinguishing between the money and the other wealth of the nation. From this it is but a step to the statement of Mun that the state's treasure may be partly in ships and stores, or the advice of Petty to invest some of it in countries where interest is high.[1] From this time on, the emphasis is shifted more and more from "treasure" to other aspects of the money economy.

Alongside of this development we note another, of perhaps less importance, but also reflecting the disintegration of the hitherto dominant theory of national wealth. Becher's discussion (1668) illustrates the new trend. Since more money leads to higher prices, he reasons, it makes no difference, within a country, how great the supply of money is. The importance of a plentiful supply arises from the greater command over commodities compared with other countries, which the richer country has.[2] Some such idea also seems to underlie the statement in the anonymous *Britannia Languens* that "the Nation and Prince which hath the greatest Treasure will finally have the Victory," but it is not clear.[3] Petty declares that the English should not rest in industry until they have more money than their neighbors — both present needs and provision for a year ahead.[4] This doubtless refers to state treasure, for Petty analyzed the question of monetary needs very differently, as we have just seen; but it is significant as another, if limited, application of the idea that the advantages of money are relative.

The two ideas just analyzed are found combined in Locke. On the one hand, as we have seen above,[5] he considers at some length the question of the amount of money needed to "drive" a country's trade, thus accepting Petty's principle that this is a pretty definite requirement; and on the other hand, he makes the point, which we noted above in Becher, that riches consist in having more money than the rest of the world, especially your neighbors. As for the quantity of money needed, he concedes that this is a matter of indifference for a country which has no trade with others; but he believes that a trading country must have enough

[1] Mun, *England's Treasure*, p. 189; Petty, *Works*, pp. 36, 446.

[2] Erdberg, *Becher*, pp. 52, 53.

[3] *Britannia Languens*, pp. 16, 17.

[4] Petty, *Works*, p. 119.

[5] Chapter XXII.

money to keep the prices of its commodities "equal or at least near" to the prices that prevail elsewhere. Otherwise it will have to sell cheap or allow part of its trade to stand idle. Thus even the quantity of money needed becomes relative. As for the other point, he explains that a country which has relatively less money will have to pay, in the exchange of native for foreign goods, "double the value" that the others do, and the latter, moreover, will be able to entice its people, command the markets, and "engross naval and warlike stores," to its great disadvantage.[1] All this argument, it should be noted, runs in terms of money, not treasure.

Of perhaps greater significance, in view of later developments, were Locke's brief references to the importance of circulation. In the midst of his discussion of the relation between velocity of circulation and the monetary needs of a country, he remarks that it would be better for trade if rents were paid more frequently; more money would thus be stirring, and less would suffice for business. Again, he notes that the multiplying of middlemen hinders trade "by making the circuit, which the money goes, larger; and in that circuit more stops." A little earlier he speaks of the evils arising from not having enough money "running in the several channels of trade" — collapse of markets, embarrassment of producers.[2] Here we seem to have something more than the familiar protest against hoarding, though probably that feeling is also involved.[3] The objection is not only to keeping money out of circulation altogether, but also to such practices as tend to make that circulation less rapid. We shall hear much of this idea later.

The emphasis placed upon money by the writers thus far discussed does not seem to have sprung from any definite belief that money is a directly productive agent; in general, it was regarded

[1] Locke, *Works*, vol. v, pp. 13, 28, 48–50, 148.

[2] *Ibid.*, vol. v, pp. 24–28.

[3] That hoarding was generally disapproved by writers in England, as elsewhere, is evident from Davenant's assertion that "'T is of such pernicious Consequence to any Nation for the Money not to circulate, that the disease cannot be cur'd at too high a Price." Quoted in Schacht, *Der Theoretische Gehalt des Englischen Mercantilismus*, p. 43.

either as wealth or as an indispensable instrument of commerce, or both. To John Law, however, it plainly means more than this. Domestic industry, he says, depends on the supply of money; a greater quantity employs more people, while a smaller sum "can only set a number of people to work proportioned to it." Every addition to the money supply, therefore, not only diminishes poverty and idleness, but it makes possible the production of a surplus for export. In another passage he argues, somewhat inconsistently, that too much money harms the moneyed man, since a given sum will buy fewer commodities.[1] Dutot repeats this point about the need of money for employing laborers,[2] and we find suggestions of it later; but it was not generally adopted.

One of the ideas developed by certain earlier writers, notably Mun and Petty, apparently did not appeal to Locke — the dangers of an excessive supply of money. We meet it again, however, early in the eighteenth century, and frequently thereafter. Cantillon, who was familiar with Petty's work, has lively fears on this score, and points out clearly the bad effects on trade of the high prices which result from an increase in a country's monetary stock, even arguing that for this reason a favorable balance of trade might spell the ruin of industry. He agrees with Locke, however, that a country which has more money than its neighbors has an advantage as long as it keeps this abundance, for in all its trade with foreigners it gives less land and labor than it receives.[3] Vanderlint also notes the effect of high prices on exports; but his discussion is confused and inconsistent, at best.[4] Berkeley thinks a country should have just enough money to suffice for the "circulating of industry," and declares that "he must be a wrongheaded patriot or politician" whose ultimate aim is to draw money into the country and keep it there.[5]

Mun and Petty, it will be remembered, had not been led by their recognition of the dangers of too much money to abandon their belief in the desirability of treasure, merely advising its withdrawal from circulation. Although there is much less em-

[1] Law, *Money and Trade*, pp. 20–28. [2] Dutot, *Réflexions Politiques*, p. 906.

[3] Cantillon, *Essai sur le Commerce*, pp. 244–250.

[4] Vanderlint, *Money Answers All Things*, pp. 17, 59, 91, 94.

[5] Berkeley, *Works*, vol. iv, pp. 447, 448, 473.

phasis on this point in these later writers, it has not entirely disappeared. In the passages just quoted, Cantillon suggests that the prince might well retire some of the money of his country as a fund for emergencies, when it becomes very plentiful; and Vanderlint says that it would be beneficial to use as much of the precious metals in "splendor" as is consistent with the needs of trade. A little later Broggia reasoned in somewhat the same way as Cantillon, though with different emphasis.[1] The accumulation of treasure, long regarded as a fundamental public policy, here seems to be reduced to a distinctly secondary position; it is no longer an end in itself.

The eighteenth century was not far advanced when other writers began to follow Locke's lead in discussing hoarding as a phase of the velocity of circulation. Lau, an obscure member of the Cameralist group, among whom the importance of circulation was already a tradition, declared that "the value of money consists solely in circulation; the oftener it passes from one hand to another, the more it brings in to its owner," and quoted Locke with approval.[2] Similarly, the unknown author of a *Lehrbuch* published in 1723 wrote that the more money circulates, the more services it performs for the community;[3] and Berkeley pointed out that silver and small money are a better kind of currency, since they circulate faster.[4] Melon held that the free and continuous circulation of money was more important for the prosperity of the country than the size of the monetary stock.[5] In Italy Broggia and Belloni also referred to the importance of circulation; but it is not clear whether they had the concept of velocity in mind.[6]

In Galiani's *Della Moneta* we find elaborate analyses of what had now become the two principal subjects of discussion — the amount of money needed, and the importance of circulation.

[1] Broggia, *Della Moneta*, vol. ii, pp. 332, 333.
[2] Zielenziger, *op. cit.*, pp. 397, 398.
[3] Böhmert, *Ein Lehrbuch über den Volkswohlstand*, p. 23.
[4] Berkeley, *Works*, vol. iv, p. 465.
[5] Melon, *Essai Politique sur le Commerce*, pp. 819, 820.
[6] Broggia, *Della Moneta*, vol. ii, p. 286; Belloni, *Dissertazione sopra il Commercio*, pp. 100–103.

With respect to the first point, he is clearly of the opinion that a country has certain definite monetary needs, but he is equally emphatic in urging the foolishness of trying to get more than this. When a country has enough money to "fill the veins of commerce," it would be neither richer nor better off through an addition to its money supply. The surplus might be used to buy foreign luxuries, to be sure, but this would mean promoting the business of rival countries. Moreover, the high prices which usually prevail where money is plentiful would diminish the sale of its goods abroad, discourage foreigners from settling in the country, and even lead some of its own citizens to emigrate. And finally, when we consider that additional money is obtained only by giving useful goods for it, the absurdity of acquiring more than is needed is evident.[1]

In a chapter evidently suggested by a reading of Locke, he criticizes current ideas concerning circulation. Rejecting the notion that money is directly productive, he declares that circulation is the effect, not the cause, of riches; unless there is already a supply of goods, money can do nothing but vainly circulate. The lack of circulation, however, impedes the conduct of industry, for it discourages the activity of important classes in the community. If circulation becomes sluggish, producers will be unable to dispose of their wares, except at a loss, and production will be curtailed. It is clear, moreover, that he is thinking in terms of velocity, for he makes an interesting computation of the rate of circulation which must be maintained if the existing money supply of his country is to do the work required of it.[2] Although these arguments involve the questionable assumption that there is an independently determined level of prices at which goods must in the long run exchange,[3] Galiani's discussion is distinctly superior to anything that had yet appeared.

Galiani was almost the last distinguished supporter of the theory that a country has certain minimum monetary needs, which had been a cardinal point of Mercantile doctrine for over a

[1] Galiani, *Della Moneta*, vol. ii, pp. 165–168.

[2] *Ibid.*, pp. 135–153.

[3] *Cf.* what is said on this point in Chapter XXII.

century. Later writers either denied it altogether or gave it only a minor place. Massie argues that any amount will do, and says that nobody can tell from Locke's rules how much money is needed, since all the bases of his computations depend on prices.[1] Hume is emphatically of the same opinion, and declares that, when money is scarce, it may still be made to carry on all the trade by mixing it with baser metal. The only advantage conveyed by a great plenty of money is in wars and negotiations with foreign princes. This is very limited. Moreover, a large supply of money may be a great hindrance to a country's foreign trade by causing high prices.[2] Ortes and Condillac also attach little importance to the money supply.[3]

There were some exceptions to this attitude of indifference. Although Harris believes that the monetary needs of a trading country will take care of themselves, he thinks it would be desirable to acquire more than this, holding the surplus, however, as "dead stock" to prevent a rise of prices.[4] Justi and Forbonnais agree that a non-trading country can get along with any amount of money, but will concede no more.[5] Sonnenfels discusses the question in much the same terms that Locke had used, but also notes the bad effects of too much money unless the excess is withdrawn from circulation.[6] Genovesi vaguely says that the money supply of a country should be less than the value of the "primary riches" needed there; then most people will not have enough money unless they work, and industry will thrive. Too much money is dangerous.[7] Steuart believes that a country's monetary needs are pretty definite, and holds that any excess simply will not circulate.[8] Even these writers, however, attach much more importance to other matters.

[1] *An Essay on the . . . Rate of Interest*, pp. 36–38.

[2] Hume, *Essays*, vol. i, pp. 310, 315, 316.

[3] Ortes, *Economia Nazionale*, vol. ii, pp. 282–288, 350; Condillac, *Le Commerce et le Gouvernement*, pp. 289, 297, 298.

[4] Harris, *Money and Coins*, pp. 80, 89, 90.

[5] Justi, *Schriften*, vol. iii, p. 385; Forbonnais, *Principes Économiques*, pp. 223–228.

[6] Sonnenfels, *Sätze aus der Polizei*, pp. 30, 31, 339, 372, 373.

[7] Genovesi, *Lezioni di Commercio*, pp. 110, 247, 248.

[8] Steuart, *Political Œconomy*, vol. i, p. 407, vol. ii, p. 171.

One fear concerning money continued to disturb many Mercantilists who had surrendered the older doctrine or ceased to emphasize it. They were deeply impressed by the importance of circulation. Postlethwayt gives a curious theory, which was probably inspired by some phrases of Cantillon's, though the latter's point of view was different. The facility of exchange, he declares, depends primarily upon the assurance of being able to exchange money and commodities at any time "on the Footing established by Custom." This assurance results from what we may call "Natural Circulation" — "the continual Presence in Trade of the Portion of Money, which each Portion of Commodities has been used to fetch." When money is hoarded, however, part of the commodities are deprived of their usual exchange, and the "Balance will incline in Favor of Money" (that is, prices will fall). In order to bring the hoarded money back into trade, people in great need will offer to pay for the use of it, and thus arises interest as part of the expenses of every undertaking. This is "Composite Circulation," and the stronger the tendency in this direction, the less will the people be able to consume.[1] The first part of this argument reminds one of Galiani, but the remainder appears to be quite unique.

Sonnenfels, like Galiani, discusses the importance of circulation in terms which show that he was thinking of velocity. The physical presence alone of money in a country does not give an adequate stimulus to industry, he says; it must circulate, and the more frequently it circulates, the greater the advantages it confers. This it does through the increase of economic activity. Here circulation is regarded not only as a necessary force in sustaining industry (as in Galiani), but also as an important factor in its increase. His elaboration of this thesis implies pretty clearly that he had simply confused monetary circulation with trade activity. These two phenomena are not unrelated, it is true, but there is no such causal connection between them as is here implied.[2]

[1] Postlethwayt, *Great Britain's True System*, pp. 335–340. It should be noted that he does not connect this with his discussion of velocity. See above, Chapter XXXIV.

[2] Sonnenfels, *Sätze aus der Polizei*, pp. 31, 335–340. It is interesting to note that Justi, from whom Sonnenfels borrowed much, does not refer to the concept of

Genovesi is more cautious. Money, he says, cannot circulate unless commodities do; circulation is therefore "nothing but the course of exchanges of what is superfluous for what is wanted," and the velocity of circulation is the course of exchanges in a given time. Hence we may say that "the effects of money" are in proportion to its circulation, and the greater circulation a state has, the richer and stronger it is. The best way to promote circulation is to remove every obstacle to trade and industry. The underlying thought here seems to be that a rapid circulation is gratifying as an evidence of vigorous trade; but there is also the implication that it is only when money attains its maximum circulation that it renders to society the greatest service of which it is capable.[1]

Beccaria follows this analysis rather closely. Strictly speaking, he says, the term circulation means going out and eventually returning. It can therefore be applied only to money. Now, since nothing is given without an equivalent, the circulation of money will be a faithful representation of the activities of the nation; the more rapidly a zecchino has passed from hand to hand, the more goods it has represented and measured. This obviously involves the fallacy that goods always exchange at the same prices, a notion which also lurks in Genovesi's reasoning. It is plain, however, that Beccaria regarded monetary circulation neither as a cause nor as a condition of commercial activity.[2]

Many writers continued to regard circulation as a factor in prosperity. Forbonnais argues, in terms suggestive of Locke, that the obstruction of circulation has serious consequences. When the receivers of money do not spend it, proprietors are worried about the sale of their products, and artisans about their wages. There is, therefore, a tendency both to produce and to consume less. Whatever quantity of money is once devoted to trade should be left there, for prices become conventionalized. In this he seems to have nothing more than hoarding in mind.[3]

velocity, merely protesting against hoarding in traditional terms. Justi, *op. cit.*, vol. i, p. 78, vol. iii, p. 354.

[1] Genovesi, *Lezioni di Commercio*, pp. 95–114.

[2] Beccaria, *Elementi di Economia Pubblica*, vol. ii, pp. 69–71.

[3] Forbonnais, *Principes Économiques*, pp. 221, 224.

In Pinto's treatise the importance of circulation is raised to the dignity of a fundamental principle. The real circulation of money, he writes, is prodigious in daily expenditures. The same crown-piece may pass through fifty hands in a day and represent fifty things, thus effecting transactions to the amount of fifty crowns. Were it not for this fact, the present money supply of Europe would be wholly inadequate for the trade which has grown up under the stimulus of the discovery of America and the mines there. Together with the existence of credit, which supports and supplements it, circulation is of the greatest service. Credit and circulation enable the English government to borrow immense sums.[1] Much of this is merely exposition, it is true, but it clearly implies that a rapid circulation contributes largely to national strength. It also involves the fallacy of the fixed price-level at which goods necessarily exchange.

Uninfluenced, apparently, by his countrymen, Galiani and Genovesi,[2] Verri analyzed circulation in a very different way. After noting that circulation increases when money is plentiful, since people are not so careful about money, he draws the conclusion that, when the money of a country is increasing, the greater circulation which results will cause production to increase more than in proportion. This is because the increase of buyers will enable sellers to get along with less profit on each article, thus lowering prices and stimulating industry. He also suggests that circulation should be speeded up by indirect means, but does not develop the point.[3]

In England, where there had been little discussion of this question since the middle of the century, we now encounter it again in the anonymous *Essay on the Theory of Money*. Since a piece of money, we read here, cannot pass from one person to another without receiving an equivalent, that is, without effecting the exchange of a "piece of industry," it is clear that the oftener a piece of money circulates, the greater will be the industry of the country, and *vice versa*. As we have already seen, such a con-

[1] Pinto, *Traité de la Circulation et du Crédit*, pp. 33, 34, 47–60.

[2] Beccaria's work had not yet been published.

[3] Verri, *Économie Politique*, pp. 86–93.

clusion does not follow unless we assume a fixed level of prices. It seems plain from some of the author's reasoning that he had derived this theory from Genovesi. It is not clear whether he considered circulation a causal factor.[1]

Ortes's discussion hardly equals the foregoing. To conceive the movement of money as more or less rapid, he declares, is "only a puerile imagination," for this movement is simply a matter of the exchange of goods. When we speak of the more or less rapid circulation of money in some countries, it would be equally correct to say that the same amount of supplies was consumed there in proportionately less time. It is true, however, that if people hoard money, the circulation of goods will be impeded to that extent.[2] It is evident that this shows no adequate conception, either of the meaning of circulation, or of its relation to trade.

We are now in a position to attempt a restatement of the Mercantile attitude toward money. Two facts seem to stand out. On the one hand, monetary problems never ceased to occupy a prominent place in analyses of national strength and prosperity — a place which often seems to us disproportionate, even when it does not involve positive error. Money and the services which money renders were so highly valued as means that they were treated as practically ends in themselves. This, of course, is not to say that these writers ignored all other factors in their problem. As active discussion and the lessons of experience revealed the sources of wealth and power more clearly, such topics as the increase of population, development of national resources, and the protection of property came to the fore; but to the end money remained among the fundamentals.

On the other hand, we observe that, in the course of time, there came profound changes in emphasis and point of view. In the seventeenth century fears and alarms about the loss of treasure gave way to concern as to the adequacy of the medium of exchange, while it came to be realized that the indefinite acquisition of the precious metals might not be an unmixed blessing, unless the excess were immobilized in non-monetary hoards. In the

[1] *An Essay on the Theory of Money*, pp. 27–39.

[2] Ortes, *Della Economia Nazionale*, vol. ii, pp. 316–318, 375.

eighteenth century the traditional aversion to hoarding, reinforced by the newly developed analysis of velocity of circulation, gradually came to outweigh other aspects of the question in the minds of many writers, and a vein of skepticism developed in others. Of course, there were overlappings of these tendencies, and crude ideas persisted until almost the very end of the period; but the general trend of opinion shows fairly well-marked stages.

In thus insisting on the importance of monetary questions in the Mercantile scheme of things I do not mean to imply that in this trait alone we have an adequate characterization of that system. We must not forget the eager nationalism which inspired their every discussion and furnished them a touchstone for every public policy, or the uncritical belief in the efficacy and justice of petty and often superficial programmes of state interference from which few of them were free. We may even concede that the significance of their work is perhaps as much political as it is economic. But the fact remains that in all their discussions of the wealth of nations they never quite broke away from the illusion that money is, somehow, *nervi rerum*.

BIBLIOGRAPHY

BIBLIOGRAPHY

Aquinas, Saint Thomas, *Opera Omnia*. Parmae, 1852–73.
Aristophanes, *Comedies*. Translated by W. J. Hickie. London, 1872.
Aristotle, *The Nicomachean Ethics*. Translated by J. E. Welldon. London, 1892.
——, *Politics*. Translated by Benjamin Jowett. Oxford, 1908.
Asgill, John, *Several Assertions Proved*. Reprint. Baltimore, 1906.
Babelon, Ernest, *Les Origines de la Monnaie*. Paris, 1897.
——, *La Théorie Féodale de la Monnaie*. In *Mémoires de l'Institut National de France*. Paris, 1909.
Bandini, Salustio Antonio, *Discorso Economico*. In Custodi collection. Milan, 1803.
Barbon, Nicholas, *A Discourse concerning Coining the New Money lighter*. London, 1696.
——, *A Discourse of Trade*. Reprint. Baltimore, 1905.
Baudeau, Nicolas, *Principes de la Science Morale et Politique sur le Luxe et les Lois Somptuaires*. Reprint. Paris, 1912.
Beccaria, Cesare, *Elementi di Economia Pubblica*. In Custodi collection. Milan, 1804.
Belloni, Girolamo, *Dissertazione sopra il Commercio*. In Custodi collection. Milan, 1803.
Berkeley, George, *Complete Works*. Oxford, 1901.
Bidermann, H. J., *Über den Merkantilismus*. Innsbruck, 1870.
Bodin, Jean, *The Six Bookes of a Commonweale*. Translated by Richard Knolles. London, 1606.
——, *Les Six Livres de la République*. Paris, 1577.
Bodin de Saint-Laurent, Jean de, *Les Idées Monétaires et Commerciales de Jean Bodin*. Bordeaux, 1907.
Böhmert, Victor, *Ein Lehrbuch über den Volkswohlstand aus dem Jahre 1723*. Leipzig, 1893.
Boisguillebert, Pierre de, *Dissertation sur la Nature des Richesses, de l'Argent, et des Tributs*. In Daire, *Économistes-Financiers du XVIIIe Siècle*. Paris, 1843.
——, *Traité de la Nature, Culture, Commerce, et Intérêt des Grains*. In Daire, *Économistes-Financiers du XVIIIe Siècle*. Paris, 1843.
Boyss, Matthaeus (editor), *Tractatus Varii atque Utiles de Monetis, eorumque Mutatione ac Falsitate*. Coloniae Agrippinae, 1574.
Brants, Victor, *Esquisse des Théories Économiques Professées par les Écrivains des XIIIe et XIVe Siècles*. Louvain, 1895.
Brehaut, Ernest, *An Encyclopedist of the Dark Ages*. New York, 1912.
Briscoe, John, *A Discourse on the Late Funds of the Million-Act, Lottery-Act, and Bank of England*. London, 1694.

Broggia, Carlo Antonio, *Trattato delle Monete.* In Custodi collection. Milan, 1804.

Burgon, John William, *The Life and Times of Sir Thomas Gresham.* London, 1839.

Cantillon, Richard, *Essai sur le Commerce.* Reprint. Boston, 1892.

Carli, Gian-Rinaldo, *Dell' Origine e del Commercio della Montea.* In Custodi collection. Milan, 1804.

Cary, John, *An Essay on the Coyn and Credit of England: as they stand with Respect to its Trade.* Bristol, 1696.

Clark, Walter Ernest, *Josiah Tucker, Economist.* New York, 1903.

Clement, Simon, *A Discourse of the General Notions of Money, Trade, & Exchanges, as They stand in Relation to each other.* London, 1695.

Coke, Roger, *A Treatise Concerning the Regulation of the Coyn of England.* London, 1696.

Condillac, E. B. de, *Le Commerce et le Gouvernement.* In Daire, *Mélanges d'Économie Politique.* Paris, 1847.

Conigliani, C. A., *Note Storiche sulla Questione Giuridica dei Pagamenti Monetarii.* Modena, 1891.

Considerations, Some, About the Raising of Coin. London, 1696.

Copernicus, Nicolas, *Monete Cudende Ratio.* Edited by M. L. Wolowski. Paris, 1864.

Davanzati, Bernardo, *Lezione delle Monete.* In Custodi collection. Milan, 1804.

D'Avenant (Davenant), Charles, *Political and Commercial Works.* London, 1771.

De Wulf, Maurice, *History of Medieval Philosophy.* Translated by Coffey. London, 1909.

Dialogue Between a Countrey Gentleman and a Merchant Concerning the Falling of Guinea's, A. London, 1696.

Douglass, William, *A Discourse Concerning the Currencies of the British Plantations in America, etc.* Edited by C. J. Bullock. New York, 1897.

Dubois, A., *Précis de l'Histoire des Doctrines Économiques.* Paris, 1903.

Dühring, E., *Kritische Geschichte der Nationalökonomie und des Socialismus.* Berlin, 1871.

Dutot, *Réflexions Politiques sur les Finances et le Commerce.* In Daire, *Économistes-Financiers du XVIIIe Siècle.* Paris, 1843.

Endemann, Wilhelm, *Studien in der Romanisch-kanonistischen Wirthschafts- und Rechtslehre.* Berlin, 1883.

Erdberg-Krczenciewski, Robert von, *Johann Joachim Becher,* Halle a. S., 1896.

Essay on the Theory of Money, An. London, 1771.

Faust ab Aschaffenburgk, Maximilian, *Consilia pro Ærario Civili, Ecclesiastico, et Militari, Pubblico atque Privato.* Frankfurt, 1641.

Forbonnais, F. V. de, *Principes Économiques.* In Daire, *Mélanges d'Économie Politique.* Paris, 1847.

Fornari, Tommaso, *Delle Teorie Economiche nelle Provincie Napolitane.* Milan, 1882–88.

Galiani, Ferdinando, *Della Moneta.* In Custodi collection. Milan, 1803.

Genovesi, Antonio, *Lezioni di Commercio o sia d'Economia Civile*. Bassano, 1788.
Gobbi, Ulisse, *L'Economia Politica negli Scrittori Italiani del Secolo XVI–XVII*. Milan, 1889.
Gómara, Francisco López de, *Annals of the Emperor Charles V*. Translated by R. B. Merriman. Oxford, 1912.
Graziani, Augusto, *Le Idee Economiche degli Scrittori Emiliani e Romagnoli sino al 1848*. Modena, 1893.
Grote, George, *Plato, and the Other Companions of Sokrates*. London, 1865.
Grotius, Hugo, *The Rights of War and Peace*. London, 1738.
Hales, John (?), *A Discourse of the Common Weal of this Realm of England*. Edited by Elizabeth Lamond. Cambridge, 1893.
Haney, Lewis H., *History of Economic Thought*. New York, 1913.
Harris, Joseph, *An Essay upon Money and Coins*. London, 1757–58.
Held, A., *Carey's Socialwissenschaft und das Merkantilsystem*. Wurzburg, 1866.
Hobbes, Thomas, *Leviathan*. Oxford, 1909.
Hodgkin, Thomas, *The Letters of Cassiodorus*. London, 1886.
Hoffmann, F., *Kritische Dogmengeschichte der Geldwerttheorien*. Leipzig, 1907.
Hornick, P. W. von, *Oesterreich über alles, wann es nur will*. Regenspurg, 1727.
Hume, David, *Essays Moral, Political, and Literary*. London, 1898.
Hutcheson, Francis, *A Short Introduction to Moral Philosophy*. Glasgow, 1764.
Ilgner, Carl, *Die volkswirtschaftlichen Anschauungen Antonins von Florenz*. Paderborn, 1904.
Inquiry into the Nature and Uses of Money, An, etc. Boston, 1740.
Jourdain, Charles, *Excursions Historiques et Philosophiques à Travers le Moyen Age*. Paris, 1888.
Journal des Économistes. Paris.
Justi, J. H. G. von, *Gesammelte Politische und Finanz-Schriften*. Copenhagen and Leipzig, 1761.
Kaulla, Rudolf, *Die Geschichtliche Entwicklung der Modernen Werttheorien*. Tübingen, 1906.
Kautz, Julius, *Die Geschichtliche Entwicklung der National-Oekonomik und ihrer Literatur*. Vienna, 1860.
Keckermann, Bartholomew, *Systema Disciplinae Politicae, Publicis Praelectionibus Anno MDCVI Propositum in Gymnasio Dantiscano*. Hanover, 1608.
Klock, Caspar, *Tractatus Juridico- Politico- Polemico- Historicus de Aerario*. Nüremberg, 1651.
Landry, Adolphe, *Essai Économique sur les Mutations des Monnaies dans l'Ancienne France de Philippe le Bel à Charles VII*. Paris, 1910.
Law, John, *Money and Trade Considered*. Glasgow, 1750.
Lenormant, François, *Essai sur l'Organisation Politique et Économique de la Monnaie dans l'Antiquité*. Paris, 1863.
Locke, John, *Works*. London, 1823.

Lotz, Walther, *Die Drei Flugschriften über den Münzstreit der Sächsischen Albertiner und Ernestiner um 1530*. Leipzig, 1893.

Lowndes, William, *A Report Containing an Essay for the Amendment of the Silver Coins*. In McCulloch's *Select Collection of Scarce and Valuable Tracts on Money*. London, 1856.

Magens, Nicolas, *The Universal Merchant*. London, 1753.

Malynes, Gerard de, *Consuetudo: vel Lex Mercatoria*. London, 1656.

Massie, Joseph, *An Essay on the Governing Causes of the Natural Rate of Interest*. London, 1750.

——, *Observations Relating to the Coin of Great Britain*. London, 1760.

Melon, Jean-François, *Essai Politique sur le Commerce*. In Daire, *Économistes-Financiers du XVIIIe Siècle*. Paris, 1843.

Mercier de la Rivière, François, *L'Ordre Naturel et Essentiel des Sociétés Politiques*. Paris, 1846.

Mirabeau, Victor Riquetti de, *L'Ami des Hommes*. Paris, 1883.

Montanari, Geminiano, *Della Moneta*. In Custodi collection. Milan, 1804.

Montchrétien, Antoyne de, *Traicté de L'Œconomie Politique*. Paris, 1889.

Montesquieu, Charles de Secondat, Baron de. *Œuvres Complètes*. Paris, 1846.

More, Sir Thomas, *Utopia*. In Morley's *Ideal Commonwealths*. London, 1885.

Mun, Thomas, *England's Treasure by Forraign Trade*. In McCulloch's *Early English Tracts on Commerce*. London, 1856.

Neri, Pompeo, *Osservazioni sopra il Prezzo Legale delle Monete*. In Custodi collection. Milan, 1804.

North, Sir Dudley, *Discourses upon Trade*. In McCulloch's *Early English Tracts on Commerce*. London, 1856.

Oertmann, Paul, *Die Volkswirtschaftslehre des Corpus Juris Civilis*. Berlin, 1891.

Oresme, Nicole, *Traictie de la Première Invention des Monnoies*. Edited by M. L. Wolowski. Paris, 1864.

Ortes, Giammaria, *Della Economia Nazionale*. In Custodi collection. Milan, 1804.

Pagnini, Giovanni Francesco, *Della Decima e di Varie Altre Gravezze Imposte dal Comune di Firenze, Della Moneta e della Mercatura de' Fiorentini fino al Secolo XVI*. Lisbon and Lucca, 1765.

——, *Saggio sopra il Giusto Pregio della Cose, la Giusta Valuta della Moneta, e sopra il Commercio dei Romani*. In Custodi collection. Milan, 1803.

Paris-Duverney, Joseph, *Examen du Livre Intitulé Reflexions Politiques sur les Finances et le Commerce*. The Hague, 1740.

Petty, Sir William, *Economic Writings*. Cambridge, 1899.

Pettyt, William (?), *Britannia Languens, or a Discourse of Trade*. London, 1680.

Philippi, Johann Albrecht, *Der Vergrösserte Staat*. Berlin, 1771.

Philips, Erasmus, *The State of the Nation, in Respect to her Commerce, Debts, and Money*. London, 1726.

Pinto, Isaac de, *Traité de la Circulation et du Crédit*. Amsterdam, 1787.

Plato, *Dialogues*. Translated by Benjamin Jowett. Oxford, 1875.

Pliny, *Natural History*. Bohn's Classical Library. London, 1857.
Plutarch, *Lives*. Clough's translation. Boston, 1906.
Pollexfen, John, *A Discourse of Trade, Coyn, and Paper Credit: and of Ways and Means to Gain and Retain Riches*. London, 1697.
Postlethwayt, Malachy, *Great Britain's True System*. London, 1757.
Prior, Thomas, *Observations on Coin in General*. In McCulloch's *Select Collection of Scarce and Valuable Tracts on Money*. London, 1856.
Pufendorf, Samuel, *The Law of Nature and Nations*. London, 1749.
Rambaud, J., *Histoire des Doctrines Économiques*. Paris, 1902.
Reflections on Coin in General, on the Coins of Gold and Silver in Great Britain in Particular; on those Metals as Merchandize, and also on Paper passing as Money. In McCulloch's *Select Collection of . . . Tracts on Money*. London, 1856.
Regulating Silver Coin, The, Made Practicable and Easie, to the Government and Subject. London, 1696.
Review of the Universal Remedy for all Diseases Incident to Coin, A. London, 1696.
Revue d'Histoire des Doctrines Économiques et Sociales. Paris.
Roberts, Lewes, *The Merchants Mappe of Commerce*. London, 1638.
Robinson, Bryan, *An Essay on Coin*. London, 1758.
Roscher, Wilhelm, *Geschichte der National-Oekonomik in Deutschland*. Munich, 1874.
Rowe (or Roe), Sir Thomas, *Speech in Parliament on the Decay of Coine and Trade*. London, 1641.
Rowe (or Roe), Sir Thomas (?), *Speech at the Councell-Table Touching Brasse-Money*. London (?), 1641.
Salmasius, Claudius, *De Usuris*. Leyden (?), 1683.
Scaruffi, Gasparo, *Discorso sopra le Monete*. In Custodi collection. Milan, 1804.
Schacht, H., *Der Theoretische Gehalt des Englischen Merkantilismus*. Berlin, 1900.
Schreiber, Edmund, *Die volkswirtschaftlichen Anschauungen der Scholastik seit Thomas v. Aquin*. Jena, 1913.
Sérionne, Joseph Accarias de, *Les Intérêts des Nations de l'Europe, Developés Relativement au Commerce*. Leyden, 1766.
Serra, Antonio, *Breve Tratto della Cause che Possono Far Abondare le Regni d'Oro e d'Argento dove non sono Miniere*. In Custodi collection. Milan, 1803.
Sewall, Hannah Robie, *The Theory of Value before Adam Smith*. New York, 1901.
Shaw, W. A., *The History of Currency, 1252–1894*. London, 1895.
——, *Select Tracts and Documents Illustrative of English Monetary History*. London, 1896.
Small, Albion W., *The Cameralists*. Chicago, 1909.
Sonnenfels, Joseph von, *Sätze aus der Polizei, Handlungs- und Finanzwissenschaft*. Vienna, 1769.
Steuart, Sir James, *An Inquiry into the Principles of Political Œconomy*. London, 1767.

Thesaurus, Gaspar Antonio, *Tractatus Novus et Utilis de Augmento ac Variatione Monetarum.* Taurini, 1607.
Thomas, Paul, *Essai sur Quelques Théories Économiques dans le Corpus Juris Civilis.* Paris, 1899.
Tucker, Josiah, *Four Tracts on Political and Commercial Subjects.* Glocester, 1776.
Turbolo, Gian-Donato, *Discorsi e Relazioni sulle Monete del Regno di Napoli.* In Custodi collection. Milan, 1803.
Turgot, Anne Robert Jacques, *Reflections on the Formation and Distribution of Wealth.* In McCulloch's *Select Collection of Scarce and Valuable Economical Tracts.* London, 1859.
Uztariz, Geronymo de, *The Theory and Practice of Commerce and Maritime Affairs.* Translated by John Kippax. London, 1751.
Vanderlint, Jacob, *Money Answers all Things.* Reprint. Baltimore, 1914.
Vasco, Giovanni Battista, *Della Moneta.* Milan, 1772.
Vaughan, Rice, *A Discourse of Coin and Coinage.* London, 1675.
Verri, Pietro, *Économie Politique.* Traduite de l'Italien. Paris, 1799 (?).
Wallace, Robert, *Characteristics of the Present Political State of Great Britain.* London, 1758.
Wirminghaus, Alexander, *Zwei Spanische Merkantilisten.* Jena, 1886.
Wood, William, *A Survey of Trade.* London, 1718.
Xenophon, *Minor Works.* Translated by J. S. Watson. London, 1878.
Zeitschrift für die Gesamte Staatswissenschaft. Tübingen.
Zielenziger, Kurt, *Die Alten Deutschen Kameralisten.* Jena, 1914.
Zuckerkandl, Robert, *Zur Theorie des Preises.* Leipzig, 1889.

INDEX

INDEX

(See also the Table of Contents)

Bei Fragen zur Produktsicherheit wenden Sie sich bitte an:
If you have any questions regarding product safety,
please contact:

Walter de Gruyter GmbH
Genthiner Straße 13
10785 Berlin
productsafety@degruyterbrill.com